Grand Piano

by the same author

THE YOUNG PERSON'S GUIDE
TO PLAYING THE PIANO

SIDNEY HARRISON

Grand Piano

FABER AND FABER
3 Queen Square
London

First published in 1976
by Faber and Faber Limited
3 Queen Square, London WC1
Printed in Great Britain by
Latimer Trend & Company Ltd Plymouth
All rights reserved

ISBN 0 571 10386 3

From SIDNEY to SYDNEY,
dear wife and companion

Contents

1. A Great Invention *page* 11

2. In Principle 14

3. Ancestry 16

4. The Defeat of the Harpsichord 22

5. New Music for the New Instrument 31

6. The Piano Meets Mozart 37

7. Mozart Meets Clementi 51

8. The Great Mogul 69

9. The Piano Promoter 81

10. The Piano Sings, Dances and Goes to War 91

11. Four Geniuses at Once 107

12. Getting On in the World 124

13. 'Con Amore' 139

14. Chopinski 157

15. The New Piano-Makers and Their Customers 169

16. He That Should Come 175

17. An American Girl Learns from Liszt 182

18. How to Make a Pianist 194

CONTENTS

19. A Thousand Kinds of Bach   204

20. No More Rules of Harmony   207

21. Strange Pianos and Argumentative Teachers   213

22. Pianos Play Themselves   228

23. The Final Romantics   238

24. Treat It Rough   242

25. Despite Everything   249

26. Teachers of the World Unite!   255

27. Before the Public   260

28. Take Care   263

   Index   267

Illustrations

PLATES

between pages 160 and 161

1. 'Piano e forte' by Bartolommeo Cristofori of Florence, *c.* 1720
2. A square piano by Longman & Broderip of London, *c.* 1795
3. A transitional giraffe piano by Van der Hoef of Amsterdam, *c.* 1810
4. A Clementi piano
5. (a) A Robert Wornum piano, *c.* 1875
   (b) Down-striker action of the Robert Wornum piano
6. A decorated Steinway in the author's home
7. A Bösendorfer (Vienna) 'Imperial' piano
8. A Steinway-Welte reproducing vertical piano, *c.* 1910
9. A Kemble upright piano
10. A modern Yamaha piano for the drawing-room

LINE DRAWINGS

Side view of the Schwander key action on a grand piano
(Figures I and II) *page* 27
Giraffe pianos in many shapes and sizes
(Figure III) *page* 84

9

Acknowledgements

I would like to convey my thanks to the following, who have kindly given me permission to reproduce copyright material: The Metropolitan Museum of Art, New York, for Plate 1 (from the Crosby Brown Collection of Musical Instruments, 1889); The Victoria and Albert Museum for Plates 2 and 3 (from Raymond Russell's *Catalogue of Musical Instruments, Vol. I: Keyboard Instruments*, H.M.S.O., London, 1968); Bösendorfer Pianos Ltd. for Plate 7; the British Piano Museum for Plate 8. The diagrams on page 27 are of a Schwander action manufactured by Messrs. Herrburger Brooks Ltd. of Long Eaton, and are reproduced from my *Young Person's Guide to Playing the Piano*, Faber and Faber, London, 1966. Extracts from Harold Schonberg's *The Great Pianists* (London, 1964) are reprinted by kind permission of Victor Gollancz Ltd.

1. *A Great Invention*

Every child knows that the great inventions of the modern world are, of course, engines—the steam engine, the internal combustion engine, the rocket engine. Or maybe radio, television and computers.

Only a rare child would dare to suggest that the piano is a great invention, and even he might hurry on to the electronics of music.

Nevertheless, let us consider the claims of the pianoforte, not only as a triumph of technology but as the greatest instrument of the most loved of all the arts. When I say the greatest instrument I am not trying to annoy the violinists, though as a dedicated pianist, I secretly think my instrument better than theirs. I base the claim on different grounds.

Certainly, it is the most necessary of all instruments. It is the necessary 'second study' of anyone who plays anything else. Without it rehearsals are impossible. The singer must provide a piano for his accompanist. The choirmaster-organist, the music mistress at school, the suburban teacher with dozens of little pupils must all have pianos. And how hard it is to be a conductor without being able to use a piano as a tool of the trade.

As for composers, only one great composer really hated the piano and that was Berlioz. All the others used pianos, some clumsily, some competently, and some at a level that allowed them to play their concertos in public. Wherever one goes in Europe to the houses of great composers the guide will show his flock the piano on which Beethoven composed his symphonies, Schubert his *Lieder*, Puccini his operas and so on. No doubt Beethoven was able to walk about the countryside muttering and cursing and singing while jotting ideas into a notebook but he had to have a piano at home, even when he was too deaf to hear it. And quite certainly Chopin had to have a piano even when he was living in a disused monastery in

Majorca where, in those days, pianos were hard to come by.

There are no great violinist-composers, no great singer-composers, no great ballerina-composers. The great master-pieces for our cathedrals, opera houses and concert halls were the works of musicians who, to some degree, were pianists.

Let me placate the objectors. Yes, the great composers of the baroque era played harpsichord, clavichord and organ. Keyboards anyway. Some later composers played a variety of instruments. For example, Gluck appeared in public as a virtuoso of the musical glasses. And the piano was a second-best instrument for Richard Strauss, who played the horn, and Elgar, who played the violin. But the piano plainly dominates the world of great composers, not only because most of them wanted to compose for it, but because the keyboard is music made visible. It is the test-bed on which everything can be tried out and evaluated, where harmony can be seen as well as heard, where modulation is a visible rerouting of major and minor scales, and where even orchestration can be suggested.

The piano admittedly has no part to play in the modern world of electronic synthesizers, but it submits stoically to having its keys played by the elbows, having ping-pong balls thrown on to its strings, and being assaulted by mallets applied to the iron frame—a species of touch that can yield a magical sound provided the sustaining pedal is down.

Until the invention of electric guitars the piano was the background for every kind of light music. It stood behind every dance-band leader. A honky-tonk piano was present at the birth of jazz. The piano was a fixture in the orchestral pit of every theatre, 'legitimate' or otherwise, and clattered non-stop from early afternoon to late night under the silver screen during the long era of silent films. When ballroom bands were organized into melody section, harmony section and rhythm section, the piano belonged to all three.

As for its domestic influence it was, over a long span of time, the source of music in every family that had raised itself even one notch above the poverty line. In the smaller home the upright piano stood against the wall. In the cook-housemaid-and-nanny home there was the sort of grand that appeared in catalogues as 'drawing-room' or (slightly smaller) 'boudoir' models. For stately homes there were spectacular grands in which the mechanism was encased in marquetry and ormolu to accord with the Louis-Quinze furniture and the Gainsboroughs of former duchesses.

Only the 'folk' were without pianos. Folk music may have influenced Dvořák and Grieg and Bartók but the piano was never a peasant instrument.

The piano has had its ups and downs, taking a beating from radio yet making an astonishing come-back. The fact remains that almost everybody would love to be able 'to sit down and play the piano'—and notice that sitting down is a significant part of the idea. Not everybody is willing to do the hard work that piano-playing entails, and not everybody aspires to fugues and sonatas rather than songs from the shows. But who is there who would wish not to play the piano if a fairy godmother offered to convey the skill with a wave of her magic wand?

Your true pianist falls in love with a piano and becomes married to it at an early age. The relationship continues as indissoluble monogamy. If, later on, he marries a woman, this is a kind of bigamy.

Your true pianist knows that his instrument is a triumph of man's genius. Why is this seldom acknowledged? Why do social historians and other such pundits never refer to the piano as one of the great influences of civilization? It is simply that the piano, unlike most mechanical inventions, crept up on us. There was no dramatic moment like Watt watching the kettle boil or the Wright brothers taking-off in a heavier-than-air machine.

When the piano was born the harpsichord was familiar. The new inventors found a new way to agitate the strings. That was all. Nothing to make monarchies totter or alter the balance of power. Just a little matter of interest to musicians and of no great consequence.

No great consequence . . . ?

2. *In Principle*

Take an iron frame shaped something like a harp. Lay it flat on a wooden plank. Stretch steel strings across it and screw them up very tight. Hit them with eighty-eight hammers.

Compose some tenderly romantic music.

A caricature? No doubt. In a piano the iron frame is not just laid on a plank: it is attached with scientific precision to a cunningly constructed sound-board. The hammers are not mere mallets: they have felt-covered heads of a shape determined by long years of experience. The 'action' that conveys the pianist's touch from key to string has been thought about by hundreds of designers for two centuries.

A concert grand, costing what many professional people would regard as a decent salary for a year, is a triumph of refined technology. So indeed is a little upright costing a tenth as much.

Nevertheless, our caricature is not altogether false. A piano does have steel strings stretched tight across an iron frame. A hammer does strike the strings—it does not stroke or caress them. No matter what is said about singing tone, every note begins with a bump of sound that immediately begins to decay. In the upper range of the instrument, where my right hand so often attempts to conjure up a singing tone, the sound dies all too soon, simply because high notes are obtained from short strings. In the lower octaves the strings are long, the tone endures, and my left hand, in the presence of a treble melody, must play with delicacy. If I move from a truly grand grand to a baby grand or an upright I must, without time for reflection, rebalance everything.

The piano-makers have done their best to minimize the problems, changing defects into qualities and characteristics. Almost from the beginning they realized that one string per note would be insufficient. There was a period when they provided two (bichord), but a modern piano provides three strings tuned to one pitch (trichord). The strings are close enough and the hammer is broad enough for this arrangement to be highly effective. However, any child who has ever pulled the front off his upright piano to see how it works will know, as I knew at the age of four, that in the deeper bass the strings are long and wound round with copper. Down there, two strings per note are sufficient, and in the deepest bass only one.

The inquisitive child will also know that if hammers are needed to make the strings sound, dampers are needed to make them stop. A damper is a small piece of felt, backed by wood, that lies on the strings of a note. Play a note, and, at the instant when the hammer flies towards the strings, the damper lifts off, allowing the string to vibrate freely. Hold the note, and the damper stays off. Remove your finger and the damper returns to the string and stops the vibration. A few of the highest notes are not provided with dampers. The strings are so short, the sound dies so soon, that a damper is not needed. But the dampers are a very important part of the action, as every inquisitive child knows when he pushes his foot on to the 'loud pedal'.

This sustaining pedal raises all the dampers at once, allowing notes to go on sounding even when one's fingers have gone elsewhere, and its proper use is almost an art in itself. The basic trick can be taught more easily to young children than to older ones, but it must be well taught. Bad habits of pedalling are very difficult to correct.

There is a left pedal, too. The piano with which I first fell in love (maker, Ebenezer Beddoe; price, probably £5 second-hand) had a crude device whereby the soft pedal caused a strip of felt to move between hammer-head and strings. This muffled the sound to the point of being nearly inaudible, but it could be kind to neighbours when scales were practised before breakfast. A later and better upright had the modern system that brings the hammers nearer to the strings. This 'half throw' reduces the leverage but it also slightly affects the feel of the action.

A better arrangement is found on nearly all grand pianos. The keyboard slides sideways a very short distance—not enough to affect one's aim—and carries the whole of the action with it. Each hammer is now off-centre. This in itself affects the lower, copper-bound strings. Where there are three strings per note, the hammer now strikes only two of them. Harking back to an earlier era when a hammer struck only one string out of two, the device is called *una corda*, though in fact it is *due corde*. The return to the normal three strings is called *tre corde*.

Just to start with, I have swiftly sketched the piano as we know it. Its life story will unfold later. To people like me the piano appeals with extraordinary power. And such is its responsiveness that one goes far beyond operating a musical machine. One almost mimes a love affair with one's mistress. If anyone challenges this statement and asks, 'What about women pianists?', I am tempted to say, dismissively, that women must learn to play music composed by men on an instrument designed by men for a man's hand. This, however, would be too sweeping. Pianists of either sex must recognize the masculine and feminine elements in each piece—to recognize the masculine and feminine elements in the composer's nature and one's own. They must also remember, when anybody talks of musical education, that a pianist is, to some degree, a wild animal dependent on instinct and on non-verbal thinking.

3. Ancestry

Piano-playing began before the piano was invented. The proof lies in the fact that keyboard music of earlier times can be played immediately on the piano. Nevertheless, when the piano was a new invention musicians soon realized that they could not just go on with the new instrument where the old one left off. They were entering a new world of sound. So fascinated were they by this that they abandoned not only the harpsichord but all its works. There was very little looking back. What about us? Can we ignore the music of the earlier eras? The obvious answer is no, but the less obvious answer is that we do ignore a great deal of it. Many a serious pianist of today follows a successful career without ever playing the virginals music that Queen Elizabeth I knew or the *clavecin* pieces that graced the court of Louis XIV. We have the volumes on our shelves. Most of us open them rarely.

But there is one great name that no one can ignore. It would be a strange pianist who was indifferent to Bach (Bach the father, though the Bach sons helped to create true piano music). In fact, so deeply do we love and reverence him that we can scarcely credit the fact that, when the fortepiano was new, Bach's music became unfashionable. For example, Mozart was a famous composer before his attention was drawn to the *Forty-eight Preludes and Fugues*. Later, the best pianists studied this music with devotion but they seldom played it in public. And this state of affairs continued until this century.

Not now. We all play Bach. Young children play from the *Anna Magdalena Notebook*. Older children approach the fugues by way of the Two-part Inventions. More advanced students attempt the partitas and toccatas and the 'Italian' Concerto. Just how all this is to be played on the 'wrong' instrument is a problem that will never (thank goodness) be finally solved. Over-edited publications are numerous, but how they came into being, and whether they are to be taken seriously, can be considered at the point in history when Bach's music began to be box-office. What we cannot do is to sweep on regardless and begin with the invention of the piano, any more than one could write a biography without mentioning the hero's parents.

Fortunately the facts are interesting; they can be summarized fairly briefly; and they are necessary to anyone who wishes to think for himself about playing Bach—and Scarlatti—on the piano. If you cannot get access to a harpsichord, there are some very useful experiments that can be made with a grand piano.

Put the lid up on its stick, take out the music desk and stand close to the keys. With the left hand push down middle C so gently as to cause no sound. Hold the key down. The damper is now off the strings and they are free to sound.

Lean over and with your fingernail pluck one of those strings. (You can see which damper is up.) Plucking illustrates the principle of the harpsichord, and the sound you hear is at least something like harpsichord sound. On a harpsichord the strings are not hammered: they are plucked by a quill taken, perhaps, from a crow.

Now for a second experiment. Once again use the left hand soundlessly to render a C string free. This time take a large coin and hold it in the fingers of the right hand. Lean over and give a slow push to a C string and do not bounce off. Just push the string, somewhere near the dampers, and hold the coin against it. You will now hear a soft sound that is higher than C. This is because the string no longer vibrates from bridge to bridge but only between the coin and the far end. When the coin pushes the string it not only sets up a vibration: it tunes the string to a new pitch. If you stretch your arm and try the experiment further along the string, the pitch will be higher because the vibrating length will be shorter.

This is the principle of a clavichord, except that the string is pushed from underneath. A key on a clavichord is a simple see-saw. The player pushes the visible end down. The invisible end, tipped with brass, goes up and pushes a string. This metal contact is called a tangent (Latin *tangere* = to touch).

The strings of a clavichord do not run fore and aft as on a grand piano: they run from left to right, parallel with the keyboard. They are thin and have no great tension. They must therefore be pushed gently since a vigorous push will make them go out of tune.

A pianist who first tries a clavichord finds the tone frustratingly feeble. Even in its own era, when silence was a common experience, the clavichord was recognized as being suitable for an audience of perhaps only half a dozen people. Nevertheless this modest little instrument had one great merit. It had nuance. To our ears its crescendo may seem to go only from *ppp* to *p*, but within its own limits it was undoubtedly expressive. It was even capable of a vibrato or an after-tone. If you vary the pressure on a held-down key the sound can be made to echo itself in an effect called *Bebung** (pronounced something like *bayboonk*).

Gentle though it was, and designed almost for self-communion,

* Literal translation is *tremor*.

18

it challenged its more brilliant rival the harpsichord which, with all its mechanical contrivances, could never deliver a run of notes with varying accent. The fact that Bach was fond of the clavichord helps to support those pianists who recoil from a doctrinaire attitude about harpsichord style.

It is one thing to reject a doctrinaire attitude: it is quite another to be content with ignorance, especially at a time when the harpsichord has gained a great deal of favour not only in the old music but also in such unforeseen fields as pop music. What then does a pianist need to know about it?

The basic mechanism is first the key—the seesaw that is common to all claviers. Standing on the far end of the seesaw is an upright 'jack' from which projects a small quill at right angles. When a note is played, the jack rises. The quill going past the string plucks it. What could be simpler? There is only one complication. Will not the quill repluck the string on the way down? To avoid this the quill is placed not into a solid jack but into a tongued section of it, hinged at the bottom. At the back of this tongue is a small spring made of bristle. When this little mechanism is properly set and balanced, the quill catches the string on the way up, but on the way down it only brushes past the string, while the tongue leans over to allow this, the bristle restoring the upright position immediately afterwards.

An absolutely basic, simple harpsichord with only one set of quills produces, for our ears, a monotonous pinging sound. However, in early days an ardent listener could find it delightful. There was, in Elizabethan times, a small instrument of this kind (the strings running parallel to the keyboard) called a virginal or, oddly enough, a pair of virginals. Either way, nothing to do with the Virgin Queen. Shakespeare loved it when the right girl played it:

> How oft, when thou, my music, music play'st,
> Upon that blessed wood whose motion sounds
> With thy sweet fingers, when thou gently sway'st
> The wiry concord that mine ear confounds,
> Do I envy those jacks that nimble leap
> To kiss the tender inward of thy hand,
> Whilst my poor lips, which should that harvest reap,

At the wood's boldness by thee blushing stand!
To be so tickled, they would change their state
And the situation with those dancing chips,
O'er whom thy fingers walk with gentle gait,
Making dead wood more blest than living lips.
Since saucy jacks so happy are in this,
Give them thy fingers, me thy lips to kiss.

Shakespeare seems to confuse a jack with a key and may be displaying the characteristic ignorance of poets about the technical terms applied to music. On the other hand it is possible that in Shakespeare's London keys were called jacks.

As time went on, makers produced two main types of quilled-instrument—those with strings running from left to right, and others with strings running fore and aft, from near the key-board to the far end. Looking back we find some inconsistency in the names applied to these different types. But generally the latter type, if it had only one string per note, was called spinet. With more strings per note, the English called it harpsichord, the French *clavecin*, and the Italians *clavicembalo*, *gravicembalo*, or simply *cembalo*. The Germans, if they did not use the word *Clavier*, said *Flügel*.

Flügel, meaning a wing, in reference to the shape of the instrument, was later applied to grand pianos—and still is. Spinet was also carried on into the piano era. Nowadays, many people think that a spinet is an old-world piano. Others, particularly in America, apply the word to very small modern uprights.

The larger harpsichords developed many varieties. For example, there might be three strings to a note, two at normal pitch and a shorter one tuned an octave higher. The jack for the octave-note remained inactive until brought into operation by a coupler, whereupon a run of notes automatically changed into a run of octaves. Borrowing the language of organists, the players spoke of normal pitch as 8-foot. The upper note was 4-foot. Modern harpsichords of the most elaborate kind also provide a lower octave (16-foot) but this seems to have been rare in period instruments.

A great many harpsichords were built with two manuals (keyboards) and with different kinds of plectra. Quills could be placed very near the keyboard end. This produced a 'nasal' tone, controlled by the 'lute stop'. Some French instruments had a set of plectra made of soft buffalo skin (*peau de buffle*), giving a softer and more tender sound. There were harpsichords with a lid made like a venetian blind. When this apparatus was gradually opened up, perhaps by a knee lever, a crescendo was produced.

Knee levers were common: so were hand levers or stops; but modern harpsichords usually have pedals, up to as many as seven, to control all the possible permutations of manuals and plectra.

It is evident that eighteenth-century musicians and makers were searching for variety of sound, even though a quilled clavier could never give them the swiftly varied, subtle nuance of which the clavichord was capable.

The pianist of today needs to understand the nature of the harpsichord without being enslaved by it. Some pianists, more argumentative than artistic, are full of self-denial. They deny themselves the use of the sustaining pedal, they deny themselves variety of accent, they seem to think that Bach should be played as to a metronome, though the metronome was not yet in existence, and in the end they are left with a monotonous, mechanical performance that pretends to be stylistic. In a sense they discard the piano without acquiring the harpsichord.

One characteristic of the harpsichord must be remembered. Its tone remains level until the player rearranges the stops or until there is a change from one manual to the other. The change of tone is immediate and abrupt—no *poco a poco crescendo*. Knowing where and when to make a change is the art of 'registration' and the player must discern very clearly the end of one musical event and the beginning of another. This introduces the concept of 'terraced' tone—so much at this level and so much at that but no gradual slopes. The notion is important; but too rigorously pursued it can make a piano seem to go against its own nature.

However, when we come to Mendelssohn's preludes and fugues or to Liszt's transcriptions of Bach's organ fugues we shall think about the problem afresh.

4. The Defeat of the Harpsichord

How did it happen that the splendid, highly developed harpsichord was so swiftly replaced by the new and imperfect piano? A few years passed and harpsichords were being relegated to cellars and attics. The musical historian, Dr. Charles Burney, writing in about 1805 when he was nearing eighty, recollected what had happened earlier, when J. S. Schroeter (not to be confused with the inventor C. G. Schröter) settled in London in 1772.

> The piano-forte was a new instrument in this country: when he first arrived the hammer instruments of a large size were bad, and harpsichord players produced no great effects upon them; but Schroeter may be said to have been the first who brought into England the true art of treating that instrument. We were unwilling to give up the harpsichord, and thought the tone of the piano-forte spiritless and insipid, till experience and better instruments vanquished our prejudices; and the expression and chiaroscuro in performing music expressly composed for that instrument, made us amends for the want of brilliancy in the tone so much, that we soon found the scratching of the quill in the harpsichord intolerable, compared with the tone produced by the hammer.

Quoting this, I have jumped ahead of the earliest days of the piano, but Burney does help us to realize how swiftly musicians changed their minds. Indeed, if the piano was so eagerly accepted we may well wonder why it was not invented sooner. The idea of a clavier with hammers must surely have been in people's minds as a possibility.

To see it all in perspective let us think back to those ancient instruments the psaltery and the dulcimer. Either instrument is basically a lyre attached to a sound-board. A psaltery-player takes into his fingers a plectrum—a small piece of shaped horn or ivory or metal—and plucks the strings. A dulcimer-player lays his instrument flat before him and beats down on it with two hammers or wands—as a cimbalom-player in Hungary does to this very day.

The harpsichord, then, is a keyboard psaltery: the piano a keyboard dulcimer. The grand piano of today seems to be a kind of upside-down dulcimer since the hammers strike upwards and fall with the aid of gravity. Indeed this was general practice from the beginning. But there were a few makers who contrived pianos with downward-striking hammers. There is a late specimen, made around 1875, to be found in the Victoria and Albert Museum in London (*see Plate 5*). The hammers, bouncing upwards and then staying up, seem to be behaving against gravity until one thinks of a seesaw weighted on one side. Press down the lighter side of such a seesaw and then let go, and it will fly up and stay up, helped by gravity. The museum piano feels very normal under the fingers.

Why were piano hammers, whether up- or down-striking, so late in being developed? Perhaps because the clavichord seemed to be a kind of dulcimer, even though its strings were pushed and not struck—the 'tangent' staying in contact with the string instead of smartly bouncing off. It must be said, however, that the name *piano e forte* was applied to some sort of new instrument as far back as 1598 by one Paliarino of Modena. At a time when virginals were in their heyday he made instruments, named in this way, one of them 'with an organ underneath'. We know about this—alas too vaguely—from some letters unearthed in 1879. There is no detailed description.

There are several claimants to the title of inventor of the piano. One is a German named Christoph Gottlieb Schröter, who never quite brought his inventions to fruition but later swore that other people had stolen his ideas. He was inspired by seeing a dulcimer virtuoso, round about 1717. What virtuosity on the dulcimer amounted to, I have no idea, but the word dulcimer has always enchanted me ever since I read Coleridge's 'Kubla Khan', and I am happy to think that a piano is a species of dulcimer.

> A damsel with a dulcimer
> In a vision once I saw:
> It was an Abyssinian maid,
> And on her dulcimer she played,
> Singing of Mount Abora.
> Could I revive within me

Her symphony and song,
To such a deep delight 'twould win me,
That with music loud and long,
I would build that dome in air,
That sunny dome! those caves of ice!
And all who heard should see them there,
And all should cry, Beware! Beware!
His flashing eyes, his floating hair!
Weave a circle round him thrice,
And close your eyes with holy dread,
For he on honey-dew hath fed,
And drunk the milk of Paradise.

Louis XIV was enchanted by a virtuoso named Pantaleon Hebenstreit who played an enlarged and developed dulcimer. The name Pantaleon makes an appearance in one of Chopin's letters (see page 114).

No dulcimer virtuoso inspired the Frenchman Jean Marius, who in 1716 submitted four kinds of 'mallet harpsichord' to the Académie des Sciences. Even earlier (1708) there had been one Cuisinié with a *clavecin* fitted up with a foot treadle operating a revolving resined bow. Somehow the player's action on a key brought a string in contact with the revolving bow. Cuisinié was born too soon. He should have worked in the era of the player-piano and the fairground organ.

In 1709 one Scipio Maffei wrote a letter after visiting Prince Ferdinand dei Medici in Florence. The Keeper of the Prince's Musical Instruments, Bartolommeo Cristofori (1655–1731), had made an instrument something like a harpsichord but with hammers instead of jacks, and Maffei describes it not only with enthusiasm but with some perception of its possibilities (*see Plate 1*).

It is known to everyone who delights in music, that one of the principal means by which the skilful in that art derive the secret of especially delighting those who listen, is the piano and forte in the theme and its response, or in the gradual diminution of tone little by little, and then returning suddenly to the full power of the instrument; which artifice is frequently used and with marvellous effect, in the great concerts in Rome. . . . Now, of this diversity and alteration of tone . . . the harpsichord is entirely deprived, and it would have been thought a vain endeavour to propose to make it so that it should participate in this power. Nevertheless, so bold an invention has been no less happily conceived than executed in Florence, by Signor Bartolommeo Cristofali, of Padua, harpsichord-maker, in the service of the most serene Prince of Tuscany.

We may notice in passing that Cristofori's name is sometimes found spelt Cristofali. Maffei continues:

The production of greater or less sound depends on the degree of power with which the player presses the keys, by regulating which, not only the piano and forte are heard, but also the gradations and diversity of power. . . . But really the great cause of the opposition which this new instrument has encountered, is in general, the want of knowledge how, at first, to play it; because it is not sufficient to know how to play perfectly upon instruments with the ordinary finger board, but being a new instrument, it requires a person who, understanding its capabilities, shall have made a particular study of its effects, so as to regulate the measure of force required on the keys and the effects of decreasing it, also to choose pieces suited to it for delicacy, and especially for the movement of the parts, that the subject may be heard distinctly. . . .

Maffei must have been a very perceptive man to have realized so much on a first encounter with what Cristofori called *Gravicembalo col piano e forte*.

I wonder who played the instrument to him. Was Cristofori a skilled player as well as inventor? It is obvious from Dr. Burney's article that the piano in England awaited an exponent, but his fellow musicians were soon converted to the new machine. Not so in Italy. Despite Cristofori's genius and advocacy the Italians were resistant, and he had to continue making harpsichords to stay in business.

The Cristofori piano was much more than a harpsichord fitted with hammers. It had the double lever that is necessary to make the hammer fly fast enough. It had a check to prevent uncontrolled bounce of the hammer. There were two strings to a note and also the sliding *una corda* device. And there was a reasonably effective escapement. Escapement was a problem that engaged the attention of inventors for generations afterwards, but Cristofori made the first important step.

The problem is this: a hammer is pushed most of the way to the string but then flies free so that it can bounce off the string. If the player is holding a key down, the hammer-pusher will be up. How, then, is the hammer to return to a position where it will be ready for a repetition of the same note? Or if the player wants to repeat a note again and again at speed, how will the action cope with that demand? Down the years that followed, many inventors worked on the escapement problem and every piano-maker had his patent method, but Cristofori led the way.

We shall discover later that Mozart particularly liked Stein pianos because of the effective escapement, but it would be a wearisome business to examine every improvement in detail. I have an old edition of *Grove's Dictionary of Music and Musicians* in which a long article is illustrated by a number of detailed drawings. One quotation, relating to the Zumpe action, will suffice to show why even dedicated pianists allow their eyes to slide down the page without digesting every detail of information.

> In the key, *c*, is fixed the jack, *g*, a wire with a leather stud on the top, known by the workmen as the 'old man's head'. This raises the hammer, *o*; the damper, *r*, is lifted by a whalebone jack, *v*, called the 'mopstick', placed near the end of the key, and is brought back to its place by the whalebone spring, *w*; a third piece of whalebone, *x*, projecting from the end of the key, works in a groove, and serves exactly as in the clavichord to keep the key steady, there being no front key-pin.*

I stop half-way. Enough is enough. But all serious pianists should surely understand how a modern action works—though many do not—and the diagrams below (Figures I and II) give clear pictures and explanation. The diagrams show only one maker's design but they illustrate a well-esteemed mechanism.

---

* The most comprehensive, detailed account of every technical improvement in piano-making up to 1851—a profoundly scholarly piece of research—is *The Piano-forte* by Rosemond E. Harding (Cambridge University Press, 1933).

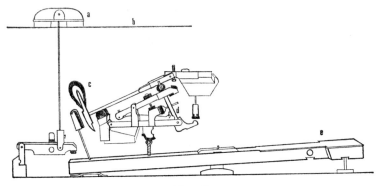

Fig. I

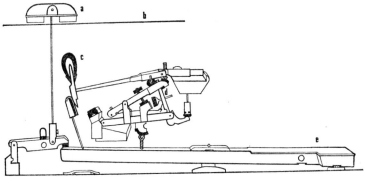

Fig. II

(The drawings are of a Schwander action manufactured by Messrs. Herrburger Brooks Ltd. of Long Eaton.)

Figures I and II represent a side view of the action of one note on a grand piano.

A key is like a seesaw. Press the visible end down and the other end goes up. In Figure I the key (e) is up. The hammer (c) is at rest. The damper (a) lies on the string (b) preventing any vibration. The rod (d) can be thought of as a sort of finger; and the finger tip is hidden in a slot in the cross piece. This finger tip touches the round piece of felt above it.

In Figure II the key has been pushed down. The other end of the seesaw goes up and, through a vertical rod, takes the damper off the string. At the same time the force is communicated to the 'finger'

(d) which pushes the piece of felt. This pushes the hammer-shank, and the hammer (c) is on its way towards the string. But now the 'finger-tip' slips to one side of the piece of felt, escaping from its original position. The hammer flies the rest of the way by momentum. It is not pushed against the string: it is *thrown* at the string, from which it bounces back. It is the escapement that makes this possible. The 'finger' of the escapement, in fact, *flicks* the hammer. (Piano-action makers call this 'finger' a hopper.)

The damper stays off the string so long as the key is held down (or so long as the sustaining pedal is down).

Returning to the eighteenth century we turn from Cristofori to Gottfried Silbermann (1683–1753), and it is through him that the piano meets Bach. J. F. Agricola's *Treatise on the Organ and Other Instruments* (1768) tells us what happened.

> Mr. Gottfried Silbermann had at first built two of these instruments. One of them was seen and played by the late Kapellmeister, Mr. Joh. Sebastian Bach. He had praised, indeed admired, its tone; but he had complained that it was too weak in the high register, and was too hard to play. This had been taken greatly amiss by Mr. Silbermann, who could not bear to have any fault found in his handiworks. He was therefore angry at Mr. Bach for a long time. And yet his conscience told him that Mr. Bach was not wrong. He therefore decided—greatly to his credit be it said—not to deliver any more of these instruments, but instead to think all the harder about how to eliminate the faults Mr. J. S. Bach had observed. He worked for many years on this. And that this was the real cause of this postponement I have the less doubt since I myself heard it frankly acknowledged by Mr. Silbermann. Finally, when Mr. Silbermann had really achieved many improvements, notably in respect to the action, he sold one again to the Court of the Prince of Rudolstadt. Shortly thereafter His Majesty the King of Prussia had one of these instruments ordered, and, when it met with His Majesty's Most Gracious approval, he had several more ordered from Mr. Silbermann. Mr. Silbermann had also had the laudable ambition to show one of these instruments of his later workmanship to the late Kapellmeister Bach, and have it examined by him, and he had received, in turn, complete approval from him.

Complete approval? Bach, as far as we know, never acquired

a piano, nor in his late years was he influenced by the new instrument. But if he did not acquire the piano, the piano acquired him. He was, however, shown some Silbermann pianos when he visited Frederick the Great at Potsdam. This visit is, perhaps, only marginally part of the history of the piano, but every pianist who has ever played to great and important music-lovers cannot help enjoying the story and wondering about Bach's secret thoughts.

Frederick of Prussia, that formidable soldier, was an amateur of the arts. He regarded most military men as uncouth. He had Voltaire to stay, he liked to speak French, he played the flute, he composed pleasant music, and at his many musical evenings he was the very picture of what an 'enlightened despot' should be. Employing Bach's son Carl Philipp Emanuel as chief harpsichordist and taking flute lessons from Quantz, he heard enough about the old composer to want to see him.

When Bach, obeying the royal command, arrived in Potsdam (1747) the king was told immediately. Interrupting a musical evening Frederick asked for Bach to come without delay, scarcely giving the traveller time to change into suitable clothes. (That, at any rate, is the popular story.) When the visitor arrived, the king was gracious and showed off a collection of instruments that according to Bach's biographer, Forkel, included fifteen Silbermann pianos. (Other writers suggest six or seven.) Then Bach was put to a test. The king had composed (unaided?) a very fine subject, put it before Bach and asked for an improvised fugue. What happened next left no doubt that Bach was the most learned musician in Europe.

It must have been a truly remarkable demonstration since the ability to improvise some sort of fugue was not uncommon in those days. A musician could hardly hope for appointment as a court Capellmeister unless he could set up a fugal activity at a moment's notice. But to do it at Bach's level . . .

Bach was not content with what he had done. When he got home he worked with great intensity on the royal theme and then sent to Potsdam a 'Musical Offering' in which the royal theme is the subject of learned fugues and incredibly complex canons in forward, backward and upside-down movement, plus a trio-sonata with a part for the royal flautist—partnered by violin and continuo. To this day the *Musical Offering* is regarded as almost unbearably learned, though occasional performances attract an audience and there have been a few recordings in versions 'realized' by quarrelling pundits, each of whom has his own idea about a score in which Bach says nothing about instrumentation except in the trio-sonata.

With the *Musical Offering* Bach sent a covering letter that to the modern reader is almost comically respectful. Did Frederick ever see it? Did he ever suspect that he would be less well remembered than Bach? Here are a few sentences.

Most Gracious King
I herewith dedicate to Your Majesty, with the deepest submission, a musical offering of which the noblest part is the work of Your Majesty's illustrious hand. It is with reverential satisfaction that I remember Your Majesty's very special royal favour, when some while ago, during my stay in Potsdam, Your Majesty condescended to play (and thereby make known to the world) the theme for a fugue on the clavier and at the same time graciously commanded me, then and there in the royal palace, to work it out. It was my humble duty to obey Your Majesty's command. But I instantly realized that, lacking preparation, the performance was not as successful as so excellent a theme deserved. I accordingly determined to set to work at once to treat this truly royal theme more perfectly. This I have now done to the best of my ability.

The *Musikalisches Opfer* is not totally inaccessible to a pianist. I have discreetly transcribed the Fuga Ricercata for three voices (*ricercata* is first cousin to researched and means learned) and have persuaded several audiences to applaud it. But, in a manner of speaking, the *Musical Offering* is 'Bach's Last Stand' even though he lived to write other pieces. The world was changing, the piano was dethroning the harpsichord, but Bach remained true to his own genius.

5. *New Music for the New Instrument*

The greatest of the baroque composers (unless you prefer Handel) sired many children, of whom three sons were men of genius, even if not on the highest level. They were Wilhelm Friedemann, Carl Philipp Emanuel and Johann Christian, and they did more than almost anyone else to create the new music that would suit the new instrument and the new taste of audiences. In doing so they relegated their father to a background from which he did not emerge for a very long time. However, they could not have done this but for a change in the climate of opinion so far-reaching as almost to persuade us that the Spirit of the Age is an objective reality and not a poetic myth. It is as though a weary Spirit had been recalled to whatever heaven such creatures inhabit and been replaced by a vigorous young rival whose wings would stir up a wind destined to intensify into the storm of the French Revolution.

But, first of all, the era of baroque was giving way to the years of rococo. The harpsichord belongs to the one: the early pianoforte or fortepiano to the other.

Baroque style, whether expressed in a great palace or a Handel opera, is very magnificent, it is imbued with grandeur, it never aspires to 'naturalness'. What could be further removed from folk-song than a Bach or Handel aria? What could be further removed from ordinary speech than its words? In the *Messiah*, the nations do not *rage* together: they *ray-ay-ay-ay-* (etc., etc.) *age* together. This is not to say that such music was totally inaccessible to 'common' people. The time was to come when farm hands and cotton operatives and coal miners would come together in great choirs to sing Handel's *Messiah* and Bach's Mass in B minor, and in his own day Handel was very popular. All the same, the grand airs of this music (in both senses of airs) led inevitably to a reaction. For example, there was *The Beggar's Opera* by John Gay. Instead of 'artificial' songs about the rulers of heaven and earth, there were popular, traditional ditties about a highwayman and his doxies. This delighted the opera lovers and the opera haters alike. It was a straw in the new wind.

In making generalizations about the baroque I have been too sweeping, but the notion of grandeur is seldom inappropriate even when applied to some small minuet or gavotte. It may not be big music or great music, but you have only to compare it with a waltz by one of the Strauss family to realize that it is written for 'the Quality'. Playing Bach one almost never thinks of the music as pretty or cosy or sentimental. Rhapsodical, yes. This may seem strange to anyone who realizes, as one must, that counterpoint imposes a severe discipline on a composer. But every time I play the highly rhetorical passages in the Chromatic Fantasia and touch those chords that anticipate Wagner I am told by my fingers (from whom I learn a great deal) that Bach was always a volcano and he erupted in this work.

Times changed, and the Quality, the arbiters of elegance, began to decree a new way of life. They moved a little nearer to what was heartfelt and touching, affecting the most refined sensibilities. Learning was less in demand: wit was more so. The houses, the furniture, the clothes, the Dresden shepherdesses, the gardens had a new, perhaps more feminine quality, to which the name rococo has been attached.

The time was ripe for the piano—and for a new kind of orchestra—and a problem of form confronted the composers. Unless we understand this we shall be like that teacher who, in my student days, said, 'Well, now, after Bach and Handel, Haydn and Mozart came along.' No doubt they did. But if their music took a certain direction there must have been some influence to account for this. The question they had to ask themselves was: how can a composer make music go on long enough to constitute a 'movement'?

At first this seems a ridiculous question. Plenty of music was already in existence that took hours to perform. But most of that large-scale music was not totally self-sufficient. Church music had prayer and ritual; opera had narrative and acting; ballroom manœuvres compelled music to behave in certain well-understood ways. Of course there was such purely instru-

mental music as the Concerti Grossi of Handel or the Brandenburg Concertos of Bach (though the Elector of Brandenburg
took no notice of the pieces sent to him); and there were the
many fugues in which composers could 'get weaving' and continue for a long time if they had sufficient industry and skill.
But none of these was quite what was wanted for the new kind
of orchestra or that fascinating instrument the fortepiano. In
this new era the violins of the orchestra were dominant, since
wind instruments were very imperfect. The pianist's right hand
was occupied with expressive line, not a complex of lines but
something almost operatic. Melody with accompaniment was in
demand, and the question of Form occupied many great minds.

Melody all too easily tends to come to an end—as any folk
tune or popular song will testify. This arises from the very
nature of the major and minor scales from which so much
material was derived. A scale runs up seven notes and is then
drawn by a powerful musical magnetism towards the eighth
note. Seven-to-eight is curiously difficult to dodge, and a couple
of simple chords, one containing the seventh and the other the
tonic, very easily suggest that a tune has reached its cadence and
that there is no need to go further.

What to do? Modulation to a new key is part of the answer.
To start with one sharp and to proceed with two was a method
of declaring that the music was on its way. The new orchestration and the new 'chiaroscuro' (Dr. Burney's word) of the
piano allowed each successive idea or melody to have its own
tone of voice, almost as though some new character had arrived.
Then there was 'development', something different from a
succession of variations on a theme but showing the composer's
first ideas in a multitude of fresh guises. Repetition played a
part too—sometimes exact repetition, sometimes recapitulation
of a sort that altered the earlier modulations and adjusted
certain shapes to make sure that the movement ended in the
key of the beginning.

Nor was one movement enough. Why not a succession of
movements that, in some mysterious way, would not be a
succession of different pieces but would add up to one work?

Several remarkable men marched into this era with a sure step, acting with a kind of unspoken agreement about general direction, as artists do, seemingly under the direction of the Spirit of the Age, when a new era dawns. There was Johann Wenzel Stamitz, from a Czech family (who would have spelt his name Jan Vaclav Stamic). Encouraged by the court of Mannheim he created the best orchestra in Europe, attracted composers who are still referred to as the Mannheim School, and has as much claim as anyone to be regarded as the father of the symphony.

As for piano music, we may say that Bach's sons were the fathers of the sonata (though multiple paternity is, I believe, biologically impossible). C. P. E. and J. C. were more influential than their eldest brother. When Mozart as a little boy went to England he met Johann Christian, who had settled in London, and was deeply influenced by the man and his music.

The music of the lesser Bachs is seldom played today, if only because the music of Haydn and Mozart overshadows theirs. But anyone opening a volume of music at random and chancing upon one of their pieces might begin to wonder if he had found some Haydn, even if further examination would raise doubts.

A word also must be spared for a rather obscure composer named Domenico Alberti (1710–40). He is said to have invented the 'Alberti bass' that figures in countless early piano pieces. Perhaps . . .

Ex. 1

The Alberti bass was adopted with astonishing enthusiasm. It provided a murmur of accompaniment. Whereas a chord might die out too soon, a broken chord, over and over again, would not only maintain a harmony but would also supply a kind of 'onwardness', a motor of energy to keep things going. At the risk of offending the many musicians who cannot bear a word of criticism about Mozart, I confess to being surprised by his lazy acceptance of this device. He covered page after page with it. But then it was part of his genius to compose music that seems uninventive, unoriginal, altogether too simple, yet miraculous.

The piano and its music marched forward triumphantly. Never mind Voltaire and his contemptuous reference to the 'boiler maker's instrument'. We have the more informed testimony of Dr. Burney, from whom I must quote a few more sentences. In his *History of Music* he writes:

> There is no instrument so favourable to such frothy and unmeaning music than the harpsichord. . . . I remember well in the early part of my life being a dupe to this kind of tinsel, this *poussière dans les yeux*. . . . At length, on the arrival of the late Mr. Bach and construction of pianofortes in this country, the performers on keyed instruments were obliged wholly to change their ground; and instead of surprising by the seeming labour and dexterity of execution, had the real and more useful difficulties of taste, expression, and light and shade to encounter.

It must have been a strange experience for a musician to discard a harpsichord and buy a pianoforte at a time when, inevitably, there were no piano teachers. How does one play softly with a clumsy, strong thumb or vigorously with the much weaker fourth and fifth fingers? Accustomed to varieties of registration, how does one balance melody against accompaniment by touch alone? In scale playing is it possible, as on a harpsichord, to put one finger over another, or shall one train one's thumb to pass underneath?

We know very little of the sort of fingering taught by father Bach but there is a fragment that is believed to be authentic, and very strange it looks to the pianist of today:

Ex. 2

Did Bach's sons finger like that? What a pity it is that there are no memoirs by people less famous than the Bachs and Burney to tell us what life was like for the customers of the first piano-makers.

If there were no piano teachers there were probably no piano tuners. Harpsichordists had been in the habit of tuning their own instruments but not all of them had adopted the system of 'equal temperament' favoured by Bach—a system necessary to anyone who might wish to play the *Forty-eight*. Even those who agreed with Bach may have found the system difficult to use, and we still find it hard to understand.

The fact is that there is a flaw in nature's tuning. Nature's fifths are a little 'out' with nature's octaves. Let us imagine the piano owner setting out to do his own tuning. He would probably begin with octaves. In terms of a modern keyboard he might start with the lowest A and go on from A to A until he reaches the highest. With every jump of an octave the vibrations will be twice as many per second as before. So if the lowest A has x vibrations per second, the subsequent As will have $2x$, $4x$, $8x$, $16x$, $32x$, $64x$ and finally $128x$.

After octaves, the easiest interval to tune is a fifth, as every violinist lets us hear when he tunes up. A pianist, tuning in fifths, will follow a route that goes A, E, B, F sharp, C sharp (D flat), A flat, E flat, B flat, F, C, G, D, A. With every jump, the vibrations will become not twice as many, as in the case of octaves, but one-and-a-half times. Unfortunately $1\frac{1}{2}$ multiplied by $1\frac{1}{2}$ again and again does not arrive at 128. It amounts to slightly more, so that the top A arrived at by this route would be sharp.

The obvious remedy is to cheat a little and make every fifth very, very slightly flat, thereby getting rid of 'the comma of Pythagoras' (the ancient Greek knew the arithmetic of acoustics); but what about all the other intervals?

Tuning by ear not only gave two different readings for top A (or would have done if the early keyboards had reached that far), it made a distinction between, say, A flat and G sharp—a very awkward distinction on a keyboard. Many solutions were proposed, but the one that triumphed was to take an octave and, within it, to tune twelve exactly equal semitones. The result is that there is no distinction between D flat and C sharp, etc., and all scales are equally (and to most ears imperceptibly) out of tune. Credit for this is generally given to Andreas Werckmeister (1691) and J. J. Neidhardt (1706). But it was Bach who settled all arguments by composing a set of preludes and fugues in every possible key (twelve major, twelve minor). This was *The Well-tempered (Wohltemperierte) Clavier*, that was later companioned by another twenty-four to make up the *Forty-eight*. Performance demanded equal temperament and equal temperament won the day.

And that is why we send for the tuner to tune our pianos out of tune.

6. *The Piano Meets Mozart*

Only one man is known to fame as both philosopher and composer, and that is Jean-Jacques Rousseau. The intelligentsia of his era were bowled over by his ideas on the nature of man and quite a number of opera houses produced his *Le Devin du Village* (The Village Soothsayer). Who, then, was better qualified to write a *Lettre sur la Musique Française*? Radical as ever, he denounced polyphony. Fugues for him had no merit 'save that of difficulty overcome'. They were a kind of clever nonsense 'that the ear cannot endure and the reason cannot justify . . . the remains of barbarism and bad taste that only persist, like the portals of our Gothic churches, to the shame of those who had the patience to construct them'.

Rousseau's ideas about education range from the profound to the ridiculous. In his book *Émile* he draws a portrait of Sophie, his vision of a well-brought-up girl. Sophie

> has contented herself with using her pretty voice to sing in tune and with taste, her feet to walk lightly, easily, gracefully . . . she has had no singing master save her father, no dancing mistress save her mother; a local organist has given her a few lessons in accompanying. . . . Gradually she became aware of harmony; finally, in growing up, she began to feel the charms of expression and to love music for itself. But it is a taste rather than a talent; she is completely unable to read music.

Sophie (wisdom) seems a strange name for so silly a child,

37

but Rousseau believed that wisdom and virtue are natural, though easily corrupted, and his enthusiastic readers accepted his notions. And, let us admit, we still do to some extent. Every piano dealer knows, when parents come into the shop to buy a small upright, that it will probably be played by a little girl who will be taught by a woman. Sons can learn if they want to, daughters should learn anyway, and 'playing for one's own amusement' is the object of the enterprise.

Let us also admit that the dealer's customers may be right in thinking that a piano in the home is a home-maker. As for Rousseau's Sophie and the thousands of Sophies who came afterwards, they were both loved and despised by manly husbands who looked upon piano-playing as suitable only for women and foreigners.

When Sophie was created Mozart was six. He had an elder sister, Nannerl, who was very talented and who had a serious musical education from her father. It was the boy, however, who became the great composer. Whether Nannerl could have developed further than she did is an open question, but until our own day and age it remained true, as we have already observed, that girls played music composed by men for an instrument designed by men to suit a man's hand.

Before we go on to think of Mozart as a great composer for the piano we must consider how the art of piano-making was getting on while he was growing up. And when we do come to the compositions we must consider how music composed for his piano for his audiences can be interpreted on pianos ten times as large in the presence of audiences ten times as numerous.

There is a legend that a piano had been built in Rome as early as 1711 by an English monk named Father Wood. In 1752, four years before Mozart was born, it was brought to England by the author Samuel Crisp who sold it for the then considerable sum of one hundred guineas to Fulke Greville. An attempt was made to copy it without success. One suspects that Father Wood was one of those ideas men who invent machines that never quite work properly.

However, pianos were, more and more, becoming objects of interest. One year before Mozart's birth the Rev. Dr. William

Mason bought a piano in Germany and wrote to the author of 'Elegy in a Country Churchyard': 'Oh, Mr. Gray! I bought at Hamburg such a pianoforte and so cheap.' Why *such* a pianoforte? Mason asserts that it was both pianoforte and harpsichord combined 'by the cleverest mechanism imaginable'. Wishing to make room for this prodigy of instruments Mason went on: 'Won't you buy my Kirkman?'

We shall hear more of Kirkman but meanwhile we may observe that pianos attracted many inventors. A sort of upright piano had been built as far back as the 1730s by Christian Ernst Friederici. It was wing-shaped like a *Flügel*, but the soundboard and strings were no longer horizontal. They were placed vertically, against the wall of a room, from keyboard level to somewhere near the ceiling. It did not occur to him, as it did to a later inventor, that the strings of an upright might start from somewhere near the floor. His piano was before its time. In the later 1700s the rival shapes were 'square' (oblong in fact) and wing-shaped. (*See Plates 2 and 3.*)

London was a great centre of piano-making, though the skills came from abroad. Clever Europeans fled from the Seven Years War, they fled from poverty and strife to the Workshop of the World and a growing, prosperous market. The first arrivals began as harpsichord-makers. There was a Fleming named Tabel whom we remember because two of his apprentices helped to found the piano trade.

There was Jacob Kirchmann, later Kirckmann and then Kirkman; and there was Burkhardt Tschudi, later Shudi. Kirkman was decidedly a smart operator. When Tabel died Kirkman proposed to the widow one morning and married her before noon on the same day. This showed considerable enterprise, but later on he was rather slow to realize that the harpsichord would have to be abandoned in favour of the piano. However, he fought a gallant rearguard action. As an advertising gimmick he gave harpsichords to girls willing to play them in the streets of London. On another occasion, finding that a craze for guitar-playing had swept through the drawing-rooms of his prospective customers, he gave a number of cheap guitars to the girls in millinery shops and thereby made the instrument vulgar. Unfortunately for him, the genteel ladies in returning to the keyboard began to think of the pianoforte rather than the harpsichord.

When he died childless his nephew Abraham and Abraham's son Joseph went over to piano-making, and Kirkman pianos were regarded with considerable respect until 1896 when the firm was taken over by Collard & Collard and the Kirkman name gradually died out.

The young Swiss who had been an apprentice alongside Kirkman in Tabel's workshop set up business on his own account with some considerable success. Like his previous master he had two remarkable apprentices. One was a Scots cabinet-maker named John Broadwood who, after working for eight years, married Shudi's daughter. The girl's father and husband went into partnership, and later generations of musicians, including Beethoven, thought very highly of Broadwood pianos.

The other Shudi apprentice was Johannes Zumpe. When he went into business he marketed a small, simple, square piano. This was so successful, not only in England but also in France, that he was unable to cope with all the orders that came his way, and a London German named Pohlmann supplied the customers who were not prepared to wait. Zumpe's piano was not of the highest class, but at £50 it was cheaper than a two-manual harpsichord which might cost as much as 85 guineas. The Zumpe action had what one authority describes as an artless escapement. For lack of a 'check' the hammer, after bouncing off the string, was liable to bounce on the bed, and this led to 'blocking' if a pianist wanted to play one note again and again at high speed. Nevertheless it was regarded as a good, reliable little piano. For a good many years the English action was established as stronger, though heavier, than the Viennese action.

If the piano attracted German makers it also attracted German musicians. Mention has already been made of the Schroeter whose piano-playing persuaded Dr. Burney to give up the harpsichord. Described as 'fascinating' and 'fawning' he married into a family who, regarding professional musicians as 'low', settled a good income on him on condition that he gave up piano-playing. Many years would pass before this attitude changed. Not until the reign of Queen Victoria would London society become accustomed to knighted musicians.

Much more important than Schroeter was the youngest of the Bachs, Johann Christian. He arrived in 1762 via Italy where (Johann Sebastian must have turned in his grave) he became a Catholic. Determined not to follow in his father's footsteps he composed Italian operas for the English nobility, gave music lessons to George III's Queen Charlotte, organized high-priced concerts in collaboration with a gamba player named Carl Friedrich Abel, and in 1768 played the piano in public, after which his compositions were published as suitable for harpsichord or piano. Before this he had met and influenced the boy Mozart.

The boy Mozart (born in Salzburg in 1756) was a great composer by the time he was six. Great? I would say yes, though biographers and musicologists just glance at the Minuet in F, exclaim with delight, and then hurry on to analyse the mature works. I do more than glance at this little piece. I also hover over a rondo composed when he was eight. Any music-lover who cannot read music—and there are plenty such in this age of recording—should persuade a piano-playing friend to play these pieces of music. The minuet is given here in full together with a fragment of the rondo and a remarkably similar phrase from the great C minor Concerto, K.491 (*see page* 42).

First the minuet. The first eight bars consist of a charming melody in the treble and a well-drawn line of notes in the bass. In the seventh bar there is a triplet. This may sound unremarkable to a listener, but anyone who has tried to teach that triplet to a child knows that it is not child's play. Then, after the double bar, the composer introduces an F sharp and an E flat. To be technical he has modulated into G minor by means of a diminished seventh chord.

The child's awareness of this chord is not in itself extraordinary. Other clever little boys (me too) have found a terrifying chord and have played it all over the piano to give themselves the same sort of shiver as comes from reading about wicked ogres in fairy tales. And other composers, on growing up, have used the diminished seventh (perhaps played by strings *tremolando*) to accompany the entry of the villain, cries of despair and revenge, and scenes of black magic.

Not young Mozart. The minuet continues, the melodic

41

Ex. 3

Minuet

Rondo by the child Mozart

Concerto in C minor K.491. (orchestra)

The Rondo transposed into the same key as the concerto

shapes are only slightly different from the ones that went before. But we have felt a momentary pang of anguish—without interrupting the graceful and courtly steps of the dance. A barely perceptible earth tremor has made the candles flicker, but the grand duchess's charming smile is undisturbed.

Did little Wolfgang never burst into tears? Or did he transform his moments of anguish into music, concealing them so cleverly that only a sensitive touch on a good piano could discover them?

Am I reading too much into innocent music? Turn to the Rondo in F, written when the boy was eight. I quote the middle section in the minor key and compare it with phrases from an acclaimed masterpiece.

The child is father to the man.

Claiming so much for Mozart I may seem to diminish his great friend and rival Haydn. Let no one underrate Haydn. There are neglected treasures in his sonatas. But Mozart very specially attracts the pianist's hand, partly because of the concertos, and partly because he is at times an opera composer conjuring the soprano voice from what seems to be a very unpromising box of hammers.

When he came to England under the control of his domineering father he met many musicians. The one he remembered with respect and affection was Johann Christian Bach. For him J. C. Bach was the 'divine' Bach. He had not yet heard of J. S.

He must have had less respect for the public. The fashionable public flocked to the great Rotunda at the Ranelagh pleasure gardens and paid half a guinea to see the prodigy. When they lost interest a less fashionable public went to the Swan and Hoop Tavern in Cornhill and paid half a crown. Wolfgang and his sister must have been disappointed children.

During his childhood the boy began to see the world as it was. He began to distinguish between the people who really understood music and the others who condescendingly viewed a travelling curiosity through their quizzing glasses. He became a hardened professional—hardened in the sense of having passed through several furnaces. By the time he was twelve he had been petted by the Empress of Austria and the Queen of France, had had two dangerous illnesses (scarlet fever and smallpox), had earned no money in some cities and a great deal in others, and had been warned by his embittered father (who failed to gain promotion beyond vice-capellmeister status) that all men are villains. He acquired a core of steel that enabled him to survive many vicissitudes and prevented him from becoming a purveyor of facile and fashionable entertainments.

The Mozart story has been told and retold a thousand times and we need not retrace his journeys in many different countries or shake our fists at the Archbishop of Salzburg and various other powerful people. What concerns us here is Mozart and the piano. In 1777, when he was twenty-one, he wrote to his father about his favourite make:

This time I shall begin at once with Stein's pianofortes. Before I had seen any of his make, Späth's claviers had always been my favourites. But now I much prefer Stein's, for they damp ever so much better than the Regensburg instruments. When I strike hard I can keep my finger on the note or raise it, but the sound ceases the moment I have produced it. In whatever way I touch the keys the tone is always even. It never jars, it is never stronger or weaker or entirely absent; in a word it is always even. It is true that he does not sell a pianoforte for less than three hundred gulden, but the trouble and the labour that Stein puts into the making of it cannot be paid for. His instruments have this splendid advantage over others, that they are made with escape action. Only one maker in a hundred bothers about this. But without an escapement it is impossible to avoid jangling and vibration after the note is struck. When you touch the keys, the hammers fall back again the moment after they have struck the strings, whether you hold down the keys or release them. . . . He often says: 'If I were not myself such a passionate lover of music and had not myself some slight skill on the clavier, I should certainly long ago have lost patience with my work. . . .' He guarantees that the sounding-board will neither break nor split. When he has finished making one for a clavier, he places it in the open air, exposing it to rain, snow, the heat of the sun and all the devils in order that it may crack. Then he inserts wedges and glues them to make the instrument very strong and firm. He is delighted when it cracks, for he can then be sure that nothing more can happen to it. Indeed he often cuts into it himself and then glues it together again and strengthens it in this way. . . . The device too which you work with your knee is better on his than on other instruments. I have only to touch it and it works; and when you shift your knee the slightest bit you do not hear the least reverberation.

Some of this letter is confusing. When Mozart says 'the sound ceases the moment I have produced it' we must assume that the sound ceased the moment he wanted it to. The 'device which you work with your knee' controlled the dampers. Foot-pedals were yet to make their appearance, but we may assume that a modern pianist is not forbidden to use the sustaining pedal in a performance of Mozart, though all the best opinion is in favour of very discreet pedalling. The letter continues further and surprisingly.

> . . . When I told Herr Stein that I should very much like to play on his organ, as that instrument was my passion, he was greatly surprised and said: 'What? A man like you, so fine a clavier-player, wants to play on an instrument which has no douceur, no expression, no piano, no forte, but is always the same?' 'That does not matter,' I replied. 'In my eyes and ears the organ is the king of instruments.'
> 'Well,' he said, 'as you like.' So off we went together. I noticed at once from what he said that he thought I would not do much on his organ; that I would play, for instance, in a thoroughly pianistic style. . . . All I said to Stein was: 'Well, Herr Stein, do you think I am going to canter about on your organ?' 'Ah, you,' he replied, 'that is quite another matter.' We reached the choir and I began to improvise, when he started to laugh: then I played a fugue. 'I can well believe,' he said, 'that you like to play the organ, when you play so well.'

Mozart cannot have been serious about the organ being the king of instruments. He composed very little for it. He was probably teasing Stein in order to astonish him. In passing, we may note that the syllable Stein accompanies the history of the piano. Think of Steinway and Bechstein.

Stein's daughter was a pupil of Mozart's. Never inclined to gloss over faults he wrote about her in a way that tells us a good deal about his pianistic ideals:

> But the best joke of all is that when she comes to a passage which ought to flow like oil and which necessitates a change of finger, she does not bother her head about it, but when the moment arrives, she just leaves out the notes, raises her hand and starts off again quite comfortably. . . . Herr Stein is quite crazy about his daughter, who is eight-and-a-half and who now learns everything by heart. She may succeed, for she has great talent for music. But she will not make progress by this method—for she will never acquire great rapidity, since she definitely does all she can to make her hands heavy. Further, she will never acquire the most essential, the most difficult and the chief requisite in music, which is time, because from her earliest years she has done her utmost not to play in time. Herr Stein and I discussed this point for two

45

hours at least and I have almost converted him, for he now asks my advice on everything. He used to be quite crazy about Beecke; but now he sees and hears that I am the better player, that I do not make grimaces, and yet play with such expression that, as he himself confesses, no one up to the present has been able to get such good results out of his pianofortes. Everyone is amazed that I can always keep strict time. What these people cannot grasp is that in tempo rubato, as in an Adagio, the left hand should go on playing in strict time. . . .

I have told her mother and I have told her, too, that if I were her regular teacher, I would lock up all her music, cover the keys with a handkerchief and make her practise, first with the right hand and then with the left, nothing but passages, trills, mordents and so forth, very slowly at first, until each hand should be thoroughly trained. I would then undertake to turn her into a first-rate keyboard player.

. . . Besides it is much easier to play a thing quickly than slowly: in difficult passages you can leave out a few notes without anyone noticing it. But is that beautiful music? . . . And wherein consists the art of playing prima vista? In this; in playing the piece in the time in which it ought to be played and in playing all the notes, appoggiaturas and so forth, exactly as they are written and with the appropriate expression and taste, so that you might suppose that the performer had composed it himself.

Every pianist and teacher must respond to this, and most of Mozart's advice is still observed. Practise with each hand separately, don't rush through a passage helter-skelter, play true time values even at sight, don't pull faces, and make the piece sound as though you yourself had written it. Yes: but what is this about 'tempo rubato'? First, it is pleasant to be assured that *rubato* did not begin with Chopin, as most people believe. But what are we to make of: 'in tempo rubato, as in an Adagio, the left hand should go on playing in strict time'?

When I first read this passage I felt sure that Mozart, like many another teacher, was expressing himself without true precision. Can one really imagine a melody that is sometimes ahead of the bass and sometimes behind it? Can one imagine an opera-house orchestra carrying on in strict time no matter what the tenor may do in the way of flexible rhythm? I was still more puzzled when I discovered that Chopin later said something on the same lines. Could it be that what they really meant is what I (and not only I) tell students: 'In a *rubato* never lose the beat, never let the listener mistake a quarter-beat for a half-beat, so that if anyone in the audience wanted to scribble the melody on paper he would not be in doubt about the note-values.'

I talked myself into believing that this was what Mozart really meant. Just as music must be interpreted, so must words. One need not understand them literally.

However, I happened to acquire an early edition of *Observations on the Florid Song; or, Sentiments on the Ancient and Modern Singers, Written in Italian by Pier Francesco Tosi, of the Phil-Harmonic Academy at Bologna. Translated into English by Mr. Galliard. Useful for all Performers, Instrumental as well as Vocal. Printed for J. Wilcox, at Virgil's Head, in the Strand. 1743.* It is addressed to 'Lovers of Musick and Perfons of Eminence, Rank, Quality, and a diftinguifhing . . .' (or so it seems until one becomes accustomed to the s's that look like f's).

Tosi has a great many interesting things to say about the decline of singing, the prevalence of poor taste, and the failure to understand that there are three kinds of ornamentation, one for the theatre (the most elaborate), one for the drawing-room (a little less so) and one for the church (the most restrained). On singing slow music he anticipates and supports Mozart. He says, 'Whoever does not know how to steal the Time in Singing, knows not how to Compose, nor to Accompany himself, and is destitute of the best Taste and greatest Knowledge. The stealing of Time, in the *Pathetick*, is an honourable Theft in one that sings better than others, provided he makes a Restitution with Ingenuity

To this there is a footnote, apparently by the translator: 'Our Author has often mentioned Time; the Regard to it, the Strictness of it, and how much it is neglected and unobserved. In this Place speaking of stealing the Time, it regards particularly the Vocal, or the performance on a single Instrument of the *Pathetick* or *Tender*; when the Bass goes an exactly regular Pace, the other Part retards or anticipates in a singular Manner, for the Sake of Expression, but after That returns to its Exactness, to be guided by the Bass. Experience and Taste must teach it.'

47

There seems no escaping the fact that, in certain circumstances, a melody could retard or anticipate in a singular manner, while the bass maintained an exactly regular pace. I doubt if I shall ever dare to play in public like this. Every member of an audience, every critic, every radio producer would accuse me of playing messily. But after some experimentation I have attempted to notate this sort of rubato. It can be seen in Example 4. Did Tosi's pupils and Mozart's opera stars sing like Bing Crosby?

Ex. 4

Mozart : Sonata in C - rubato

If, in the face of all this evidence, anyone should still believe that the music of Mozart's time should be played with strictness and austerity, we can bring one more authority into the witness box. This is C. P. E. Bach who, in 1753, published his *Essay on the True Art of Playing Keyboard Instruments*.* Like all teachers he can seem to contradict himself at times but he is in no doubt about tempo rubato. 'When the execution is such that one hand seems to play against the bar and the other strictly with it, it may be said that the performer is doing everything that can be required of him.' Then, a few sentences later, he tells us 'as soon as the upper part begins slavishly to follow the bar, the essence of rubato is lost, for then all other parts must be played in time.'

He is constantly in search of *affekt*. He assures us that 'purposeful violations of the beat are often exceptionally beautiful' and, while despising ugly grimaces, believes that 'those who maintain that all of this can be accomplished without gesture will retract their words when, owing to their own insensibility, they find themselves obliged to sit like a statue before their instrument.' Add to all this the author's belief that discords

* Quotations from the translation published by Ernst Eulenburg, London, 1974.

should be played more loudly than concords and we may well wonder about present-day notions of interpretation.

If a Wellsian Time Machine were available and we could go back to the eighteenth century to hear Mozart playing an adagio on a Stein, we might scuttle back to the twentieth century with relief, but I would certainly attempt the journey.

Mozart's letters show that he was very self-satisfied about his own performances and scornful about anyone else's. But throughout his childhood and beyond he had excited wonder wherever he went. Nobody knows for certain just where or when he abandoned the harpsichord or how he found the time to practise amidst all the travelling and composing, but in that era, when the piano was new and the later developments of pianism were still unthought of, his prowess at the keyboard seemed unchallengeable. When he was ten, after the first long tour, and the family was for a while settled in Salzburg, his father took him through Fux's *Gradus ad Parnassum*. Maybe that was the time when serious work was done on the piano, but genius children have their own mysterious ways of learning, and we must accept that, somehow or other, he became a master.

Leopold Mozart's employer, the Archbishop of Salzburg, must have been remarkably tolerant. Soon the Mozarts were off again. At twelve the boy was in Vienna, at fourteen travelling far and wide in Italy (acquiring the Order of the Golden Spur from the Pope *en route*). After a short return to Salzburg, off again . . . and so on.

Alas, the accommodating Archbishop died. His successor, Hieronymus, Count von Colleredo, is often depicted as an unreasonable tyrant, but for the first ten years of his reign he saw precious little of the young genius. He insisted that if the boy was to go on travelling his mother should accompany him while Leopold remained to fulfil his duties in the court orchestra. The Archbishop was undoubtedly disagreeable—he said afterwards that he could not bear people going about begging in that fashion—but he was not totally unreasonable. As for going about begging, free-lance artists have been doing that ever since—in the grandest way, of course.

Munich, Augsburg, Mannheim. In the last of these cities he

heard the greatest orchestra in Europe and became aware of
the clarinet. In Paris his mother died. He was twenty-two.
J. C. Bach, in Paris at that time, was, as ever, kind to him.
However, it was time to go home—not in a hurry but by way
of Strasbourg, Munich and Mannheim.

He was by now a very famous composer and performer. Life
in Salzburg was irksome, he was too near the father who until
then had controlled his every movement and thought, and the
Archbishop was not only unhelpful but abusive. To the Archbishop, Mozart was a member of the household who, of course,
would dine with the servants. To the Countess Thun in Vienna,
Mozart was a great artist whom one invited to dinner.

It was the Archbishop's visit to Vienna in 1781 that brought
matters to a head. To the Archbishop the musician was a man
who could be displayed to one's friends in public and sworn at
in private. The Archbishop was not the first or last nobleman
who would expect a member of his household to remember his
place and not answer back. Mozart, who could also be rather
grand and, on his own admission, refused to associate with a
good many people in Salzburg, was in a state of unendurable
frustration when the household returned to Salzburg. He had
written to his father about the man he sometimes called Arch-
booby: 'I shall certainly hoodwink the Archbishop, and how I
shall enjoy doing it!' It came to an interview, the Archbishop
swore at his court organist, and the Court Chamberlain, Count
Arco, kicked Mozart out of the door. Whether Mozart was
quite literally booted is a question that need not bother us.
What does concern us, as students of pianos and pianists, is the
advice that Count Arco gave to the young musician:

> Believe me, you allow yourself to be too easily dazzled in
> Vienna. A man's reputation here lasts a very short time. At first,
> it is true, you are overwhelmed with praise and make a great deal
> of money into the bargain—but how long does that last? After a
> few months the Viennese want something new.

This advice was given in Vienna shortly before the last interview in Salzburg and the words are from one of Mozart's own
letters. Having quoted Arco, Mozart goes on, in the same
letter:

It is perfectly true that the Viennese are apt to change their affections, but only in the theatre, and my special line is too popular not to enable me to support myself. Vienna is certainly the land of the clavier! And even granted that they do get tired of me, they will certainly not do so for a few years, certainly not before then. In the meantime, I shall have gained both honour and money. There are many other places; and who can tell what opportunities may not occur before then?

It is interesting that Mozart does not dismiss Arco's advice with contempt. The subsequent sentences are far from cocky. The young artist was not a green beginner: he had seen the world. He had, however, burned his boats, and he was off to the land of the clavier.

Where he was to meet Clementi.

7. Mozart Meets Clementi

Many rich Englishmen in the eighteenth century went on the Grand Tour. The young ones went to improve their minds and manners. The older ones went shopping. They bought pictures, they engaged craftsmen to decorate stately homes, they sought the best voices for the opera in London.

In 1767 one Peter Beckford, nephew of a Lord Mayor of London, owner of sugar plantations in Jamaica and extremely rich, was in Rome. There he heard of a prodigy, fourteen or fifteen years old, named Muzio Clementi. Beckford was impressed, went to the boy's father, a silversmith, offered a sum of money, and acquired the young genius. Indeed, in after years, he spoke of 'the celebrated Clementi whom I bought from his father for seven years'. It was a strange transaction but not out of character for a slave-owner who, so they say, 'would bag a fox in Greek, find a hare in Latin, inspect his Kennels in Italian, and direct the economy of his stable in exquisite French'.

Beckford installed the boy in his fine house—Steepleton

House, Iverne, Dorset—and gave him every chance to study and mature. One must suppose that there were visits to London, since Iverne was not a centre of learning or culture, but Muzio Clementi was under the control of his patron until the age of eighteen. Beckford,* who in the meantime had become a member of Parliament, used his influence and wealth to launch his young genius in 1770, and from then on Clementi was a celebrity.

At the age of twenty-one Clementi published a set of sonatas for harpsichord or piano. At the age of twenty-five he was cembalist at the Italian Opera in London. In those days, before baton-conducting was established, orchestras were propelled by a keyboard-player, even though no keyboard part was written in the score. Clementi kept the job for three years.

It was time to spread his wings and fly abroad. He played in Paris, Strassburg and Munich and then went on to Vienna where he made the acquaintance of Haydn. Hearing about this, the Emperor Joseph II conceived the idea of inviting Clementi to come to court and play in a kind of competition with Mozart. Why not? There were two clever young men—Mozart twenty-five, Clementi twenty-nine—and Joseph II, being an emperor, assumed that he would be fully qualified to decide the issue.

What happened is described by Mozart in a letter to his father, dated 16 January 1782, a little while after the event. He begins by refuting Leopold Mozart's accusations against the family into which Wolfgang was to marry: 'It hurts me very much to think that you could believe etc. . . .' Then:

> Now a word about Clementi. He is an excellent cembalo-player, but that is all. He has great facility with his right hand. His star passages are thirds. Apart from this, he has not a farthing's worth of taste or feeling; he is a mere *mechanicus*.
>
> After we had stood on ceremony long enough, the Emperor declared that Clementi ought to begin. '*La Santa Chiesa Cattolica*',

* Beckford's cousin William later became famous for a novel, somewhat in the manner of the *Arabian Nights*, called *Vathek*. This Beckford was even more outrageous than Clementi's patron. He was involved in a scandal about a boy, built a 'folly' called Fonthill which later fell down, and startled even such characters as Byron and Lady Hamilton. He wrote the adventures of the Caliph Vathek, in French, when he was twenty-one, completing it (so he claimed) in a single sitting of three days and two nights.

he said, Clementi being a Roman. He improvised and then played a sonata. The Emperor then turned to me: '*Allons*, fire away.' I improvised and played variations. The Grand Duchess produced some sonatas by Paisiello (wretchedly written out in his own hand), of which I had to play the Allegros and Clementi the Andantes and Rondos. We then selected a theme from them and developed it on two pianofortes. The funny thing was that although I had borrowed Countess Thun's pianoforte, I only played on it when I played alone, such was the Emperor's desire—and, by the way, the other instrument was out of tune and three of the keys were stuck. 'That doesn't matter,' said the Emperor. Well, I put the best construction on it I could, that is that the Emperor, already knowing my skill and my knowledge of music, was only desirous of showing especial courtesy to a foreigner. Besides, I have it from a very good source that he was extremely pleased with me.

Two years later, still hating Italians in general and Clementi in particular, Mozart writes to his father:

Well, I have a few words to say to my sister about Clementi's sonatas. Everyone who either hears them or plays them must feel that as compositions they are worthless. They contain no remarkable or striking passages except those in sixths and octaves. And I implore my sister not to practise these passages too much, so that she may not spoil her quiet, even touch and that her hand may not lose its natural lightness, flexibility and smooth rapidity. Supposing that you do play sixths and octaves with the utmost velocity (which no one can accomplish, not even Clementi) you only produce an atrocious chopping effect and nothing else whatever. Clementi is a *ciarlatano*, like all Italians. He writes *Presto* over a sonata or even *Prestissimo* and *Alla breve*, and plays it himself *Allegro* in 4/4 time. I know this is the case, for I have heard him do so. What he really does well are his passages in thirds, but he sweated over them day and night in London. Apart from this, he can do nothing, absolutely nothing, for he has not the slightest expression or taste, still less, feeling. . . .

Without anticipating the later history of Clementi we may reflect that playing sixths and octaves with the utmost rapidity after sweating day and night was to be the pattern of the future. As for the worthlessness of the sonatas, Beethoven bought a number of them for his surprisingly small library.

53

Clementi was much less self-satisfied than Mozart. Fifteen years after the contest he talked to a pupil named Ludwig Berger (afterwards one of Mendelssohn's teachers) who asked if in the days of the contest he had treated the piano in his present style. Clementi answered no, and said that he had formerly cultivated a brilliant execution, especially in double notes, hardly known then, but had later achieved a more melodic and noble style after listening to famous singers and taking advantage of improvements in English pianos.

He seems to have made no bitchy remarks about Mozart. The nearest he came to it was a sentence printed in the first edition of the sonata that he composed specially for the contest: 'Cette sonate, avec la toccata qui la suit, a été jouée par l'auteur devant Sa Majesté Joseph II en 1781, Mozart étant présent' (This sonata, with the toccata that follows it, was played by the composer before His Majesty Joseph II in 1781, Mozart being present). In this way he laid prior claim to a theme that Mozart afterwards appropriated for the *Magic Flute* overture. It is, however, only fair to Mozart to say that he used the theme unaccompanied as the start of a fugato, making such a delightful and original effect as to make the charge of plagiarism stupid. The two versions are given here (Example 5).

One need not doubt that Mozart was by far the greater composer, but Clementi must not be underrated. He was destined to have a profound and far-reaching influence on pianos and piano-playing and no small influence on the art of composition.

Few people influenced Mozart once he had reached maturity. The great Bach is an exception. A year after the famous contest Mozart wrote to his sister. He had written a fugue for her.

> . . . The reason why I did not reply to your letter at once was that on account of the wearisome labour of writing these small notes, I could not finish the composition any sooner. And, even so, it is awkwardly done, for the prelude ought to come first and the fugue to follow. But I composed the fugue first and wrote it down while I was thinking of the prelude. I only hope you will be able to read it, for it is written very small; and I hope further that you will like it. Another time I shall send you something better for the

Ex. 5 (a and b)

(a) Clementi : Sonata in B flat

(b) Mozart : Magic Flute Overture

clavier. My dear Constanze is really the cause of this fugue's coming into the world. Baron van Swieten, to whom I go every Sunday, gave me all the works of Handel and Sebastian Bach to take home with me (after I had played them to him). When Constanze heard the fugues, she absolutely fell in love with them. Now she will listen to nothing but fugues, and particularly (in this kind of composition) the works of Handel and Bach. Well, as she had often heard me play fugues out of my head, she asked me if I had ever written any down, and when I said I had not, she scolded me roundly for not recording some of my compositions in this most artistic and beautiful of musical forms and never ceased to entreat me until I wrote down a fugue for her. So this is its origin. I have purposely written above it *Andante maestoso*, as it must not be played too fast. For if a fugue is not played slowly, the ear cannot distinguish the theme when it comes in and consequently the effect is entirely missed. . . .

This letter is extraordinarily revealing. To think that Mozart was largely ignorant of Handel and Bach until he was twenty-six—even though he could play fugues out of his head! To think that he could compose a fugue for his sister and, while writing it down (was it already complete in his head?), start to think of the prelude! To think that he wished 'to distinguish the theme when it comes in'—a technique frowned on by some present-day pundits!

The Baron van Swieten was himself a recent convert to the music of Bach. He had had an audience with King Frederick the Great and wrote about it to Count Kaunitz:

> He spoke to me among other things of music, and of a great organist named Bach, who lived for a while in Berlin. This artist is endowed with a talent superior, in depth of harmonic knowledge and power of execution, to any I have heard or can imagine, while those who knew his father claim that he, in turn, was even greater. The King is of this opinion, and to prove it to me, he sang aloud a chromatic fugue-subject which he had given this old Bach, who on the spot had made of it a fugue in four parts, then in five parts, and finally in eight parts.

The Berlin Bach was, of course, Carl Philipp Emanuel, who had been on the King's staff, but the King had no doubt that the composer of the *Musical Offering* was the greatest of all the Bachs.

Mozart's response to the music was to arrange some of the fugues for string trio or quartet. Such an arrangement can be startlingly attractive, rather like seeing a long-admired building floodlit for the first time. This is not to say that buildings should always be seen floodlit, but to make the point that there are still hidden beauties in Bach's music waiting to be revealed.

It cannot be said that Bach 'shows up' much in Mozart's piano music. What one *is* tempted to say is that Beethoven does. Chronologically this is absurd, but when Beethoven was fourteen or fifteen and living in Bonn, Mozart in Vienna composed a Sonata in C minor (K.457) that has a decidedly Beethovenian flavour. He went on to compose a Fantasie in C (K.475) in the same vein. The Fantasie, the later of the two works, is often played as an introduction to the sonata and serves very effectively in this role.

Since Beethoven cannot literally have influenced Mozart one could argue that these works, and only these, influenced Beethoven. Maybe; but this was a moment in history when the Spirit of the Age was particularly active. Trite though the phrase has become, it is true that 'coming events cast their shadow before'.

Mozart, as he grew older, was the prey of many conflicting feelings. He was a Catholic who, against the teaching of his Church, became a Freemason. As a Mason he could be 'brother' to princes, yet he admired the character of Figaro, the valet who outwits his master. *The Marriage of Figaro*, based on a Beaumarchais play banned by the Vienna police, would, he hoped, please the Emperor. He was not the first, nor would he be the last, artist to be buffeted by the storms of opinion that culminate in the tornado of revolution. He could not have foreseen the French Revolution that broke out soon after the end of his short life, yet he was, in a sense, involved in it.

Some of this is apparent in his larger works—the Catholic Requiem, the Masonic *Magic Flute*, the radical *Figaro*—but in the piano music, in the absence of words, these things cannot be found in any specific way. No doubt the Vienna police would have been glad to find cause for complaint, but crotchets and quavers are not subversive.

Mozart is the composer most admired by other composers perhaps because of the way he achieves great effects with apparently no effort. But this very perfection (and even the pieces I would dare to call trivial have an air of perfection) can sometimes make one resistant. In the present climate of opinion one hardly dares to say that a page here and there is of no great consequence, but even the dissenter must agree about the greatness of the best works.

The music seems to yield no explanation of why the greatest composer in Europe should have been buried in a pauper's grave. He was a very famous man, but where were his friends? Where were his brother Masons, or the Baron van Swieten, or members of his own or his wife's family? Some blame his wife as feckless, some commiserate with her and say she was ill at the time. Some blame the weather. Some point out that fashionable people regarded funeral rites as ridiculously superstitious. Indeed the Emperor thought funerals a waste of time and money and even ordered that dead bodies should be put in sacks and consumed by quicklime. But the Emperor's order had to be withdrawn because of public anger, and the weather is insufficient excuse for non-attendance at a funeral, and a wife is not a man's only relative. We, who love the Mozart we hear, cannot bring ourselves to admit that the musicians of Vienna may have thoroughly disliked the Mozart they met.

Is the Mozart we hear the music that Mozart composed? And how shall we play it?

Mozart never fought against the piano he knew. The music doesn't collide with the limits of the instrument: a Mozart *sforzato* does not threaten to break strings or hammers. So we pianists must restrain ourselves. No doubt: but an audience needs something more than restraint. A concerto designed for an audience of 150 is played on a concert grand to perhaps two or three thousand people. The orchestra, even a chamber orchestra, is playing on instruments of a sonority Mozart never knew. Even the violins have steel strings and strengthened bass-bars.

How shall we deploy our modern technique and touch? We are apt to assume that Mozart was a fine pianist (*he* certainly thought so), but Beethoven remembered Mozart's piano-playing as 'a mere dance of the fingers'. And Clementi could not produce the *cantabile* he wanted until the action of English pianos had been improved. Inevitably—there is no escape from it—we listen with ears accustomed to the music of Beethoven, Brahms, Chopin and many others. So when we play a slow movement and try to make the piano imitate the sound of a great soprano singing a Mozart aria, there will be some slight element of Nocturne in the performance. And when we play other movements there must be a slight element of Beethoven. Certainly we must seek a truly Mozartian style, but if we try over-conscientiously to exclude anything that even slightly suggests Beethoven or Chopin we shall finish with a restrained, finicky, bloodless performance that will have little merit other than 'good taste'.

And what of taste in Mozart's own sense of the word? Shall

we add ornaments to taste? Shall we elaborate some of the cadences? And shall we fill in those concerto phrases in which a high melody is accompanied by a very few bass notes and no harmonies? (See Example 6.) Some authorities tell us that we

Ex. 6

from Concerto in C K.503

Variant by
Mozart's pupil
Philipp Karl
Hoffmann

Mozart's own
text

should: most pianists are satisfied to let the orchestra supply the harmonies. The fact is that any pianist who tries to fulfil the requirements of Mozartian taste, as understood by Mozart himself, is met with a certain degree of critical respect but no enthusiasm.

In the first editions of Mozart's music we find very few marks of expression. Many of us now use an 'Urtext' based on those editions and are surprised to find no mark of *forte* or *piano* at the start of a movement. A mature pianist can use his experience and judgement to decide the issue, but what is a child pianist to do, and can he rely on his teacher to know best?

Over the years, many publishers have appointed eminent professors and performers to produce 'authoritative' editions. Examination boards have indicated 'recommended' editions. Footnotes indicate how certain ornaments may be performed. Fingerings are added. How helpful! How confusing! No doubt a return to an Urtext is desirable, but every teacher knows that in every lesson he will, in effect, edit a pupil's copy.

One of his tasks will be to explain the meaning of the slurs. These curved lines placed over groups of notes may mean: play these notes *legato*. Or they mean: 'sing' the notes in one breath and regard them as a phrase. Mozart, however, meant something different. So did Haydn and Beethoven and even later composers. Accustomed to the orchestra, they applied slurs as though indicating bowing to string players: up-bow for this slur, down-bow for that. In good string playing, a change of bow-direction does not break the smoothness of a line but it may impart slight accentuation to the first note of a 'new bow'.

Imagine four short notes followed by a long one—corresponding, if you like, to *Figaro is here*. A singer's slur would cover all five syllables, and this is the sort of slur that has now come into favour in piano music. But a violinist would probably play up-bow for *Figaro is* and then tug on a down-bow for *here*, giving the last word its due accent.

It is this violinistic slurring that we often find in classical Urtexts. We ought to understand all this, but many pianists work from editions that have been, as the publishers say, 'critically revised' by well-known pianists, teachers and other authorities. These editors in improving the phrasing have concealed that element of accentuation that, in all its subtlety, cannot be shown by printed accent-signs.

The problems remain and there is no final solution. We play square-piano music on a concert grand. We deploy a technique developed by Clementi and his pupils. We attempt restraint knowing that we need intensity. We half guiltily allow ourselves some 'discreet' pedalling and *rubato*. Loving Mozart so much, we devote infinite pains to every boring Alberti bass, every perfunctory scale, every conventional cadence and are never sure at the end whether we have elevated certain pages to an eminence they do not deserve or have truly discovered a unique beauty. As the art of music evolves we inevitably recompose the masterpieces we admire.

What of Haydn? Every child is brought up on the easier pages of Haydn's sonatas—a minuet from one, a rondo from another.

In due course several sonatas emerge as favourites for study in their entirety. But a great many are ignored. No doubt some deserve to be ignored. Haydn's piano music is not consistently at masterpiece level. But there are some sonatas that get less than their desserts because we pianists cannot easily discover how to play them. No doubt a revised edition can offer suggestions, but the plain text can be deceptive. To make the point I offer a quotation from the beginning of the Sonata in A flat (Hob. XVI:46):

Ex. 7

Haydn: Sonata in A flat ,Hob. XVI:46
Allegro moderato

What does *allegro moderato* mean? The sound of the music tells us immediately that *allegro* does not carry its literal meaning of merry. Nor—so the music seems to say—does it mean fast. Perhaps Haydn is saying: this allegro is *moderato*. (The first movement of a sonata was often referred to as the opening allegro.) There is no word of advice about loudness or softness. The first note is A flat but, because of the inverted turn, we begin on a G. The next melody note is an E flat on paper that begins as an F on the keyboard. The little grace-note F (appoggiatura) is printed as a semiquaver, but is that its real length or should it last for the whole of the third beat? We go past the bar-line and are a little surprised to find trills not on the first and third beats, where they might lend emphasis to the rhythm, but on the 'shaded-off' weak beats. Bar 4 arrives and there is a run that can sound as though one had stopped practising one's piece and decided to practise one's scales. . . .

What shall one do? After a great deal of experiment one discovers that the music requires a constant variety of nuance that almost defies the musical dictionary—a little loudness here, a certain degree of softness there, a slowing down that would certainly be too obvious if anyone wrote *rall* or even *poco rall*, every beat different, no 'pulling it about', lightness with warmth, slowness on tiptoe. . . . One must multiply the contradictions and arrive at simplicity.

What one says about Haydn may seem interchangeable with what one says about Mozart, but one cannot assume that a good Mozartian will play Haydn well. Admittedly the two collections of sonatas have many points of resemblance. Certainly if you switch on your radio in the middle of a piece you might mistake one composer for the other . . . for a while. But the differences are important. Of the two men Mozart seems more up to date because he was a concerto man and a theatre man. His music more than Haydn's has acclimatized itself to our century, which is why some writers seem to suggest that the real Haydn is in the symphonies and the chamber music.

There is some very real Haydn in the piano music.

The spread of Mozart's music has depended, of course, on publishers. In Leipzig, long before Mozart's time, there was a well-established printing firm named Breitkopf. The son of the founder, in 1750, invented a means of printing music from movable type (later to be superseded by engraving), and in the year of Mozart's birth he published a full score of a now forgotten opera. A few years after Mozart's death he started to bring out the works of Mozart in seventeen volumes, of Haydn in twelve volumes, of Clementi in thirteen volumes. This Immanuel Breitkopf had two sons, but the future of the firm was in the hands of a friend named Gottfried Härtel. He not only continued in music publishing, he was for a while a piano-maker until the ever-growing publishing business demanded the workshop space occupied by pianos.

Who were the most numerous customers of Breitkopf & Härtel? The pianists, both amateur and professional.

Seeing which way the wind was blowing, Clementi went into business. He returned to London from a tour of the Continent in 1785 and decided to invest some money in the firm of Longman & Broderip, publishers and instrument-makers. Their catalogue offered 'Glove Horns, Sticcado-Pastorals (forerunners of the modern xylophones), Pipes and Tabors, Upright Harpsichords with curious newly invented swell* (upright harpsichords come as a surprise), and Portable Clavecins agreeable for travelling with, they may be carried or even performed on in a coach'.

The 1789 catalogue of publications had 1,668 items, 565 of which were for 'harpsichord or pianoforte'. There were hundreds of songs and dances (minuets, cotillions, country dances) and a good supply of pieces for various instruments. The public evidently had a taste for descriptive pieces, one of which attempted to depict the flight of the first balloonist over London. This 'Lunardi's Flight', by Corri, was not the only flight of fancy. There were 'Pigmy Revels' and 'The Enraged Musician'. As for airs with variations—particularly Scots airs—there were dozens of titles, not to mention piano arrangements of popular overtures whether from light entertainments or Italian operas. Sonatas, 'Lessons' and concertos abounded. As music sellers to His Royal Highness the Prince of Wales, the firm had two shops, one in the City in Cheapside, the other in the fashionable part of town in the Haymarket.

It must have cost Clementi a sizeable sum of money to buy his way into a firm of this importance, but he had amassed some capital. His trips abroad had been successful, he was a popular pianist and, perhaps, the most expensive teacher in London. In those days, when taxes amounted to almost nothing and servants were cheap, a successful professional could save. His investment was a shrewd move, even though he was embarking on a business voyage that would encounter a few storms. The music trade was booming. Furthermore Longman & Broderip had amongst their employees a young man named Frederick William Collard who knew as much as anybody about the manufacture of pianos.

* A swell effect, normally unobtainable in a harpsichord, could be provided by making the lid of the instrument in the manner of a venetian blind. When the louvres opened, more sound emerged. An adaptation of this to an upright harpsichord may well have been curious.

Clementi had plenty of rivals. In 1786 a Frenchman named Sébastien Érard arrived in London to patent certain improvements in the construction of harps and pianos. In some respects he was like Clementi. He was born in the same year. His father, like Clementi's, was a craftsman—a cabinet-maker who died when Sébastien was fifteen. The boy left his native city of Strassburg, went to Paris, and apprenticed himself to a harpsichord-maker. As in Clementi's case, rich patronage suddenly materialized. The Duchesse de Villeroi gave the young man living quarters and a workshop in her own chateau and for her he produced the first piano not imported into the country. It was a square, built naturally enough in imitation of German and English examples.

A good beginning. Then he and his brother Jean-Baptiste set up shop in Paris. This annoyed other instrument-makers who surprisingly enough, belonged to the Fan Makers' Guild—the Luthiers' section. Taking advantage of regulations they seized the interlopers' workshops. However, Sébastien Érard had friends at court, and King Louis XVI, no less, intervened. He conferred a *brevet* on Sébastien that made the firm independent of the Guild but, with great tact, required the Érards to employ only such workmen as satisfied the Guild's regulations. If only His Majesty had been equally clever in all his dealings with his subjects the French Revolution might never have happened.

However, it did happen, and Sébastien returned to London, remaining until the Terror was over. He went back, sized up the situation with his customary shrewdness, and was soon supplying the most important people. Even Napoleon acquired an Érard in 1801—no doubt a presentation model.

It must not be thought that the best pianos in the best houses were devoted to the best music. The Érards, helped by a law that forbade the importation of English pianos, were making instruments, not deciding public taste in music.

The public ran after a German pianist named Daniel Steibelt.

Steibelt was one of the first, and certainly not the last, of a line of bogus Great Pianists who thrilled ignorant audiences. But let us not be too hard on our ancestors. The growing army of piano owners, from small shop keepers to noble dukes, knew next to nothing of Mozart or Haydn or their great contemporary, Beethoven. How many people were there who could play the great sonatas? How many teachers were there who understood the technical demands of this music? How were the provincial butcher, baker and candlestick-maker to acquire appreciation when even the richest sophisticates went to the opera house to stroll about, converse with friends in the boxes and make assignations, pausing to listen only when some expensive singer embarked on some exciting piece of coloratura?

No: their wives and daughters played their airs and variations and were only too ready to applaud anyone who could play faster and louder than themselves.

There was a great demand for 'effects'. Some of the ideas came from Vienna. The Austrian military bands (and military bands were a fairly recent institution in Europe) imported boys from North Africa and the Middle East, dressed them in colourful uniforms, gave them drums, cymbals and gongs, and in this way entertained the populace with what was called Turkish music. Even Mozart composed an *Alla Turca* for his Sonata in A (K.331), and this is still able to bring some rather knockabout fun to a serious recital.

The piano manufacturers began to add drums and cymbals, etc., to their instruments. Extra pedals produced the noises where desired. They were, in fact, anticipating what is now common on pop electronic organs—what, indeed, is remembered from those mighty Wurlitzers that relieved the silence of silent films.*

Clementi went even further. His firm built a large upright piano that incorporated, between the pedals and the keyboard, a large cylinder with pins, actuated by clockwork, that converted the piano into a musical box. (*See Plate 4.*)

It was for a mostly uncultured audience that Steibelt composed duets that he played with his English wife—he playing the piano, she the tambourine. He made full use of the sustaining pedal and a tremolo from a not very skilful left hand. He was up to all the tricks of 'personality', including a very late

* In 1796 in Prague there was an instrument with 230 strings, 360 pipes, and 105 assorted effects.

start of the programme. A rival pianist named Tomaschek has left us an account of a Steibelt concert in Prague in 1800:

> After the nobility . . . had exhausted itself in French in all kinds of indignation, and the orchestra was ready to go home with its job undone, the long-yearned-for virtuoso finally came, one hour after the appointed time. He arrived nearly out of breath, distributed the parts, and gave the signal for the overture. . . . As a pianist he has a neat yet rather firm touch. His right hand is excellent in its cultivation. . . . On the other hand his left hand stood in no harmonious relationship whatever to his right: clumsy, almost imbecile, it hobbled along. . . . He had with him an Englishwoman whom he introduced as his wife and who played the tambourine. . . . The new combination of such diverse instruments so electrified the gentlefolk that they could hardly see their fill of the Englishwoman's pretty arm, and so it came about that Steibelt's female friend was easily persuaded to give lessons on it. . . . Steibelt remained in Prague for several months and in due course sold a large wagonload of tambourines.

The fact remains, however, that Steibelt composed, amongst a deal of rubbish, some pieces of distinction, one of which, known only by hearsay, was a piano concerto (No. 8) with a choral finale. Later in life he settled in St. Petersburg where they took him very seriously and produced a number of his operas.

However, before this he had met Beethoven—twice. The first time Beethoven played the piano in his own Trio in B flat. Then Steibelt played—no comment from Beethoven. The second time Steibelt played a fantasy for piano and strings on a theme taken from the Beethoven trio. At the end of it, Beethoven went to the piano, picking up the cello part of Steibelt's fantasy on the way, put it on the music-desk upside down, played a theme with one finger, and then delivered himself of such an improvisation that thereafter Steibelt never played in Vienna without making sure that Beethoven would not be present.

All this might seem to show that there was nothing in common between Beethoven and the composers of storm rondos, battle pieces and the like. Not so: apart from the storm in the Pastoral Symphony and the warlike music of *Wellington's Victory* (or *The Battle of Vittoria*) there is a great deal of Beethoven's music that can be described as stormy and combative. If anyone should argue that a Beethoven sonata is more likely to depict the storm in a man's soul than a storm in the sky, it is fair to answer that nobody would apply the word storm to the emotions if he had never heard thunder or seen lightning.

Beethoven's contemporary pianists were not all Steibelts. One of the finest was Dussek, born in Bohemia (Czechoslovakia to us) in 1761 and therefore five years younger than Mozart. His name is generally remembered as Johann Ludwig Dussek, but the name Ludwig was originally Ladislav, and his surname was sometimes spelt Dussik or Duschek. He finally settled on Dussek and pronounced it Dooshek. He was a prodigy—the son of a distinguished organist—and was soon an expert in church music. Indeed he wanted to become a Cistercian friar. However, he was soon on his travels through various countries. At the age of twenty-two, in Hamburg, he had the good fortune to be taught by Carl Philipp Emanuel Bach. Then he went on to Berlin, astonishing the *dilettanti* with his performances on the piano and the harmonica. This harmonica was invented by one Hessel—it was probably an elaborate set of musical glasses. We do not now know whether it resembled the glass harmonica invented by Benjamin Franklin who, in about 1792, had invented an instrument in which the pitch was governed not by the level of water in each glass but by the size of each glass revolving in water. In fact the conventional glasses were replaced by basins turned on their side and threaded on a long spindle. Big basins at the left for bass notes, little ones towards the right. A foot treadle spun the spindle and the basins, with their lower edges all dipping in a common trough of water, were ready for the player's touch.

Hessel's harmonica proved popular when Dussek went to Italy but was abandoned when he arrived in London in 1790. There he was immediately successful and well liked. Haydn, then composing symphonies for the concert promoter Salomon, wrote from London to Dussek's father, telling the old man 'you have one of the most upright, moral, and, in music, most eminent of men for a son'.

Despite an unlucky venture in a music shop that compelled him to go abroad temporarily, Dussek spent some twelve years in London, where he was tremendously admired as pianist, composer and teacher.

More travels. At the age of forty-two he became a close friend of Prince Louis Ferdinand of Prussia, himself a considerable pianist. Also with a well-known pianist named Himmel. The three men were boon companions in music and drink, and Dussek lived in the Prince's house. Alas, the Prince went to war and was killed in battle. Dussek composed an effective *Élégie Harmonique* and found other patronage.

Once again we are struck by the freedom of travel in Napoleonic times. The pianist who as a young man had enchanted Marie Antoinette was welcome in Napoleon's Paris where his performances were remembered in after years by that eminent authority, Fétis.*

> Until then the pianoforte had only been heard to disadvantage as a concert instrument, but under the hands of Dussek it eclipsed all that surrounded it. The broad and noble style of this artist, his method of singing on an instrument which possessed no sustained sounds, the neatness, delicacy, and brilliancy of his playing, in short, procured him a triumph of which there had been no previous example.

Powerful aid was again at hand. Dussek resided for the rest of his life with Talleyrand. He must have been very compelling. His rival, Tomaschek, said that his fingers were like 'a company of ten singers, endowed with equal executive powers and able to produce with the utmost perfection whatever their director could require'. He goes on to say: 'Dussek was the first who placed his instrument sideways upon the platform, in which our pianoforte heroes now all follow him, though they may have no very interesting profile to exhibit.' Interesting in profile or not, we imitate Dussek so that the lid of the piano will open towards the audience.

---

* François Joseph Fétis (1784–1871), from whom issued operas, dogmatic theories, unreliable history and prejudiced criticism.

8. *The Great Mogul*

Greatest of all was Beethoven. Nobody doubted this. He was one of those compelling people who shoot up to the top in early manhood and are never displaced.

When he went to Vienna from Bonn he had only to play in a few great houses to convince everyone that a force of nature had arrived. He smashed his hosts' pianos, but they realized it was not so much he who did the damage as his music. *It* smashed the pianos. They were inadequate. Pianists' hands were inadequate. His audiences' ears were inadequate, needing to be opened to new sounds and thoughts.

Even as a child he had been a prodigy—an unhappy one. His father was a drunkard earning a poor living in the Prince-Elector of Bonn's orchestra as a horn player (alongside a second-horn named Niklaus Simrock who later founded a great publishing house). Young Ludwig was noticed by the Elector (brother to the Emperor) and by Count Waldstein, a friend not only of the royal family but of Haydn and Mozart. The two noblemen saw to it that he had good lessons from Christian Gottlob Neefe, a man whose character comes out in his apostrophes to Music: 'Imitator of human passions, artistic union between contradictory dissonances, source of completeness!' Beethoven wrote in this same vein later.

When the boy was fifteen the Prince and the Count made it possible for him to visit Vienna, where he played to Mozart, then about thirty or thirty-one. What Mozart said of him has been variously reported but it was something like, 'This young man will make a noise in the world.' Exactly so!

Back in Bonn Beethoven was befriended by a cultivated family named Breuning from whom he learned something of how to behave in society—though he was always capable of social gaffes. He heard poems and plays read aloud and fell in and out of love, but he did not quite outgrow the poor boy's resentment in the presence of easy wealth. He was young and

69

impressionable when the French Revolution proclaimed Liberty, Equality, Fraternity, and he was touchy about being patronized. Fortunately his friends were tactful.

Mozart had died. Waldstein urged Beethoven to go to Vienna. 'Mozart's genius bewails and grieves his death. It sought refuge in Haydn, but found no place there. . . .'

Very soon 'all Vienna'—in fact a small, tight community of well-born music-lovers—became aware of the young man whose performances were commonly followed by a visit from the piano repairer. The music demanded a piano not yet in existence. It demanded a new tone, a new technique and a new kind of piano lesson.

Years later there were old aristocratic ladies in Vienna who would say '*I* knew Beethoven' and would feel ennobled by the memory, even though he was, by their standards, ill-bred, uncouth, poorly dressed and often 'impossible'. He was so obviously a genius that they ignored his clumsiness, his pock-marked complexion, his unkempt hair.

This is not to say that his music is totally without precedent. No new music ever is. We have already noticed that Mozart's C minor sonata seems to prophesy how Beethoven would compose. That late Mozart sonata and Beethoven's first have something in common. Both begin with the sort of upward marching arpeggio that had been a favourite opening gambit in the days when composers wrote for Elector Theodore's orchestra. It was a cliché nicknamed the Mannheim Rocket. Beethoven inherited this rocket technology and launched a good many missiles to begin his sonatas. It was evident, however, that Beethoven's rocketry was more fiery, more explosive than anything known before.

We pianists are aware of this through our hands. Much of Mozart's piano music can be played by well-taught, gifted children, sometimes at a surprisingly high level. Beethoven is another matter. It is true that children can play his sonatinas, some of the Bagatelles, his 'für Elise' and some carefully chosen sonata movements, but only a true prodigy can attempt the larger works.

I was myself a near-prodigy and could beat any rivals for a hundred miles around, and what my eleven-year-old fingers told me about Beethoven has remained with me ever since. I had a go at a number of sonatas—not the frightening ones at the end of my prize volume but anything up to and including the Moonlight—and Beethoven's message came to me through my fingers, up my arms, into my ears, into my brain, passing thence into my guts. I did not listen to Beethoven, think about Beethoven and then put my thoughts into practice. I left that sort of thing (and still leave it) to musicologists. I played Beethoven in a way that cannot be described, since it is a non-verbal experience: one might as well try to explain what it is like to sniff a rose. At the risk of making an apparently stupid statement I must say that my fingers told my mind what to think.

Of course I played Beethoven badly, judged from a critic's standpoint. But I played him well from my own standpoint since he not only 'came over loud and clear' to me but he became a family favourite in a not specially musical home.

This personal recollection is unimportant in itself but it is worth making because, as I now know, I felt what thousands of other boys and girls have felt and will feel in the future. If Beethoven's music seemed grander than most of the other music I then knew, there must have been something in it that 'told' me about life and death, man and woman, joy and sorrow, journeys and homecomings. What I heard (and I say this as an agnostic) was the voice of God and the Ten Commandments. Interestingly enough, in spite of what the music seemed to 'say', I never felt the need to invent stories to go with the music. I was just aware that at one moment a voice spoke with resolution, that at another there was a pleading note, that Beethoven was hesitating or planning a surprise, that in a journey a new landscape had opened, that the skies had darkened or brightened. Later I played as though I heard the strings of an orchestra, I let fly with massed brass, I traced a line of wood-wind, or thumped the timps. The marks of expression took on meanings not to be found in a glossary. *Con brio* meant stand tall and go at it. *Pianissimo* might mean softness: it might mean the tread of a distant enemy. Form was not a matter of themes and developments: it was more concerned with actions and their consequences. A bridge passage was one that went on and on while I wondered what lay over the hill. And the proof of the greatness of the music was that even when I knew very well what lay ahead it always surprised me, and still does.

Beethoven accepted the sonata form that Mozart and Haydn had used with such ease and effect. It is also true to say that he never accepted it. Sometimes he moves with grace and cunning through an elegant bridge passage to a new idea: at others (particularly in the later sonatas) he seems unwilling to bother with such niceties, jolts to a standstill, does a clumsy sidespring and is off in a new direction. Formal analysis for such music often seems a pointless exercise, but the ground plan of Exposition, Development and Recapitulation is always there. Before the exposition there may be an Introduction, long or short, and at the end there may be a Coda of a few bars or of several dense pages. One accepts that, however it is done, the result is fairly named sonata. This plan applies particularly to first movements, but it is apparent to some degree in many others.

In two of the sonatas Beethoven began, unconventionally, with a slow movement and he called Nos. 1 and 2 of Op. 27, 'Sonata quasi una fantasia'. The second, later called Moonlight by an astute publisher, must have surprised Beethoven himself. He never wrote another piece like that first movement. I have sometimes described it as the greatest work that Schubert never wrote and it illustrates once again how great composers sometimes foreshadow what lies ahead. (Schubert was a child at the time.) How can it be played except in Schubertian style and with the kind of touch that was later to be developed by Liszt and Chopin and subsequent great pianists? Furthermore it is the first of Beethoven's sonatas to mention the sustaining-pedal though, instead of saying with pedal (*con pedale*) he asks us to play without the dampers (*senza sordini*).* He says nothing about the exact behaviour of the pedal-foot, nor does he resolve the contradiction of asking for *pianissimo* tone while confronting us with long notes. The instrument being what it is, long notes must always be loud enough to last their length. But from that day to this, we have dodged the issue by saying that the long notes are not loud (or even loudish) but *cantabile*.

* The word *sordino* is sometimes found applied to a special mechanism for muting the tone, recalling a lute stop on a harpsichord. Beethoven's *sordini* were the dampers that are part of every piano action.

Rigorously scientific people will smile at this, but musicians are much governed by the 'as if' principle. We play the Moonlight first movement as if the melody came from a beautiful voice; as if an expensive piano stood a few feet behind a singer; as if the accompanist possessed a sensitive touch and a subtle technique of pedalling; as if pianos had no hammers, and as if key-beds were upholstered. We play, if you like, as if in love.

Biographers never fail to tell us that Beethoven intended to dedicate the music to someone other than the Countess Julie Guicciardi and then changed his mind. Never mind! He was at least a little in love with this pupil of his, and (avoiding *schmaltz* and *kitsch*) we may play the music as if giving a *Lieder* recital. When the young woman married (disastrously) a man of her own class, Beethoven said angrily something like, 'I loved her more than he did, but he was more her lover than I was, if you know what I mean.'

After the slow movement, Beethoven glances back to a world passing away and gives us a minuettish movement, but then he is launched into a violent piece that must have astounded his patrons. Who before then had composed violent music? Who had assaulted the piano? To this very day what pianist would be so stupid as to begin the Hammerklavier Sonata with 'a nice tone' even though he would avoid the karate chop that defeats even the biggest and best concert grand? Again and again one encounters Beethoven's violence and must accept its challenge.

One cannot avoid the comparison with Napoleon. Both men were upstarts, guided more by genius than training. Both put their rivals to flight. When Napoleon made himself Emperor, he angered Beethoven, who regarded himself as a democrat and a republican. But Beethoven was the uncrowned emperor of music—nobody could dispute it. After some twenty years of war the great powers defeated Napoleon and marooned him on the island of St. Helena. Long before this, Fate marooned Beethoven in an island of deafness. Napoleon was a defeated man. Beethoven was always victorious.

How did all this affect his piano-playing? He had his own, highly individual technique. Not for him Clementi's stillness of hand or the kind of playing that Mozart praised by describing

73

it as flowing 'like oil'. He used the airspace above the keys and 'went for them'.

He never played a piece twice in the same way. This makes nonsense of the idea that, for every work, there is some ideal performance to which we must all aspire. It also makes nonsense of the claim that a particular pianist is *the* Beethoven player. Beethoven would never have subscribed to the modern idea that each piece has some perfect tempo. It is true he used the metronome, invented by his friend Maelzel, to suggest speeds, but can anyone imagine Beethoven sitting in his music room and playing to the wagging and ticking of this piece of clockwork?

Something of his pianistic behaviour can be learned from his friends. Anton Reicha:

> He asked me to turn pages for him. But I was mostly occupied in wrenching strings of the pianoforte which snapped, while the hammers stuck amongst the broken strings. Beethoven insisted on finishing the concerto, and so back and forth I leaped, jerking out a string, disentangling a hammer, and I worked harder than Beethoven.

Czerny refers to 'titanic execution' and inadequate pianos. Anton Schindler, who deeply admired Beethoven, says that 'he played like a composer' and, with respect to such as Liszt and Rachmaninoff, we know what he means. His observations have been much quoted and are set out fully in that excellent book *The Great Pianists*, by Harold C. Schonberg.* I shall quote Schonberg's version of Schindler, partly because it is excellent and partly because, with respect, I slightly disagree with some of his comments.

> I will now, as far as verbal description may permit, endeavour to convey an idea of the manner in which Beethoven used to play the two sonatas contained in Op. 14.† His wonderful performance of these two compositions was a sort of musical declamation in which the two principles were as distinctly separated as the two

---

* Published by Victor Gollancz Ltd., London, 1964.

† Earlier Beethoven sonatas were described by his publishers as written for 'Clavecin or Piano Forte'. They were, of course, composed for the piano. The Op. 14 sonatas abandon all mention of the *clavecin* (harpsichord).

parts of a dialogue when recited by the flexible voice of a good speaker.

Schonberg suggests that the two principles are contrasting principles of sonata design. My own guess is that they refer to a masculine–feminine contrast. Beethoven was very aware not only of women but of Woman.

He commenced the opening allegro with vigor and spirit, relaxing these qualities at the sixth bar, and in the following passage.

Ex. 8 (a)

Here a slight *ritardando* made preparation for gently introducing the entreating principle. The performance of the phrase,

Ex. 8 (b)

was exquisitely shaded, and to the following bars,

Ex. 8 (c)

Beethoven's manner of holding down particular notes, combined with a kind of soft, gliding touch, imparted such a vivid colouring, that the hearer could fancy he actually beheld the lover in his living form, and heard him apostrophizing his obdurate mistress. In the following groups of semiquavers,

Ex. 8 (d)

he strongly accented the fourth note of each group, and gave a joyous expression to the whole passage, and, at the succeeding chromatic run, he resumed the original tempo, and continued until he arrived at this phrase,

Ex. 8 (e)

which he gave in tempo *andantino*, beautifully accenting the bass, and the third notes of the upper part of the harmony,* as I have marked them in the last two bars of the above example, thereby rendering distinct to the ear the separation of the two principles [two phrases?]. On arriving at the ninth bar,

Ex. 8 (f)

he made the bass stand out prominently, and closed the succeeding cadence on the dominant in the original tempo, which he maintained without deviation to the end of the first part [to the double bar?].

In the second part, Beethoven introduced the phrase in A flat major by a *ritardando* of the two preceding bars. He attacked this phrase vigorously, thus diffusing the glow of colour over the picture. He gave a charming expression to the following phrase in the treble by strongly accenting and holding down longer than the prescribed time the first note in each bar,

Ex. 8 (g)

while the bass was played with gradually increasing softness, and with a sort of creeping motion of the hand.

*Schindler's outline of melody assumes that the reader knows the supporting harmony.

The passage next in succession was touched off brilliantly; and in its closing bars the *decrescendo* was accompanied by a *ritardando*. The following phrase was started in *andante* tempo,

Ex. 8 (h)

At the fifth bar, there was a slight *accelerando*, and an increase of tone. At the sixth bar, the original tempo was resumed. Throughout the remainder of the first movement, Beethoven observed the same tempo as that which he had taken in the opening bars.

Various as were the tempi which Beethoven introduced in this movement, yet they were all beautifully prepared, and if I may so express myself, the colours were delicately blended with one another. There were none of those abrupt changes which the composer frequently admitted in some of his other works with the view of giving a loftier flight to the declamation. Those who truly enter into the spirit of this fine movement will find it advisable not to repeat the first part: by this allowable abridgement, the gratification of the hearer will be unquestionably increased, while it may possibly be diminished by frequent repetitions of the same phrases. . . .

It is now the fashion to observe all repeats, but I have been known to swim against this tide.

With regard to the second sonata in E major (Op. 14), the subject of which is similar to that of the first, I shall confine my description of Beethoven's manner of performing a few passages. In the eighth bar of the first *allegro* movement,

Ex. 8 (i)

as well as in the ninth bar, he retarded the tempo, touching the keys more *forte*, and holding down the fifth note, as marked above.

77

By these means he imparted to the passage an indescribable earnestness and dignity of character.

In the tenth bar

Ex. 8 (j)

the original tempo was resumed, the powerful expression still being maintained. The eleventh bar was *diminuendo* and somewhat lingering. The twelfth and thirteenth bars were played in the same manner as the two foregoing.

On the introduction of the middle movement [second subject, not second movement of sonata]

Ex. 8 (k)

the dialogue became sentimental. The prevailing tempo was *andante,* but not regularly maintained; for every time that either principle was introduced, a little pause was made on the first note, thus,

Ex. 8 (l)

At the following phrase

Ex. 8 (m)

a joyous character was expressed. The original tempo was taken, and not changed until the close of the first part.

The second part, from this passage

78

Ex. 8 (n)

forward was characterized by an increased breadth of rhythm, and augmented power of tone, which, however, was further on shaded into an exquisitely delicate *pianissimo*; so that the apparent meaning of the dialogue became more perceptible without any over-strained effort of imagination.

The second movement *allegretto* was, as performed by Beethoven, more like an *allegro furioso*; and until he arrived at the single chord,

Ex. 8 (o)

on which he made a very long pause, he kept up the same tempo.

Many pianists have felt that the word *allegretto*, nearly always associated with *grazioso* movements, is inappropriate here. To the *allegro furioso* I should like to add *non presto*.

In the *maggiore*, the tempo was taken more moderately, and played by Beethoven in a beautifully expressive style. He added not a single note; but he gave to many an accentuation which would not have suggested itself to any other player. On the subject of accentuation, I may state, as a general remark, that Beethoven gave prominent force to all appoggiaturas, particularly the minor second in running passages; and in the slow movements, his transition to the principal note was as delicately managed as it could have been by the voice of a singer.

In the rondo of the sonata to which I am here referring, Beethoven maintained the tempo as marked until he arrived at the bars introducing the first and third pauses. These bars he made *ritardando*.

Schindler goes on to say, of several other sonatas, that in every movement Beethoven varied the tempo as the feelings changed.

No wonder he despised those pianists 'who only run up and down the keyboard with long-practised passage-work, *putsch*!, *putsch*!, *putsch*!'

No wonder he despised the pianos of the day. In 1796 he wrote to the piano-maker Johann Streicher complaining that too many instruments were like harps. 'And I am delighted, my dear fellow, that you are one of the few who realize and perceive that, provided one can feel the music, one can also make the pianoforte sing. I hope the time will come when the harp and the pianoforte will be treated as entirely different instruments.'

Streicher had married the daughter of Mozart's piano-maker, Stein, the girl whose playing had aroused Mozart's contempt. She grew up in the business and was a friend and confidante of Beethoven's. It was the Streichers who made a piano for Beethoven of more than six and a half octaves compass. Other manufacturers courted the great man. In 1802 Érard sent him an instrument. In 1818 Broadwood put his best and strongest piano on a sailing ship that took it to Trieste whence it was hauled by horse power to Vienna. Of this Beethoven wrote: 'I shall regard it as an altar upon which I shall place the most beautiful offerings of my spirit to the divine Apollo.' In pursuit of more and more tone Graf of Vienna made a piano for Beethoven with four strings to a note.

At this time the left pedal must have offered pianists more choice of action than we enjoy today. In the Adagio of Op. 101 Beethoven asks for *eine seite* (one string), then more and more strings, culminating in *tutto il Cembalo ma piano* (the whole instrument but softly). The instructions in two languages leave us in some doubt as to how this was done.

The piano of Beethoven's era—the grand, not the square—is often called fortepiano. In the mouths of modern musicians this can sometimes seem slightly affected, since the word pianoforte was never abandoned. For example, in Clementi's business letters we find the abbreviation P.Forte. However, fortepiano* appears in many publications of the time, and the word reminds us of instruments that had wooden, not iron,

* *Fortepiano* is the standard word in Russian.

frames, had two, not three, strings to a note and had leather, not felt, on the hammer-heads.

Whether Beethoven's music sounds most authentic when played on a fortepiano is arguable. There are times when the performance is pleasing, carrying us back into a long-vanished world, but we can never quite forget that Beethoven was always demanding bigger and louder pianos or that his sonatas often have an orchestral character.

9. *The Piano Promoter*

In 1800 Bonaparte (at that time Bonaparte was a more familiar name than Napoleon) revised the constitution of the Paris Conservatoire. It had been established five years earlier as a free school by the National Convention. There had been previous royal and national institutions, but the republican conservatoire was the first great school of its type. It started very grandly with 125 professors, 600 students, a printing works and the publication of *Méthodes du Conservatoire*. No doubt there were difficulties of organization and General Bonaparte imposed a system of ranks: a director, five inspectors of tuition, thirty first-class and forty second-class professors. Something of this kind exists in all such places to this day.

There were no fee-paying places. One cannot apply *égalité* to musicians, but at least there was the *fraternité* of ability. Bonaparte's motto was 'careers open to talent', a good motto for musicians and not at all a bad one for armies.

The conservatoire remained unique for many years. In other countries students continued to take lessons from individual teachers not attached to institutions and in some cases virtually apprenticed to their masters. One such was John Field.

John Field was born in Dublin and was destined to acquire a European reputation as Irish Field, but in fact he spent only his childhood in his birthplace. At the age of ten, and pretending to be eight, he played a concerto composed by his Dublin teacher, Tommasso Giordani. Later, in London, he was praised by Haydn, Dussek and Cramer. When he was fifteen the *Morning Chronicle* declared that he had been esteemed by the best judges to be one of the finest performers in this kingdom.

By now Field's father was settled in London as a violinist at the Haymarket Theatre, and he asked the great Clementi to take the boy on as pupil, assistant, apprentice or whatever. This Clementi agreed to do but not until the boy's father had paid 100 guineas, a sizeable sum for those days. (Clementi was always acquisitive.) Thereafter the boy was worked hard by his demanding master but he learned a great deal from one of the foremost composers and pianists of the age, he learned the technology and salesmanship of the piano trade, and he travelled far and wide.

Clementi's energy was astounding. In the midst of his commercial activities he found time to compose, assemble and publish his *Gradus ad Parnassum*, a compendium of his studies and other pieces amounting to a comprehensive education in the techniques of piano-playing. He was not, of course, the inventor of the *étude* or the first composer-teacher to write a treatise. C. P. E. Bach had written a considerable work of the kind, and the great Bach's Preludes may be regarded, as Schumann regarded them, as the first true studies. But *Gradus* is extraordinarily forward-looking. Beethoven admired the work. In the age of Liszt and Chopin it was standard teaching material. And in our own age I have played a page or two to unsuspecting colleagues, asked them to guess the composer and heard them suggest Mendelssohn (not yet born).

In the exercise and study market Clementi had his rivals, including his own pupil Cramer and Beethoven's pupil Czerny, but *Gradus* is, somehow, a historic event. Clementi, with his ambitious sonatas and his still-charming sonatinas, never became, as Czerny did, a kind of young pianists' bogy-man. Czerny terrorized thousands with his School of Velocity, School of Finger Perfection and the Hundred and One Exercises.

It is, of course, unfair to suggest that Czerny's music is invariably dreary and mechanical, but exercises are, by definition, a kind of pianistic square-bashing. And until Chopin and Liszt ennobled the *étude* a study was often not much more than an extended exercise spread over several pages with the help of a few modulations and pretending to be a piece of music. The value of sheer mechanical finger-drill will always be argued, but a pianist must be an athlete and it is difficult to see how anyone can become an athlete or gymnast without going into training.

In Clementi's day the piano was becoming the indispensable instrument. The *Allgemeine Musikalische Zeitung* declared 'Everybody plays the piano', meaning, no doubt, everybody who was respectable, educated and genteel. And although almost everybody played easy little pieces* there were in 1800 at least a few customers for the *Well-tempered Clavier*, not previously published in its entirety.

In that same year Matthias Müller produced a true upright piano. In previous vertical pianos the grand piano had had its tail put up in the air, which left the hammers striking from behind. Now the hammers were placed in front, and the strings ran from floor level (or thereabouts). A very similar kind of piano was invented in the same year in America. John Isaac Hawkins of Philadelphia, not himself a piano-maker and therefore not hampered by tradition, persuaded a piano-man to build an instrument to his design. He used more metal than other makers would have thought proper, put his tuning pins in a metal wrest-plank and coiled his bass strings like springs. The metal wrest-plank and the coiled bass strings are now forgotten, but Hawkins was one of the many inventors who, over the years, have tried to improve the piano, and we are in his debt. The piano did, in fact, need a more secure fixing for tuning pins; also a method of making bass strings heavier to avoid making them longer. In due course bass strings came to be weighted by having copper wire coiled round them; and a wrest-plank was made by glueing together lengths of very hard wood, with the grain of alternate layers running at right angles to one another. But Hawkins was going in the right direction. Other inventors were not. There was a vogue for upright pianos that retained the wing-shape of the grand and were called

* In 1777 Dr. Burney composed the first duets to be played on one keyboard. He cannot possibly have guessed how much pleasure duets would give to amateurs at home for generations to come.

giraffes (*see illustrations*), and very elegant they looked in the high-ceilinged rooms of the gentry. Some of them supported sculptured excrescences in the way of columns or urns or scrolls.

The giraffe piano became an extinct species, but the customer of today must at times long for a revival of a little of the fancy work and elegance that graced pianos in the days before the notion of functionalism was invented.

Functionalism is a recent consequence of industrialization. But, even in the first decade of the 1800s, industry was creating a large output of pianos. By 1802 Broadwood was making 400

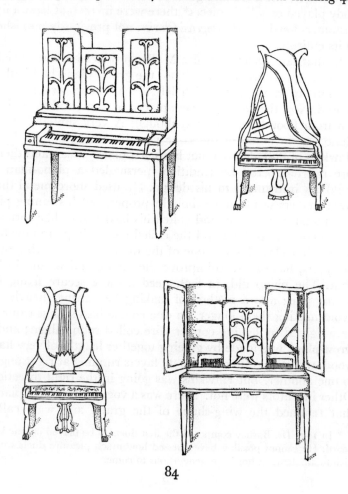

pianos a year. In Paris the Érard factories were noted for the organization of the labour force, each man to his own speciality. No longer did a man make a piano on his own. Exports were governed by the availability of water transport and the power of the purse—for example of the Russian nobility. The industry was on the march and it would be quite possible to fill pages and pages with statistics about its progress.

But what must interest us much more is the character and life style of the pioneers, and here we must return to Clementi and his letters from abroad. With them, suddenly, the picture comes to life. In 1803 he was in Leipzig negotiating with Härtel of the firm of Breitkopf & Härtel which as we have already seen, was one of the pioneers and leaders of music publishing. As far back as 1750 J. G. I. Breitkopf, son of the founder, with his invention for printing music from movable type, had built up a sizeable business. It proved too much, however, for his son who, in due course, handed it over to a friend named Gottfried Christoph Härtel who began to publish collected editions of the great masters (including Clementi). Abandoning movable type he took up Senefelder's invention of engraving music on pewter plates and, for a while, was a piano manufacturer. Härtel and Clementi were just the men to do business together, and Clementi wrote from Leipzig to London as follows:

> 1803—Härtel who is a man of great sense and probity has written to you. He is likely to become exceedingly useful to us; pray neglect nothing to satisfy him. His dealings with Authors are *liberal* by which means he has lately got the preference before the other German Editors. He has promised me to engage Beethoven to send him all his new MSS. and we shall have them for the *British Dominions* for *half the price* he gives him. He is to have all that Haydn means to publish, and has likewise promised to send you whatever he gets from his pen. He has shown me the two songs which the good Doctor Haydn gave me a sight of, with the promise in his usual polite way, I mean the Doctor's, that I should be the *sole* possessor. Writing to him or *Beethoven* has now become superfluous to say no more, since my conference with Härtel, for now with *less* trouble and *much less* expense we shall get all we want.

The two songs of Haydn's were dedicated to an Englishman, and Clementi makes his characteristic comment:

85

. . . dedicated to Dr. Harrington by Dr. Haydn. The 1st Dr. having bestowed much well-earned praise on the 2nd Dr., the said 2nd Dr., out of *Doctorial* gratitude returns the first Dr. thanks for all favours recd. and praises in his turn the 1st Dr. *most handsomely*. Shall I ever be a Doctor? Don't laugh now.

From Leipzig to St. Petersburg, with his apprentice. While he was there the famous violinist and composer, Ludwig Spohr, arrived and called on Clementi, finding maestro and apprentice at the washtub. Clementi, it seemed, distrusted Russian washerwomen . . . or was he saving a few roubles? Anyway he was soon busy selling his pianos.

1804—General Markloffsky wants such an instrument (a Grand Pfte. with additional keys) as last mentioned. John Field is in his house on my recommendation. Pray be most particular for the General minds no expense, and he is a warm good fellow.

Before this he had played to the nobility. A letter dated 1803 paints the picture:

Dear Collard, I am alive! But without making long winded apologies for my silence, I shall please you and myself better by proceeding at once to business.

At Petersburg I found no *real* lovers of good music except amongst some foreigners, which disgusted one so much that after some few trials I refused to play unless they paid me down 100 ducats when with company, or 100 rubles without; but more of this *viva voce*. As for the Emperor nothing less than a trumpet would make its way through his obtuse tympanum; and his avarice is a doleful example too willingly followed by his more than half-ruined nobility. . . . Remember once for all that the Russians in general possess good ears for *sound* though they have none for *sense and style*.

He establishes agencies in Moscow and Petersburg and finds useful friends amongst bankers and customs officials.

Hoeke is in Moscow, what Faversear is in Petersburg, and I believe, by what he said, he may become a very considerable correspondent. Hoeke said he would send for a small quantity at first, but afterwards by the dozen, for in Moscow they want instruments extremely, and the people in general are much richer than in the Capital. Pray send good stuff, and let the wood be well seasoned.

Clementi usually asked London to send copies of his own compositions as, what he called, Evangelists for the Art.

In 1805 he is in Berlin: 'Did you tell Field of my intentions in regard to money? How does he go on? Has he sent you his Concerto in E-flat? Get it soon and pay him well, for I think 'twill sell.'

The apprenticeship was now at an end. Field had decided to settle in Russia where he could easily become the top man as pianist, composer and teacher. Nevertheless he retained a kind of partnership with his master, and did not immediately cease to be a salesman. 'How much of Field's money is in your hands? . . . I hope you were not fools enough to pay him commission on that last sale . . . it was sold before he touched it.'

It seems that new music was bartered for a new piano. From Leipzig in 1804: 'Has Field sent you the Concerto, the Quintette, and *something more*, as I had agreed with him, for his Grand Piano? If not pray write (by Faversear) to him. He is a lazy dog. I'll endeavour to write to him too.'

Clementi was not the only person to regard Field as a lazy dog. In later years, Field thought nothing of having a nap in the middle of a piano lesson or at least would lie down in an adjacent room and call out occasional instructions to the pupil in the music room. And perhaps it may be said of some of his music that it had a lazy charm. It also exerted great influence, as we shall discover.

In St. Petersburg Clementi persuaded two Berlin pupils to set up in business.

1806—I have procured them plenty of scholars, and as they will now and then want instruments to sell, I have persuaded them to send for ours on their own account, and to encourage them I have promised to furnish them for £50 each grand (good plain mahogany). . . . Send them by the 1st opportunity 6 grand and 2 square patent, with pedal. The small you'll charge as low as you can. But pray, pray, pray now let me entreat you to pick out as excellent in tone and touch as you possibly can, from which you may in future expect great orders, for they'll push like the devil;

as they love and want money. Rather don't hurry in the choice; and keep them sometime in a very warm room, in order to discover whether the wood won't warp, or any other mischief don't ensue.

Clementi was sharply aware of criticism. He knew how Germans compared Vienna and London as providers of pianos.

... the *price*, the heaviness, and the *depth of touch* are the general objections throughout Germany to English P.Fortes; but especially the *first* sticks most confoundedly in their gizzard. Poor devils!

The eminent musician, Prince Louis Ferdinand, paid a visit.

He played a couple of hours to me, for which I gave him only 3 dishes of tea. He said he had 3 gr.P.fortes of ours, of which the first was much the best; concluding our manufacture to have considerably suffered *by my absence*, and as the Devil would have it, he had some plea to confirm his assertion. . . .

In the midst of all these travels Clementi suffered a setback that would have destroyed a lesser man. His London factory went up in flames in 1807 and the damage is said to have amounted to £40,000. Fortunately for him, Collard was resourceful, and his powerful rival, Broadwood, was a man of principle. The Broadwood firm helped to fulfil Collard's orders, and the Broadwood workmen had a whip-round to provide their fellow workmen with new tools of their trade.

At about this time Clementi visited Beethoven in Vienna. With infinite guile he managed to meet the great man and do a deal.

By a little management, and without commiting myself I have made at last a compleat conquest of that *haughty beauty* Beethoven; who first began at public places to grin and coquet with me, which of course I took care not to discourage; then slid into familiar chat, till meeting him by chance one day in the street— 'where do you lodge?' says he, 'I have not seen you this *long* while.' Upon which I gave him my address. Two days after I find on my table his card, brought by himself, from the maid's description of his lovely form. This will do, thought I. Three days after that, he calls again and finds me at home. Conceive then the mutual extasy of such a meeting! I took pretty good care to improve it to *our house's* advantage. Therefore as soon as decency would allow, after praising very handsomely some of his compositions, 'Are you engaged with any publisher in London?' 'No,' says he. 'Suppose then, you prefer *me*.' 'With all my heart.' 'Done.' 'What have you ready?' 'I'll bring you a list.' In short, I agreed with him to take in MS. three *Quartetts, a Symphony, an Overture, a Concerto for the Violin* which is beautiful, and which, at my request, he will adapt for the Pianoforte with and without additional keys; and a *Concerto for the Pianoforte.* For all which we are to pay him two hundred pounds sterling. . . . The Symphony and Overture are wonderfully fine, so that I think I have made a good bargain. To-day the courier sets off for London via Russia. . . .

The symphony was No. 4 and the overture was *Coriolanus.* Truly Clementi got a good bargain. What did he mean by a piano arrangement of the Violin Concerto with and without additional keys? For this arrangement, by the way, Beethoven composed a cadenza. Did he have to take into account varying lengths of keyboard?

It was part of giving Clementi and the public their money's worth that in every concerto the composer had to provide—or leave space for—a cadenza. I have to confess that when, as a student, I first encountered Beethoven's cadenzas I thought them a terrible lot of noisy nonsense. Later I found them more acceptable. First, they are more impressive, on sheer merit, than I at first realized. Second, they give us a sense of history. A cadenza composed by Beethoven was almost certainly in the same style as one that he improvised and we get a glimpse of what Beethoven must have been like when let loose on a cowering piano and an affrighted audience. We are left, however, with an insoluble problem. Where the composer did not write a cadenza—where there is nothing to guide us but the chord on which the orchestra stops, the word *cadenza*, and the trills that tell the orchestra that the pianist has finished at last and would like them to pick up their instruments—we must find suitable music. Shall we attempt to imitate Beethoven? Shall we use a cadenza provided by Hummel or Clara Schumann? Or shall we insert a modern and highly personal flourish into Beethoven's music? Hummel is probably the best bet. His life overlaps Beethoven's by a considerable span of years and he was a highly skilled musician.

89

It was during his travels, and at the age of fifty-four, that Clementi at last decided to marry.

> Berlin 1804—Dear Collard, I shall be married on Saturday next—you see I come plump to the point, and don't go about and about it. A charming young lady whom I have known fourteen months, of excellent disposition and angelic temper, has at last fixt my mercury. After the ceremony we set off for Italy. But I am in a confounded borrowing condition and unless the notes I begged you to send arrive I shall be put to my last shifts, and not only to borrow—but beg and steal—for off I will be.

No traveller's cheques or credit cards smoothed his way, but Clementi managed. In due course he looked forward to becoming a father, preferably of a son: '. . . make haste with the Gr.P.forte, for no doubt he'll want to play as soon as he is born —or I'll cut him off with a shilling for a bastard. . . .'

Alas, his charming Caroline died in childbirth and he gave the Gr.P.forte to the girl's parents. 'I shall set off for Riga . . . as soon as I am a little recovered and will give the final touches to my 3 new Sonatas.'

How like an artist! Later he married again—some say twice —and had daughters.*

Clementi never went to America but the piano thrived there. It was perhaps in 1774 that a set of 'hammer harpsichords' went under the hammer after being taken off a wrecked ship, and a few years later a privateer brought a piano to Boston. In 1883, John Jacob Astor, the immigrant fur merchant who founded a dynasty of millionaires, imported pianos while exporting skins. Earlier, in 1785, a Scotsman, Charles Jarvis, started to make pianos in Philadelphia. Not everybody was pleased. One Brissot de Warville wrote in Boston, 'God grant that Bostonian Women may never, like those of France, acquire the malady of perfection in this art. It is never attained except at the expense of domestic virtues.'

* A descendant of a daughter took legal steps to call himself Clementi and there are several distinguished Clementis today.

10. *The Piano Sings, Dances and Goes to War*

In 1801 a boy of fifteen who, two years earlier, had heard his opera, *The Forest Maiden*, performed eight times in Vienna, wrote to the publisher, Artraria, in that same city offering a lithographic invention. 'I can engrave music on stone in a manner quite equal to the finest English copper-plate engraving, as the enclosed specimens will show. . . . Two men can take as many thousand impressions a week as in common printing. One hundred thalers will cover the whole outlay for machinery.' He also offered several compositions for strings and for piano. Artraria took no notice. The boy was Carl Maria von Weber.

He wrote music, he engraved music, he studied piano music according to the principles of C. P. E. Bach, he planned a history of music, and started a musical novel. He criticized Beethoven and admired Hummel. He changed his opinions about both in due course, but at the age of twenty-three he was able to say of Beethoven:

> His fervid, almost incredible inventive powers, are accompanied by so much confusion in the arrangement of his ideas, that his early works alone interest me; the later ones are to me a bewildering chaos, an obscure straining after novelty, lit up it is true by divine flashes of genius, which only serve to show how great he might be if he would but curb his riotous imagination.

Weber's own imagination and life style were somewhat riotous largely because his father was a bit of a musician and a bit of an old soldier (falsely calling himself Major) and a bit of a rascal, fiercely desirous that the boy would turn out to be a prodigy. Perhaps the fact that Carl was first cousin to Mozart's wife had something to do with this notion. The boy grew up on the road, in theatres, in aristocratic households (some providing a liberal education in depravity) and, whenever possible, in the company of great musicians. He learned a great deal from the celebrated teacher Abbé Vogler—a fellow student was

91

Meyerbeer—and learned how to fascinate audiences by singing to his own guitar accompaniment and improvising on the piano. As a teenager he travelled about Germany giving concerts—as far as Napoleon's campaigns would allow—and then spent some time as private correspondent to a spendthrift and dissipated duke. By the time he was twenty-four he had experienced a short imprisonment and banishment from the Kingdom of Württemberg.

Gradually he settled down more and more to serious work, becoming in due course the great composer who may be said to have founded German romantic opera. His imagination never settled down. Over the short span of his life he poured forth ideas in the fields of concert music, patriotic music to celebrate Napoleon's downfall, and piano music.

Naturally we think of him as an opera composer, and *Der Freischütz* is the work that still fascinates. But he is more important in the story of the piano than many now realize.

When he was twenty-three he wrote the *Invitation to the Dance*, and this was an enormous success amongst pianists. Only a brilliant pianist could have written it and it foreshadowed much music that would be written by composers who were still children. The waltz was beginning its long era of triumph (Johann Strauss the elder was fifteen) and the new dance halls of Vienna and elsewhere were thronged. What gave Weber's waltz added enchantment was that it told a story. The introduction conjures up a vision of a young man approaching a charming girl and asking her, perhaps through her chaperone, for the pleasure of the next waltz. All is expectancy. Then the waltz itself strikes up and, in the midst of its brilliancy and gaiety, suggests phrases of conversation between the enchanted dancers. The dance ends in a way that invites the audience to applaud. But no: the music is not finished. In a postlude, almost a *reprise* of the introduction, the young man sees the young girl to her seat beside her chaperone, restoring her from giddiness to decorum.

Nowadays this piece is more often than not heard in an orchestral version, but it held its place for generations in the repertoire of great pianists, and who can doubt its influence on Chopin?

Then there were the four sonatas. The C major was perhaps the favourite, and its last movement, a *moto perpetuo*, was often played separately as a display piece. Some pianists later played Brahms's variant on this piece in which the endless semiquavers are transferred from the right hand to the left, making the whole thing more than ever a display of confident virtuosity.

We know that Liszt was excited by Weber's sonatas.

Weber is, in some respects, a link between Beethoven and the romantics. He came to admire Beethoven's music profoundly; he is said to have played the great man's sonatas magnificently; he conducted *Fidelio* in Dresden. He longed to arouse the musical world to all the possibilities opened up by Beethoven and, in 1810, founded a musical society to promote 'the elevation of musical criticism by musicians themselves'. This society was fashioned as a kind of secret society, and the members adopted *noms de plume*. All this almost uncannily foreshadows Schumann's *Davidsbündler*, even though Weber never portrayed himself and his friends in his piano music, as Schumann was to do. Alas, he was consumptive and died in London after conducting twelve performances of his new opera *Oberon*. (It continued up to twenty-eight performances.) He was forty.

We pianists may not play much of Weber now, but we owe him a great debt. And, in so far as we are accompanists, we should recall the fact that he composed seventy-eight *Lieder*.

Lieder! On the face of it, the piano seems an unlikely instrument for the support of the voice. If one did not know about its great success in this matter one might well imagine that the best way of accompanying a singer would be to use a string quartet. But no: it is precisely the instrument with eighty-eight hammers banging steel strings that the greatest song-writers have chosen to support, illumine and enhance the sung poem.

There is something about two hands on a keyboard that is peculiarly sympathetic to the voice, and we can easily see why.

Put two fingers on your lower lip and say 'I love thee'. Say 'speak' and notice how one senses the 'sp . . .' before the outburst of '. . . eak'. Say 'moon' and make your fingers aware of the closed-lip hum at the beginning of the word and the open-

93

lip hum at the end. Feel the breath passing your fingers through the long *oo*-sound.

If one has the right empathy, the quick hearing, the heart-to-heart sense of the singer's breathing, one's hands join the voice not only as a matter of timing but in the very air-pressure of utterance, almost as though the singer's breath were linked by some invisible system of pneumatic tubing to the muscles of the arm and hand.

I became very aware of this when, as a schoolboy, I accompanied the singing of drawing-room ballads, in our best room, on an old upright piano that sprouted the brass candlesticks of the period. In the first stage of my development, before I learned better, I would play a chord to support a word and, holding it with my foot, would place my fingers very near the next chord with the object of being 'spot on' when the singer arrived there. This was not a bad piece of juvenile cunning, and some element of it perhaps remained to be used on occasion. But, more and more, I learned to flow with the processes of singing. When the singer breathed in, my hand became airborne. When the singer's diaphragm began to press the air out, energizing the tone, my hand went down, energizing *my* tone and using, as it were, the singer's degree of air-pressure.

This was not altogether a one-way signalling system from singer to pianist. There was an element of feedback. If I judged the introduction aright I propelled the song into motion and, to a degree, energized the singer.

This understanding of accompaniment as something more than merely accompanying was useful to me when, as an episode in an all too versatile career, I conducted a short season of ballet. Did the music accompany the dancers, or did the dancers accompany the music?

When Schubert brought his incomparable genius to the composing of songs he discovered in the piano a power of suggestion that no one had suspected before. Nobody has ever been able to explain how he did it. It is easier to say what he did not do. He did not compose pretty little trills to illustrate a reference to the birds in the air. He did not compose rumbling up-and-down arpeggios to illustrate a storm at sea or the wind in the trees.

We play a cluster of notes at the beginning of a song and wonder—and never cease to wonder—why just *that* is incontestably perfect.

Franz Schubert was born in Vienna (it now seems inconceivable that he should have been born anywhere else) in 1797—eleven years after Weber. And he, too, lived his childhood in the war-torn years when Napoleon was teaching the emperors a lesson they never properly learned. There was little money in the home of a parish schoolmaster whose first wife bore ten children, of whom half died in infancy, and perhaps even less when the father married again and had five more children. But the whole family was united and affectionate, and Franz, the genius child, always had what we now call background—books, music and a general desire to develop understanding.

His gifts got him into a good school named—strangely to our ears—the Imperial Convict School. He became an imperial chorister, he played in the school orchestra, he played chamber music at home. And he wrote and wrote, always begging for more paper to write on. He grew up in the shadow of Beethoven and, like Weber, did not at first come to terms with the titan's music. At the age of nineteen, by which time he had himself composed several masterpieces, he was still able to write of Beethoven's '*bizarrerie* which unites the tragic and the comic, the agreeable and the repulsive, the heroic and the petty, the Holiest and a harlequin; infuriates those who hear it instead of dissolving them in love, and makes them laugh instead of raising them heavenwards'. He adored Mozart—'what countless consolatory images of a bright better world hast thou stamped on our souls'.

Later he was to change his mind, and still later Beethoven, almost at the end of his life, was to discover Schubert's songs and admire them, but we cannot too often remind ourselves that Beethoven's later music frightened even the best minds out of their wits. And it still puzzles the sort of concert-goer and record buyer who is just fond of music.

All his life Schubert was inured to hardship. While still a schoolboy he wrote to his brother:

You know from experience that we all like to eat a roll and a few

95

apples sometimes, the more so if after a middling lunch one may not look for a miserable evening meal for eight and a half hours. This wish, which has often become insistent, is now becoming more and more frequent, and I had willy-nilly to make a change. The few groats I receive from Father go to the deuce the very first days, and what am I to do for the rest of the time? 'Whosoever believeth on Him shall not be put to shame.' I thought so too.—How if you were to let me have a few kreutzer a month? You would not so much as know it, while I in my cell should think myself lucky, and be content.

He signed this 'Your loving, poor, hopeful, and again poor brother', and for the rest of his life he was loving, poor, hopeful and again poor. But he was never gutter-poor or destitute and he was never without many friends.

In his Vienna there was an ever-increasing number of music-lovers—serious amateurs whose idea of a pleasant Sunday was to spend the day in playing chamber music and singing songs and trying over the newest symphonies four-handed on the piano. In such company Schubert would find a better piano than he could ever afford and an understanding audience. Schubert parties became known as *Schubertiades*, and there were many, many people who would say, simply and sincerely, that they loved dear Franz. But, alas, their daughters did not fall in love with him, and the countless love songs flowed from the pen of a man whose own love life was full of frustration.

In the story of the piano we see Schubert again and again taking his music to a party and spending most of the evening at the keyboard. Sometimes his friends listened to a long and profound sonata (and sometimes they complained that it was too long and that their dear friend ought to omit some of the repetitions). Sometimes they played chamber music. Sometimes they persuaded him to improvise waltzes for the younger people to dance to. (Can I not myself remember playing a sonata followed by fox-trots and blues?) What they almost certainly remembered in after years when their dear Franz was dead was the songs, especially when Vogl sang them.

Johann Michael Vogl was a great baritone who, after an operatic career, became a *Lieder* singer. Thirty years older than Schubert he was at first, almost inevitably, a bit patronizing.

'There is some stuff in you,' he said, 'but you are too little of an actor, too little of a charlatan. You squander your fine thoughts instead of developing them.' Soon he became a devoted champion of his young friend, and no one who heard Vogl sing *Erlkönig* ever forgot it.

This song, written when Schubert was eighteen, must make us stop and consider Schubert's extraordinary use of the piano. Goethe's poem tells of a man riding through the dark forest with his little son in his arms. The forest is sinister and stormy and the child is frightened. The father asks the little boy why he is afraid and the child says he can hear the Erl-King, the wicked ogre who steals away the souls of children. The word 'Erl' is probably derived from *Elle* meaning elf, it being understood that elves in the old legends were not delightful 'elfin' creatures. Alternatively the word may come from *Erlenbaum*, the alder tree that has ancient associations with witchcraft.

As in all such stories the question is asked three times. First, 'I can hear the Erl-King. . . .' The child hears the voice inaudible to his father; and *we* hear it enticing the boy away. Then, 'Father, father, I can see the Erl-King. . . .' 'Nay, 'tis but the shadow cast by the moon'; but we have heard what the child hears. The third time, the Erl-King's voice becomes menacing. 'If thou wilt not come willingly I must take thee by force.' The father rides faster than ever but when he reaches his own door the child in his arms is dead.

It seems obvious enough that a song called 'The Erl-King' should have a piano part that suggests the galloping horse, but since when has a four-legged horse made a sound anything like triplets? Since when has a frightened heart hammered three to a beat?

The figure for the pianist's left hand runs up six notes of a minor scale and then returns through five, three and one. Is that the sound of wind in the trees? Yet the young man who was too little of an actor, too little of a charlatan, found a pattern of notes that would never have occurred to a sophisticated practitioner of the arts of programme-music. I know of no better example of what we helplessly call a stroke of genius, the shaft of lightning, the thunderbolt that brings inspiration (whatever that is) from on high (wherever that may be).

It would be idle to suggest that every one of Schubert's hundreds of songs leaves us thunderstruck, but the great ones that constitute such a large part of the *Lieder* repertoire have this magic. We gaze at some simple, apparently innocent collection of notes, we wonder how they can possibly apply to the title of the song, we play them, and we immediately know, before the singer has formed the first syllable of the poem, that these notes have been waiting since poetry began—waiting for the birth of Schubert. Make your audience weep with Gretchen at the spinning wheel; lull them with 'To be sung on the waters'; raise them on wings of joy 'To the Skylark'; and follow all the vicissitudes of the unhappy young man who loved the pretty daughter of the miller, and you will find again and again something that not only belongs to Schubert and to his chosen poets but half persuades us that the Spirit of the Piano had at last fallen in love and would never fall out of it.

Sometimes we arrange the events of history too tidily and may give the impression that the classical era ended on a Saturday night and the romantic era began on a Sunday morning, but I retain the notion, formed very early in my student life, that Schubert really did begin a new era. No doubt a *Lieder* recital may include some Mozart and Beethoven, but Mozart was above all an opera composer, and Beethoven confessed to a lack of enthusiasm for song-writing.

Schubert's early masterpieces of song are the true point of take-off in the history of the *Lied*. They are also—and the point is seldom made—the point of take-off for the drawing-room song, the sentimental 'ballad', the song that makes a fortune for the composer of operetta, and the hit-number of a film musical. No doubt the Vienna Strausses and Lehár are nearer relatives than London Sullivan and Paris Offenbach, and perhaps Gershwin's kinship is somewhat remote, but Schubert affects them all.

As for the song-writers of today, high and low, they severed themselves from the Schubert family when they gave up the piano.

Schubert's sonatas and other piano music did not galvanize piano-makers and inventors into new activity. They did not help to create a new school of piano-playing. Schubert wrote no studies, transcendental or otherwise, no concertos, no 'war-horse' pieces. Since public pianists are vain creatures (how can one acquire virtuosity without some degree of vanity?) there has been a long-standing tendency to regard Schubert's sonatas as not box-office. This is not to say that they are neglected masterpieces. The musical personality that attracts us to Schubert's symphonies and quartets is clear in the piano music and this piano music is deeply loved. But a Schubert sonata is not display music. As Vogl said, 'You are too little of an actor, too little of a charlatan.' And perhaps the great pianists of the world have been too much actors and charlatans. Only those who have cared for chamber music and *Lieder* (a great soloist *can* be a fine accompanist) have deeply devoted themselves to the sonatas; and the point must be made that one cannot play Schubert melodies with a vague sentimental expressiveness: one must play them as though one knew the non-existent words.

This is Schubert's great contribution to piano-playing. We must pause to consider it and, in the process, unlearn childish notions. A child pianist 'does theory' and learns that *crescendo* means gradually louder, by which he understands that each note is louder than the previous one. To show that this is not necessarily so I have a favourite illustration which is to say the word 'louder' in a crescendo manner. And what do we find? One says 'louder' and '*loud*-er' and 'LOUD-er'. 'Louder' is, in any case, a strong–weak word, and even when it is shouted at the end of a crescendo, the final *er*-sound will be relatively soft.

Sometimes in the company of gifted children I give them a simple test. 'Can you play an ordinary C major scale so as to sound like a love song? Can you make the scale seem to say *Tell me, O tell me you love me?*' A little experiment shows—and the experiment is by no means easy—that the scale is accented on C, F and B.

'Now make the scale seem to say *I never shall forget the day.*' This time the scale is accented on D and A, and that last note is well held.

This is also the moment to make the youngster realize that the composer may give no help to the pianist. All he will write in the score is *cantabile*. But how can one play in a singing style unless there is a suggestion of words? (And, by the way, to do this with Schubert's music you do not need to know German.)

I first discovered this when, as a student, and the champion sight-reader of my year, I was in constant demand to play for my singing friends. In Schubert, more perhaps than with any other composer, I constantly found the piano phrase that echoes the singer's most heartfelt utterance. It was not enough to lean on the keys and look soulful. In a song the piano had to sing the words too. And in Schubert's piano music the piano must sing the poem that never was.

This is the essence of romantic music, and from Schubert's time onwards, thousands of piano pieces called Romance, Intermezzo, Caprice, Prelude could have been called by the title 'patented' by Mendelssohn: Song without Words.

In Russia, John Field, seldom a song composer, was also making the piano sing in a way that was to have great consequences. The Muscovite nobility admired their Irish piano teacher and depended on him as they depended on their French cooks and dressmakers, their German administrators, their British businessmen and engineers (Clementi and Collard) and their Italian singers. Russian opera was not yet in existence. It awaited the work of Glinka—a Field pupil. But an Italian style of coloratura singing was greatly admired. Field, without perhaps being a conscious imitator, brought coloratura singing to the keyboard. Like several other outstanding pianists of his time he had discovered the conjuring tricks of sensitive touch, and as a composer he was alive to all the possibilities of the ever-improving piano. His left hand knew how to spread harmonies over wide distances and keep them all sounding with the help of the sustaining pedal. His right hand had command of nuance. He also developed decorations that were more than ornaments and less than cadenzas. Ornaments are often no more than trills and shakes and turns: cadenzas are interruptions, exciting and dazzling maybe, but temporarily stopping the onward flow of the 'argument'. But Field's *fiorature* were small, brilliant sprays and showers of notes that seemed to enhance an otherwise simple melody. The rhythm was unhindered, needing only that slight, subtle flexibility of beat that we call *rubato*.

We can never hope to describe precisely how to be imprecise, and the word *rubato* has given rise to pages of not very helpful 'fine writing' about ebb and flow, give and take, and the swaying of trees in the breeze. But *rubato* can be seen to be done when we watch the hand of an opera conductor persuading his players to be at one with a singer in the throes of a passionate aria. We certainly see the beats but we do not see a metronome.

Rubato was not invented by Field (we have noticed Mozart's awareness of it), but his new kind of music, for which he invented the title Nocturne, called for a special sensitivity to this element in piano-playing, and we shall find it spoken of, again and again, by Chopin and Liszt.

Field is now a half-forgotten composer. His seven concertos may occasionally be taken off the library shelf to help a radio producer to build a series of historical programmes. Like any other pianist I sometimes play a Field nocturne as though to say 'Yes, but before Chopin's nocturnes there were . . .'. I also go back to Field's Op. 1, No. 1. How quickly he found his own unique voice! He must have written this two-movement sonata under the tutelage of Clementi and, sure enough, the first movement bears the stamp of the apprentice's sorcerer. But the second movement is a gay, jaunty, amusing rondo such as nobody else could have written. Has it an Anglo-Irish flavour? I have known my friends, invited to guess the composer, offer Percy Grainger . . . who was Australian.

The genteel and polite houses that were furnished with elegant pianos heard little enough of Beethoven, Weber, Field and Schubert. What happened in families of quality is portrayed unerringly by Jane Austen, and I quote from quotations in that excellent book, *Men, Women, and Pianos* by Arthur Loesser. Jane Austen was herself lukewarm about music, though she could play country dances to amuse her nephews and nieces, and she had a sharp eye for those who pretended to be enthusiastic. She is indulgent to her heroine, Elizabeth, in *Pride and Prejudice*, but not to sister Mary:

> Her performance was pleasing, though by no means capital. After a song or two, and before she could reply to the entreaties

of several that she should sing again, she was eagerly succeeded at the instrument by her sister Mary, who having, in consequence of being the only plain one in the family, worked hard for knowledge and accomplishments, was always impatient for display.

Mary had neither genius nor taste; and though vanity had given her application, it had given her likewise a pedantic air and conceited manner, which would have injured a higher degree of excellence than she had reached. Elizabeth, easy and unaffected, had been listened to with much more pleasure, though not playing half so well; and Mary, at the end of a long concerto, was glad to purchase praise and gratitude by Scotch and Irish airs, at the request of her younger sisters. . . .

I wonder about the 'long concerto'. Was Miss Austen herself ignorant enough to use the word concerto to mean anything loud, long and important-sounding? However, I love the portrait of Lady Catherine de Bourgh: 'There are few people in England, I suppose, who have more true enjoyment of music than myself, or a better natural taste. If I had ever learnt, I should have been a great proficient.'

Jane Austen never mentioned the Napoleonic wars, but I wonder if her characters ever played *The Glorious Battle of Trafalgar*. The title page in a fine variety of letterings—plain, italic and copperplate—tells of: '*The Cruising of the British Fleet off Cadiz*—The Signals—*Bearing-down in Two Columns on the Enemy, Clearing Ship for Action. Drum beating to Quarters*—Lord Nelson's Signal—"*England Expects that every Man will do his Duty*", THE ENGAGEMENT, *Boarding &c. an Elegy on the Death of* ADMIRAL LORD NELSON, *Commander of the British Fleet, Together with Beginning & Concluding Songs, Composed (for the* PIANOFORTE *&* VOICE) *& respectfully Dedicated to* ADMIRAL LORD COLLINGWOOD BY JOHN WATLEN, *Composer of the Celebrated Sea Piece* THE SURRENDER OF TOULON. *Formerly an Officer on Board the Defence 74 Guns one of the above Fleet. Price 5s/–.*'

The songs inveigh against 'the murd'rous thraldom-making Tyrant' and assure Nelson that 'thy very name shall strike with dread the Foe'. At every change in the music the composer tells us what it all means. A plain C major scale over four octaves is 'The Blowing up of the French'. Broken chords in F major suggest 'The Victory close engaged with Two Ships of the

Enemy'. Every thump on a bass octave is marked 'Cannons', and a descending B flat scale, becoming slow and quiet as it nears its end, is 'Lord Nelson mortally wounded by a Musket Shot from the Enemies Top'.

A similar piece—and it had enormous vogue—was *The Battle of Prague* by Katzwarra. This one has a Heavy Cannonade; also Cries of the Wounded.

We laugh at this nonsense, but Beethoven's *Wellington's Victory* or *The Battle of Vittoria*, sometimes called the Battle Symphony, is of the same genre. In it the French are represented by the song 'Marlbrouck s'en va-t-en guerre' which sounds odd to English ears since 'Marlbrouck' refers back to the earlier wars of the Duke of Marlborough and the melody is now used on convivial occasions in Great Britain, and perhaps beyond the seas, to the words 'For he's a jolly good fellow' or 'We won't be home till the morning'. The English forces in the *Battle of Vittoria* are represented by 'God Save the King', a tune greatly admired by Beethoven (and me). It has grandeur and brevity and manages to be royal and impressive without being a march. Amongst national anthems it has no rivals on a musical level except *La Marseillaise*, which is the greatest day-of-glory song of all time.

In the same category as the Battle Symphony but composed much later is Tchaikovsky's *1812*. In this the enemy song is *La Marseillaise* and the Russian patriotic song is a national anthem that was composed long after 1812. It is still box-office.

These two works do not, perhaps, belong to the story of the piano, but in my own personal story of the piano I still treasure a ninepenny piano version of 1812 that made our family piano rattle. Piano, piano, piano—everything was played on the piano.

There must have been a time when the battle pieces aroused patriotic, nationalistic and military fervour in their players. One wonders about Beethoven's feelings. This former Bonapartist conducted his battle piece in the presence of all the crowned autocrats in Europe, assembled at the Congress of Vienna, and they sent him presents of money that he invested in shares in the Bank of Austria.

Let us refrain from condemnation. The musicians of today have read their history and recall, if they are old enough, how feelings can change as war and revolution and counter-revolution and the downfall of empires succeed one another. Perhaps for this reason no battle pieces now shake our pianos with patriotic ardour.

In 1812 a new ardour was sweeping across Europe, never mind the war. This was a rage for dancing the waltz, and very shocking it seemed in its intimate embracings and its giddy whirlings. It was denounced in pulpit and newspaper article. Even in earlier days of the waltz, before it became a kind of fever, Burney had said 'we could not help reflecting how uneasy an English mother would be to see her daughter so familiarly treated', but now Byron had a few lines to write on the subject:

> Round all the confines of the yielded waist
> The strangest hand may wander undisplaced . . .
> Till some might marvel, with the modest Turk,
> If nothing follows all this palming work . . .
> Something does follow at a fitter time;
> The breast thus publicly resign'd to man,
> In private may resist him—if it can.

Quite certainly the waltz, which is now thought of as cosy and old-fashioned, had for a long time the reputation of being dangerous and seductive, and the great waltzes of musical history should be played accordingly. The best were yet to be composed, by the Strausses, by Chopin and many others, but already the pianos of the world were stirring up passions on the ballroom floor, and whether God or the Devil inspired the musicians must be left open to question.

Certainly the waltz did nothing to diminish the demand for pianos. Broadwood went on from strength to strength. Clementi, back from his travels, saw some of his pianos exported to America. The French pianist and composer, Ignaz Pleyel (born in Austria), followed Clementi's example by going into business. As far back as 1797 he had become a publisher. Later he sold some Clementi pianos in Paris and sent compositions to London, but by 1813 he was making, not hundreds or thousands of pianos but certainly dozens, and his firm was to become one of the most famous in Europe.

As for Érard, he was busy improving the escapement by providing what he called double-escapement. This mechanism affected the behaviour of the hammer while a key was being held. The hammer stayed near the string until the key was released and only then fell back to its bed. This meant that repetition on one note could become swifter than ever before, and Dussek proved the point in an impressive recital in 1808. Indeed nuance of touch was altogether improved.

In 1821 Érard patented the action in England, but this did not prevent other makers from devising something similar for top-class instruments.*

Clever engineering could improve pianos. Could it improve pianists? Why not? While the Broadwoods and the Érards were organizing piano factories, and well-meaning educationists were organizing conservatories (1808 Milan and Naples, 1811 Prague), John Baptist Logier was promoting practice machines. Born in Alsace he settled in Dublin, played in a military band, ran a Music Saloon, and, a little ahead of Beethoven, composed a *Battle of Vittoria* performed by 'upwards of 150 performers'. He then began to organize piano classes for children playing on up to ten pianos at a time. Many historians have made fun of this—Schonberg and Loesser among them—but in these days when Suzuki in Japan teaches thousands of tiny tots to play difficult music on half-sized violins—getting them to stroll about, playing Bach with wonderful unanimity—we should not condemn the idea, even if Logier was a bit of a charlatan. His prospectus claimed too much, promising that pupils of ordinary capacity and ordinary industry could be made to emulate Mozart, but class piano teaching is a perfectly respectable idea with only one disadvantage. The clever children soon begin to outdistance the others. For them Logier organized individual lessons.

There was money to be made, and Logier soon had a new

* Some inventors persisted in trying to improve duration of sound by means of repeating hammers or bowing devices. Even Érard patented a toothed cylinder that agitated the hammers, and another device, invented by one Alexander in Paris, had a great future foretold for it by Berlioz. Such inventions were soon forgotten.

idea. He invented a 'Chiroplast', a means of holding the student's hands and fingers in what was conceived to be the ideal shape and position. Rods and adjustment-screws and brass plates with holes through which the fingers might be thrust were guaranteed to prevent any untoward movements. One fears that they may have constricted movement altogether. The hands could slide sideways along the rods but could not assist the fingers to produce tone.

Some very distinguished musicians took it up. We may think that Clementi, always on the make, was less than honest in giving it his 'warmest approbation and recommendation' especially as he took up its manufacture, but the great Parisian pianist and teacher, Kalkbrenner, used some sort of version of the Chiroplast, and his rival, Henri Herz, produced a Dactylion in which the fingers worked against suspended springs.

In Dublin Logier organized a Chiroplast Club at Chiroplast Hall and put its members into uniform (no doubt getting a commission from the outfitter). In due course Logier academies spread to London, Berlin, New York, Philadelphia and Calcutta. Inevitably the Logier craze petered out, especially as the machine positively prevented the thumb from passing under the fingers and was therefore useless in scale-playing; but it is still possible to believe that traditional ways of teaching are not necessarily the last word.

In any case, it was an era of experiment and uncertainty. Long and earnest, and sometimes malicious, were the comparisons about the studies of Czerny and Cramer, the playing of Hummel and Field and Moscheles. Should one take lessons in London or Paris or go on to Vienna where, in 1818, there was a new conservatory? What about Berlin—where, Spohr complained, there was no concert hall? Were Hummel's Twenty-four Preludes worth studying? Were Field's new pieces, the Nocturnes, worth buying? Could one take women pianists seriously?

And, from the composer's point of view, what could audiences be expected to accept—or endure? Beethoven wrote to Ries about the Hammerklavier Sonata:

Should the sonata not be suitable for London, I could send you another one; or you could omit the Largo and begin straight-away with the Fugue, which is the last movement; or you could use the first movement and then the Adagio, and then the third movement, the Scherzo—and omit entirely No. 4 with the Largo and Allegro Risoluto. Or you could take just the first movement and the Scherzo and let them form the whole sonata. I leave it to you to do what you think best.

I tell this to my students and they cannot believe their ears. Certainly no Ferdinand Ries of today would dare confront the critics with bits and pieces of the Hammerklavier, and perhaps the original Ferdinand Ries was uneasy. Interestingly enough, it was just before then that some of the best musicians and music-lovers of London formed the Philharmonic Society. In 1813 the time had come to promote serious music seriously.

11. *Four Geniuses at Once*

1809 Mendelssohn. 1810 Schumann and Chopin. 1811 Liszt. Were the stars in some favourable conjunction? Could the pianists who bought the music of Beethoven, Schubert, Field and Weber reasonably hope for more? The four babies of un-suspected genius were destined to grow up in homes where, of course, there was a piano; of course there was a love for learning and art; of course parents would know where to find good teachers.

Of the four of them, Mendelssohn was born with a silver spoon in his mouth. He was of distinguished descent. His grand-father, Moses Mendelssohn, at a time when Jews were at last emerging from the ghettos of Europe, made a reputation as philosopher and man of letters. Moses's son went into business and made a fortune in banking. Whether out of conviction or to make himself more acceptable socially, Abraham became a Christian. He became a Protestant after his sisters had become Catholics. Also, following the example of his wife's brother, he added the name Bartholdy to Mendelssohn.

His wonderfully gifted child was baptized Felix Mendelssohn-Bartholdy and was nurtured in an atmosphere of love and money, not over indulged but greatly encouraged. Perhaps it was fortunate for Felix that his father was not a professional musician. There were none of the pressures that Leopold Mozart exerted on Wolfgang. And we may guess that Abraham Mendelssohn was not too puffed up by his own success in the world of business. We remember that charming remark: 'Formerly I was the son of my father, now I am the father of my son.' But we cannot doubt that Mr. and Mrs. Mendelssohn (never mind the Bartholdy hyphenation) had the customary Jewish attitude to the upbringing of a brainy boy. In passing it is interesting to know that Felix and his younger brother Paul were baptized before their parents took the plunge (if that is the apposite expression) and Mother then called herself, besides Lea, Felicia Paulina.

Besides Felix there was a clever daughter. When Fanny and Felix were old enough to take music seriously, their mother taught them for five minutes every day until they were ready for eight or ten. And later when they had professional lessons she remained at hand, knitting while they practised.

They had three music teachers—for piano, for violin and for harmony and composition; another for drawing and painting (Felix remained a competent sketcher of holiday scenes); and another for Greek. They got up at five and set to work. Only on Sundays did they lie abed longer.

By the time he was nine Felix was astonishing music-lovers with his piano-playing—the family home was open to many visitors—and at eleven he was systematically composing. It all sounds too much, but nobody has suggested that the boy was overdriven by stern parents. There seems to have been great love and confidence in that remarkable family.

Whereas his as yet unknown rivals, Schumann, Chopin and Liszt, began with little else but piano music, young Felix was composing symphonies, operatic fragments, cantatas, organ pieces, songs and chamber music.

The early piano pieces are astonishing. At fourteen he composed the Andante and Rondo Capriccioso that to this day is a standard work in the piano repertoire. Anyone who knows this delightful piece should not be surprised by the *Midsummer Night's Dream* overture that he composed a few years later. The Rondo is a happily youthful work, but not in a single phrase does it sound juvenile. It has total professional certainty. It is enough to make even a prodigy despair.

Yet perhaps it is a pity that he advanced so far so soon. He well knew how to write for the piano, and his 'piano writing' never went further. As inventors of pianism his rivals out-distanced him. Interestingly, they all wrote *études* that were transformations of mere studies. Mendelssohn never did. He became a great favourite with pianists for whom the great *études* would have been too hard.

As a business-man August Schumann was nowhere near as successful as Abraham Mendelssohn, but by great effort he had brought himself to a condition of modest prosperity. He was a bookseller who was also something of a novelist, poet, translator and biographer. Indeed he would have liked to be altogether a man of letters rather than a shopkeeper, but he learned the hard way that while it was pleasant to translate Byron it was more realistic to publish *Portraits of Contemporaneous Celebrities*. Indeed as a young man he had written several books with the object of being able to buy a business and get married.

He must have been a curious and interesting mixture of sensibility and what's called good sense. He had three sons and a daughter before Robert was born and they were all given the advantages of a good home and a decent education. And when it became obvious that the youngest was a born musician, father, of course, looked for a teacher. This teacher, one Johann Gottfried Kuntsch, was no great master but he was affection-ately remembered in later years by Schumann—as many of us remember with kindness the 'little' man or woman who first opened our ears and energized our fingers.

Very interestingly, at the age of seven or thereabouts, Robert revealed a knack of inventing little pieces that were supposed to portray the people around him, and this knack never deserted him.

At the age of nine, the child was taken by his father to hear the great pianist Moscheles—who later gave piano lessons to

Mendelssohn—and Robert was deeply impressed. He kept the programme as a 'sacred relic'—or so he told Moscheles many years later. Another two or three years and the boy was playing in public—also giving recitations. It was obvious that he needed lessons from a true master, and August Schumann approached Weber, who was too busy.

What of the recitations? The fact is that the boy was as interested in poetry as in music. He joined his school's German Literary Society and found himself able to offer opinions on Sophocles, Homer, Horace, Plato, Cicero and other classic writers. He loved Schiller, failed to love Goethe, and was overwhelmed by Jean Paul Richter, under whose influence he was liable, in letters to his friends, to write this sort of thing: '. . . a last kiss from glowing lips was touching the sweetly fading green of the wooded heights; golden cloudlets floated in the pure aether. . . .'

Good! Any youngster who does not go through some such phase will never write. He began to fall in love. At one moment he would 'gladly die on her eyelash, and gladly, gladly, be no more'. At another he would romp with the girls at a wayside inn: '. . . we rejoiced and rushed about, staggering among the legs of the clodhoppers, and then took a tender farewell of the whole company by imprinting smacking kisses on the lips of all the peasant girls. . . .'

Alas, at the time when a teenager is very vulnerable, one of his sisters committed suicide, and shortly afterwards his father died. He was sixteen. It was all too easy for him now to swing between morbid melancholy and the sort of gaiety that he could feel amongst congenial friends. In his home town, Zwickau, there was a merchant named Carus, and in the Carus home he met artists, music-lovers and a young woman (wife of Carus's nephew) who sang well. Here was his escape to happiness, but the future was dark and uncertain. At the Caruses there were champagne and cigars (of which he grew fond); at home there were discussions with his mother and his guardian about the advisability of adopting a safe profession.

Over-persuaded, he went off to Leipzig to study law. He was eighteen. Beethoven had recently died. Schubert, aged thirty-one, was to die a few months later.

In 1787 a young Frenchman, aged sixteen, left his native Lorraine and went, nobody seems to know why, to Poland. There he learned the language and became as Polish as could be, to the extent of joining the National Guard and fighting against the Russians when the Tsar seized the largest part of the country, leaving the rest to be divided between Prussia and Austria.

He became a tutor to various distinguished families. In those days French was the polite language. Anyone who did not speak it was simply not well bred. He taught the little girl who later became known to history as Maria Walewska, mistress of Napoleon. He taught the children of a family named Skarbek and he married a poor relation of theirs—Tekla-Justyna Krzyzanowska. He had put down roots and he seemed positively disinclined to refer to his French origin. Indeed, later, when Frédéric Chopin was a celebrity in Paris, two of Nicholas's sisters, living quietly in a French village, did not know that the great composer was their nephew.

Nicholas and Justyna had four children: a girl, the genius boy and two more girls, and they seem to have been a united, affectionate family. They were all clever: the eldest girl, Louise, composed some good mazurkas. Furthermore their father's scholastic career brought them into contact with people of education and influence. Nicholas became professor of French in the new Lyceum (High School) in Warsaw, took in boarders to supplement his income, and then taught also at the School of Artillery and Military Engineering. No wonder young Frédéric grew up with the outlook and manner that made some people later nickname him the prince.

At a very early age young Frédéric* showed that he was extraordinarily gifted. He went to the family grand piano at the age of six, found a few notes, and wept with excitement.

This in itself is not unique. There is a legend in my own family that at a similar age I was liable to weep if I played a particularly affecting chord, and I am no Chopin. I record the fact merely to say that Chopin's tears seem convincing to me, not a pretty story invented by a romantic biographer. Soon he was

* His Polish names were Fryderyk Franciszek. In Paris he was usually addressed as Frédéric.

having lessons with a competent musician named Zywny. Just as Schumann remembered Kuntsch, Frederick later remembered Zywny, particularly because of his enthusiasm for Bach.

That Bach should have been second only to Mozart in Chopin's estimation comes as a surprise to many people who do not realize how contrapuntal Chopin's music is, even though it is never *fugato*.

Very soon the child was being listened to with astonishment by distinguished people who wondered if another Mozart had come into their midst. He composed a march, played it to the Grand Duke Constantine, had it written out by his teacher and then heard a version of it played by a military band. At the age of eight, and with his name spelt Schoppin in the programme, he played a concerto by Gyrowetz (whoever he was) at a charity concert and soon was noticed by such great people as the Radziwills, Potockis and Czartoryskis. At the age of ten he played to the great prima donna, Angelica Catalani, and she gave him a gold watch.

He outgrew Zywny, and his father saw to it that his general education should not be neglected. But he worked at harmony and managed to have lessons with Joseph Elsner, founder and head of the Warsaw Conservatoire. In due course he would outgrow Elsner, but meanwhile this excellent man was to be a good and important influence. As for the quality of his compositions it is hard to credit that at the age of, perhaps, fourteen he had produced a draft of the Mazurka in A minor, later published as Op. 17, No. 4. It is a heartbreakingly sensitive piece, probably the mazurka I care for most.

At this time he had begun to write long, gossipy, amusing letters to the young men who were his close friends. He addresses them with endearments and showers them with 'kisses'—not to be misinterpreted. (I have distant foreign nephews who still think it appropriate to touch cheeks with their London uncle.) Artlessly they provide us with a self-portrait. Translations into English of letters written in colloquial Polish with odd sentences in French can never be precise, but I quote from the Opienski collection translated, very readably, by Voynich. In one, young Frédéric refers to

... how many shelves, and boxes, and cupboards there are, how many hundreds of pieces of music all in disorder on the piano, like peas and cabbage—even not counting the Hummels, and Rieses and Kalkbrenners (to whom fate has doubtless allotted a place, in so large a community, with Pleyel, Hemerlyn and Hoffmeister) —all lying in wait for me.

Like any student, any time, anywhere, he notices his teacher's eccentricities.

... I was reading ... to Zywny, as he sat over Gorski, who was falling asleep at the piano, wiping his nose, twisting his handkerchief into a roll, poking it into the pocket of his clumsily made green coat ... adjusting his peruke. ...

He boasts of his sister's mazurka, tells of seeing *The Barber of Seville* and composing a *polonaise* on one of its melodies, eagerly awaits *Freischütz*, and remarks on every performer who comes to Warsaw.

He mentions an instrument called a choraleon, made by one Brunner. It was on this instrument, also called aeolimelodikon, that he played to Tsar Alexander I, newly arrived in Warsaw to open the Polish Diet. The Poles may not have been greatly delighted by the festivities in honour of their conqueror, but it was an honour for the fifteen-year-old boy to play to the Emperor, who graciously bestowed diamond rings on pianist and manufacturer, and it was a further honour to be 'noticed' not only by Prince Antoine Radziwill but by the Leipzig journal *Allgemeine Musikalische Zeitung*. Just who invented the new instrument is a mystery. Arthur Hedley in his *Chopin* (Master Musicians series) gives Brunner as 'constructor' and describes the machine as 'a kind of piano-organ'—whatever that may mean. Hedley knew more about Chopin than any man alive, but I never heard him speak with any special knowledge of pianos. In Chopin's *Letters* a footnote says that the choraleon or aeolimelodikon was invented by a Polish professor named Hoffmann and made by Brunner. But one of Chopin's letters says that on a visit to a friend's house he spent nearly the whole evening in admiring Dlugosz's eolipantaleon, and a footnote in the *Letters* says that this was a combination of choraleon and pianoforte invented by the skilled artisan Dlugosz and made by Brunner. The name recalls the Pantaleon Hebenstreit* who brilliantly played a large, developed dulcimer to the pleasure of Louis XIV.

When Chopin was seventeen, in the midst of a mostly rather jolly letter he suddenly turns to this:

> We have illness in the house. Emilja has been in bed for 4 weeks; she has got a cough and has begun to spit blood and Mamma is frightened. Malcz ordered bloodletting. They bled her once, twice; leeches without end, vesicators, sinapisms, wolfs-bane; horrors, horrors! All this time she has been eating nothing; she has grown so thin that you wouldn't know her. . . . You'll have to imagine it, because I can't describe it for you. Now about other subjects.

No wonder he could scarcely bear to write of his dying sister. Not long before, he had been sent to the Silesian watering-place, Reinertz, to take the cure and improve his health. He followed a strict regime, and though he enjoyed walking in the countryside he was forbidden the more strenuous excursions.

It was at this time that he composed his Variations on 'La ci darem la mano' from *Don Giovanni*, a work that, a few years later, was to cause Schumann to exclaim, in print, 'Hats off, gentlemen! A genius!' We never play it now: it is too full of the fashionable 'passage-work' that Chopin soon outgrew. But Schumann was right. The genius is there, and the more mature style is already apparent. Particularly striking are the moments when Mozart's aria is transformed into a Chopin *étude*, a Chopin nocturne, a Chopin *polonaise*. This was undeniable quality: nobody thought him overrated.

In 1828 Hummel came to town. Every such visit was grist to Chopin's mill. He could never have enough of new piano music, new operas. And it was the prospect of hearing even more that made him so glad to go off to Berlin with a colleague of his father's—the older man to a scientific conference, the younger to concerts and operas. Strangely—since he generally had self-confidence—he writes from Berlin: 'I have seen Spontini, Zelter, and Mendelssohn, but I did not speak with any of them as I felt shy about introducing myself.'

* See page 24.

One result of the Berlin visit was deep admiration for Handel's *Ode to St. Cecilia*. He found it near 'to the ideal I have formed of great music'. But he is soon back to pianos and piano music. He refers to some pianos as pantaleons. It is possible that downward-striking hammers were prevalent in Poland at this time, but the name is probably used ironically to suggest something less than the newest and best. He writes to his close friend Titus Woyciechowski about another young man who was to be a lifelong companion, Juljan Fontana.

> The orphaned Rondo for two pantaleons has found a stepfather in the person of Fontana; perhaps you have met him at our house; he goes to the university. He has been over a month learning it, but he has learned it, and the other day, at Bucholtz's we tried what effect it *might* produce. Might, because, as the pantaleons were not quite in tune, the emotion didn't always come off. . . . Wherever you go there are Leszczynski's bad instruments. . . .

There is no mention of Beethoven, recently dead. Schubert was probably unknown. Chopin's genius was too confined in Warsaw—once the capital of a kingdom but now only a provincial centre in the vast Russian empire. The young man's father addressed a petition to the Minister for Public Instruction, Grabowski:

> I have a son whose innate musical gifts call out for him to be educated in this art. His late Imperial Majesty Tsar Alexander, of blessed memory, graciously deigned to present him with a precious ring as a mark of His satisfaction when my son had the honour to be heard by the Monarch, His Imperial Majesty. His Imperial Highness the Grand Duke, Supreme Commander of the Army, has often been most graciously pleased to allow him to give proofs of his growing talent in His Most Serene presence. And lastly, many of the highest personages and musical connoisseurs can support the view that my son could be a credit to his country in his chosen profession if he were given the opportunity to pursue the necessary studies to their conclusion. He has completed his preliminary studies; all that he now needs is to visit foreign countries, especially Germany, Italy and France, so as to form himself upon the best models. For the purposes of such a journey, which might last three years, funds are required which

my modest resources, based exclusively on my salary as a teacher, are insufficient to provide.

The minister forwarded the petition and supported the figure of 5,000 zlotys a year. The family waited. Meanwhile the new Tsar, Nicholas I, came to Warsaw to be crowned King of Poland. And Paganini came to give ten concerts.

This extraordinary violinist is of great importance in the history of the piano since, to Schumann, to Liszt, and to Chopin he brought the realization of just what virtuosity could be. His violin seemed to say to the piano, 'Match that if you can.' And the piano (through Chopin) provided such *études* as had never been composed before.

Nothing could now hold Chopin in Warsaw, even though the petition for financial help was rejected. 'Public funds cannot be used for this class of artist.' ('Cannot be used' replaced the first draft—'cannot be wasted'!)

In 1830, aged twenty, he gave two public performances of his Concerto in F minor and, later, of the one in E minor. It was enough. The time had come to go, even without a grant, and he set out on his first professional foreign tour.

In Vienna his success was immediate and extraordinary. Evidently he possessed not only genius but presence—charisma. He called on the powerful publisher, Haslinger:

> . . . while showing me his finest editions, he informed me that my Variations will probably appear in a week's time in the *Odéon*. I didn't expect that.
>
> He wants me to play in public. They tell me here that it would be a great loss for Vienna if I were to leave without being heard. All this is incomprehensible for me. Schuppanzigh, to whom I also had introductions, told me that, though he is not giving winter quartets any more he would try to arrange one during my visit to Vienna.
>
> I have been once to the Hussarzewski's'; the old man was enthusiastic about my playing and asked me to dinner. At the dinner there were a lot of Viennese folk, and, as if he had arranged it with them, they all told me to play in public. Stein wanted at once to send one of his instruments to my lodging, and then to the concert, if I give one. Graff, who, by the way, makes better instru-

ments, made the same offer. . . . They are awfully pleased with the Variations. . . .

P.S. I have decided. Blahetka says that I shall cause a *furore*, that I'm a virtuoso of the front rank, that I count with Moscheles, Herz and Kalkbrenner. Würfel today introduced me to Count Gallenberg, Kapellmeister Seyfried and everyone else he encountered, as a young man whom he was persuading to give a concert (*nota bene* without any pay), which greatly pleased Count Gallenberg, as it is a question of his pocket. . . . Würfel really is making everything easy for me; he will come to the rehearsal and is genuinely taking trouble over my début. . . . I have chosen one of Graff's instruments for the concert; I'm afraid Stein will take offence, but I shall thank him warmly for his kindness.

I hope the Lord will help me.—Don't worry!

Another letter, written four days later, suggests that the Lord did help and that there was indeed no need to worry:

As soon as I appeared on the stage, the bravos began; after each variation the applause was so loud that I couldn't hear the orchestra's tutti. . . .

The journalists have taken a fancy to me. . . . Gallenberg likes my compositions. . . .

My friends and colleagues spread themselves over the hall to listen for opinions and criticisms. . . . Some lady said, 'A pity the boy has so little style.' If that is all the fault anybody found—and otherwise they assure me they heard only praises, and that they never started the bravos themselves—then I don't need to worry. . . . My spies in the stalls assure me that people even jumped on the seats. . . .

All the same it is being said everywhere that I played too softly or, rather, too delicately for people used to the piano-pounding of the artists here.

Further letters continue the tale of triumph:

. . . Today I met Count Lichnowski. . . . It's the same who was Beethoven's greatest friend. It's said everywhere here that the local nobility likes me. . . . Countess Lichnowska and her daughter, with whom I had tea today, are greatly delighted that I am to give a second concert next Tuesday. She told me, if I go to Paris by way of Vienna, not to forget to call on them, and they will give me a letter to some *comtesse*, Lichnowski's sister. They are very kind. Czerny has paid me a lot of compliments. . . .

I shan't give a third concert, and would not even give a second but they insist on it; besides, it occurred to me that people might say in Warsaw: 'What is it? He gave only one concert and went away; perhaps it was a failure.'

This time too I shall play for nothing; but that is to please the count, whose pocket is emaciated.

The second concert was, if anything, even more of a success than the first:

The moment I appeared on the stage there were bravos, repeated three times; and there was a larger audience. Baron— I don't know what his name is: the financier of the theatre, thanked me for the receipts. . . . All the professional musicians are captivated with my Rondo. Beginning with Kapellmeister Lachner and ending with the pianoforte-tuner, they are surprised at the beauty of the composition. . . . No one here wants to take me as a pupil. Blahetka said nothing surprised him so much as my having learned all that in Warsaw. I answered that under Zywny and Elsner the greatest donkey could learn.

I have captured both the learned and the emotional folk. . . . My finances are all right. I have just been to Schuppanzigh and Czerny. Czerny is more sensitive than any of his compositions. I have packed my bag. . . .

He had slightly bitchy things to say about the musicians he met. 'Thalberg takes tenths as easily as I do octaves, and wears studs with diamonds'; 'Moscheles does not at all astonish me'; 'Czerny has again arranged an overture for eight pianos and sixteen performances and seems to be very happy over it.'

He wrote in the same vein when, on the way home, he heard Pixis in Prague. 'He plays well but I should have liked him to play better (hush).'

Chopin knew his own worth. It may be that in choosing extracts from his letters referring only to his career-making I have given the impression that he was snobbish and self-satisfied. But he had to seek the approbation of the 'best' people and it has to be said that, as pianist and composer, he was totally uninterested in 'broad appeal'. He could be contemptuous of some of his rivals, but artistically he was never self-satisfied.

On his return home he fell in love with a talented and attractive young singer named Constantia Gladkowska.

Is this relevant to our story of the piano?

The great loves of the great musicians have been recounted many times and we need not dwell on them yet again while we follow the development of pianos and pianism. But we cannot ignore them altogether. A piano is a pianist's mistress, and his love relationship with the instrument that he touches and caresses and strikes with passion is coloured by his love affairs. Chopin as a young man believed in woman as inspiration. He wrote to Titus Woyciechowski:

> It is perhaps my misfortune that I have already found my ideal, whom I have served faithfully, though without saying a word to her, for six months; whom I dream of, to whose memory the adagio of my Concerto is dedicated, and who this morning inspired me to write the little waltz I am sending you. Notice the passage marked with an X. No one but you will know what it means. . . .

The concerto is the one in F minor; the waltz, in D flat, has a middle section in G flat, and that is the passage marked with an X. Published after Chopin's death it bears the deceptively high opus number 70 (No. 3).

I cannot help reflecting that the modern reader, almost embarrassed by Chopin's letters to Woyciechowski, turns to the music and is once again enchanted. We love what that means and prefer not to know *exactly* what it means. Other days, other customs; and we must accept a letter that ends: 'Forgive me for sending you the waltz; perhaps it will make you angry with me, but really I did it to give you pleasure, for I do love you desperately.'

Not only women but politics can affect the pianist. I am not the only pianist of this era who remembers the countries one could not visit, the fees that could not be brought past exchange control, the refugees from this tyranny and that, and the wars. Chopin, determined to go abroad again, wrote:

> It is true that Father did not want me to leave a few weeks ago because of the disturbances taking place throughout Germany. In addition to what happened in the Rhineland, in Saxony, which has also got a new king, in Brunswick, Kassel, Darmstadt etc., there were rumours that in Vienna too a couple of thousand

people were growing restive on account of flour. I don't know what the flour had to do with it, but I do know that there was something.

The widespread unrest had been triggered off by the fall of the Bourbons in Paris and their replacement by Louis Philippe, whom the Tsar described as king of the grocers. Chopin composed heartfelt music—for example the Étude in E major, Op. 10—he gave farewell performances, he exchanged rings with Constantia, he waited for the moment when he could take wings again.

At last the stage-coach bore him away. As it arrived in the Warsaw suburb of Wola, there was Elsner with a male-voice choir, with guitar accompaniment. His faithful teacher had composed a little cantata in which the refrain went:

> Although you leave our native land
> Still will your heart remain with us,
> And the memory of the genius within you.
> And so, from the bottom of our hearts, we say,
> 'Good luck wherever you go.'

In this fashion Chopin, aged twenty and full of high hopes, left Poland. He never returned.

In Hungary a frail little boy took to music so violently that he nearly died of piano-playing. When this was temporarily discouraged he became immersed in religious imaginings. He returned to music and, by the time he was nine, attracted the attention of three noblemen—Counts Apponyi, Szapary and Erdödy—who clubbed together to guarantee an income for six years that would support the best kind of education. When the boy was eleven the family moved to Vienna and the young prodigy took lessons with Czerny for piano and with Salieri for harmony and composition. Hummel was too expensive.

The boy, of course, was Liszt, and we may pause at the moment of his removal from home to consider his background. He was, as everybody knows, Hungarian. Yes, but his Austrian mother never spoke the language and always called him Franz, not Ferencz. His setting was rural. Yes, but his father, a farm-steward, was employed by the son of that great Prince

Esterházy who 'discovered' Haydn and supported the great composer as princes ought always to support genius. He was aware of the music of Haydn, Mozart and Beethoven. Yes, but a different kind of music was in his ears and his heart, and in his later years of grandeur he retained something of the sex appeal and allure of the 'raggle-taggle gipsies, O!'

He never had the sort of settled home life or serious education that was enjoyed by Mendelssohn, Schumann or Chopin. He was trained to be the darling of audiences.

Czerny was delighted to teach his little 'Putzi' and refused to accept a fee. Within two years the child was a celebrity, a phenomenon. Even Beethoven, very deaf and living in seclusion, was persuaded to take notice. Liszt later claimed to have been kissed by Beethoven and spoke of it as though it were a sort of apostolic blessing. The boy also met Schubert, but we know nothing of what was said.

We might well think that no city could be more important for a musician than Vienna, but then and for many years thereafter, Paris was the place that set the seal on artists who wanted to make their fortunes. Franz's father decided that the boy should seek enrolment at the Paris Conservatoire.

Armed with a letter from Prince Metternich (no less) father and son presented themselves to the Director. Cherubini explained that the regulations did not permit a foreigner to take lessons.

Anybody who serves on a music faculty knows the tiresomeness of rules imposed by ministries and education authorities and usually develops some cunning in circumventing them where necessary. That so great a man as Cherubini should have been unable (unwilling?) to bend the rules in favour of so astounding a student seems beyond belief. However, teachers were found outside the Conservatoire, and soon Franz was a lion in the *salons*. He toured the French provinces at the age of thirteen, and he crossed over to London where he is said to have improvised a fugue on 'Zitti, Zitti' from *The Barber of Seville*.

A likely tale! I would believe it about Mendelssohn, but I suspect that Liszt merely gave an impression of a man improvising a fugue, to the delight of a fashionable audience.

In the next year he toured France again, appeared at

Windsor before George IV (who thought himself qualified to decide that the boy was better than Moscheles and Cramer), and then went off to the provinces and to Ireland. At the Theatre Royal in Manchester, the fourteen-year-old artist, advertised as twelve years of age, played an Air with Grand Variations and Orchestral Accompaniment by Czerny, the Concerto in A minor by Hummel, and an Extempore Fantasia on a theme provided 'by any person present'. A nine-year-old violin prodigy was also in the programme.

Meanwhile he had composed a one-act operetta, *Don Sanche*, and this was given on his return to Paris, without any great success. He would never be an opera composer. What he would be was a composer of stunning studies, and at the age of fifteen he found a publisher for *Études en Douze Exercices pour le Piano*—an Opus 1 that would be reworked in later years as the *Études d'Exécution Transcendante*.

The extraordinary career continued. Another visit to England followed, this time to play for the Philharmonic Society. It was (for a while) too much and, suffering from exhaustion, he went in for prayer and fasting and thought again of a life of religion. In later years he reminded his mother of how 'during many years of my youth, I dreamed myself incessantly into the world of the saints. Nothing seemed to me so self-evident as heaven, nothing so true and rich in blessedness as the goodness and compassion of God.'

His father, however, said, 'You belong to Art, not to the Church', and took him to the seaside at Boulogne for a complete rest. Franz grew better but his father became ill and died, perhaps from typhoid.

Accounts of 'last words' are notoriously unreliable, but Adam Liszt's are supposed to have been, 'Je crains pour toi les femmes.' Liszt later said:

> This prevision was strange, for at that time, at the age of sixteen, I had no idea what a woman was, and in my simplicity I asked my confessor to explain the sixth and ninth Commandments to me, for I was afraid I might have broken them without knowing I had done so.

Did Liszt expect anyone to believe this?

After the death of his father, Franz sent for his mother, found an apartment in Paris and was soon making a good living as a teacher. He fell in love with Caroline de Saint-Cricq with a passion that, before long, caused her father to terminate the lessons. The girl, sixteen years of age, was already promised to a Count. Being shown the door was a traumatic experience for Liszt and may have had some bearing on his many later conquests of aristocratic women. Like many another man he never quite forgot his first love.

Once again he abandoned himself to religious and philosophical ideas, and he was further tormented by the thought that he should devote more time to composition and forget the lure of applause.

He reckoned without Paganini. He had only to hear this wizard of the violin, this gaunt figure who seemed to live out the legend that he had sold his soul to the devil as the price of virtuosity, to decide on mounting to greater and greater heights of pianism.

Schumann, Chopin, Liszt—all of them were deeply influenced by Paganini, and it may be that Liszt was influenced not only by Paganini's virtuosity but by his success—a success that produced shop windows full of hats, dresses, perfumes, gloves and walking sticks *à la Paganini* and made the concert promoters come running with fantastic offers. (In one year in England Paganini amassed some 16,000 eighteenth-century golden guineas.)

In a new fever of self-improvement Liszt read the Bible and the works of Homer, Plato, Locke, Byron, Lamartine and Chateaubriand, and studied the music of Beethoven, Bach, Hummel, Mozart and Weber. He worked for hours at exercises. He wrote a piano version of the *Symphonie Fantastique* of Berlioz, having developed a deep appreciation for the man and his music. He resumed concert-giving with such intensity that on one occasion he is reported to have fainted and been carried out in a fit of hysterics.

He was soon to meet Chopin.

12. *Getting On in the World*

While Mendelssohn, Schumann, Chopin and Liszt were growing up, the piano-makers, the publishers, the inventors were as
busy as ever. For the pianist it was: take your pick. Moscheles
describes a London concert in 1822.

> The strong metal plates used by Broadwood in building his
> instruments, give a heaviness to the touch, but a fullness and vocal
> resonance to the tone, which are well adapted to Cramer's legato,
> and those fingers softly gliding from key to key. I, however, use
> Clementi's more supple mechanism for my repeating notes, skips
> and full chords.

In 1825 Clementi produced (as has already been mentioned)
an 'automatic' piano. I once used one of these in a television
children's programme and, for the occasion, wore period
costume. In this guise I was able to talk of the miracles of
modern science. The piano was an upright of beautiful appearance and splendid workmanship. Going down on my knees I
removed the upright board that stands between pedals and
keyboard and revealed a large drum studded with pins. This
could be set in motion by clockwork, and therefore the piano
was also a musical box, making use of the conventional strings
and hammers. (*See Plate 4.*)

In Paris Jean-Henri (formerly Johann Heinrich) Pape
abandoned leather hammer-heads and patented felt coverings.
Beginning as an employee of Pleyel's he set up on his own and
was almost too busy throwing out new ideas. He seems never
to have made a piano that attracted the virtuosi, but some of
his ideas spread far and wide—ideas like crossing one set of
strings over the others—the low strings running from s.w. to
N.E., as it were, while the others went s.E. to N.w. This over-
strung piano allowed for longer strings without lengthening
grands or raising the height of uprights. He invented round and
hexagonal pianos, he tried double sound-boards and extra

resonators, and extended the keyboard to eight octaves. (We are content with less.) He invented a gauge so that tuning could be done by sight rather than by ear—an idea only now brought to fruition by electronics.

About the time when Schumann and Chopin were fifteen, American piano-making made a great advance. A Bostonian named Alpheus Babcock was granted a patent in 1825 for an iron frame cast in one piece. He designed it for a square piano (squares were still popular in the States) but he had little success in promoting it commercially. It was Jonas Chickering who later was able to establish a modern kind of iron-frame piano. He was granted a patent in 1843 and, with the help of an astute business partner, and taking advantage of the ever-growing wealth of Americans, dragged piano-makers into a new era.

Concert-giving was on the increase. Pleyel built a hall in Paris and named it after himself; and in the years and decades that followed this enterprise many a famous maker built his own hall in the great capital cities.

Private concert-giving gave opportunity to many artists but also put them in their place. Countess Marie d'Agoult left a description of such occasions in the fashionable Faubourg Saint-Germain:

> Composers and singers had their place apart; in spite of the eagerness to have them, they appeared in the salons only on the footing of inferiors. If somebody wanted to give a fine concert, he sent to Rossini, who, for a recognized fee—it was small enough, only 1,500 francs if I remember rightly—undertook to arrange the programme and to see to its carrying out, thus relieving the master of the house of all embarrassments in the way of choice of artists, of rehearsals, and so on. The great maestro himself sat at the piano all evening accompanying the singers. Generally he added an instrumental virtuoso—Herz or Moscheles . . . or the wonder of the musical world, the little Liszt. At the appointed hour they arrived in a body, entering by a side door; in a body they sat near the piano; and in a body they departed, after receiving the compliments of the master of the house, and of a few professed dilettantes. The next day the master sent Rossini his fee and believed he had discharged his obligations toward them and him.

The time was soon to come when Rossini and Chopin and Liszt would establish themselves on a different footing, but for many a year afterwards and right on into the present century there was an uneasy relationship between host and pianist in a private house. Great personages would refrain from inviting a pianist to dinner: if he was paid how could he be a guest? And great pianists, invited to dinner, refused to play unless given a large fee.

(When I was a student the musical 'At Home' had almost died out in London; but I remember a few; and to this day I feel a surge of reminiscent rage if some grand woman peers at me through a lorgnette.)

In Moscow, however, Field enjoyed considerable prestige. He was paid large fees for concerts, and pupils came from far and wide if only to boast that they had studied with him. We have already noted the story that, when bored by a poor pupil, he went into the next room and had a nap. What is certain is that his bohemianism caused offence in a society that was not unfamiliar with infidelity and drunkenness. Nevertheless, from his distant vantage point, he commanded the interest of pianists all over Europe.

We cannot doubt his influence on the boy Chopin. Many Chopin biographers gloss this over, but I go along with David Branson's arguments in *John Field and Chopin*. Branson makes an immense number of close comparisons, one of which strikes me with some force. Years before I read this book I had taken Field's and Chopin's Nocturnes to a television studio and opened them both, side by side, at Nocturne in E flat. Glancing first at one and then at another, to and fro, I found it easy to play a composite Field-Chopin nocturne, to the astonishment of my viewers.

In 1831 Field decided to make a long tour and reappeared in London, playing his Concerto No. 3 in E flat at a Philharmonic concert. It was during this visit that Clementi died, aged eighty. The old man, a year earlier, had been given a complimentary dinner in London and then went off to retire. He had continued active. People sometimes found him at the piano, playing away while reading a book propped on the music desk.

He was held in such esteem as to rate burial in Westminster Abbey, where his epitaph describes him as Father of the Pianoforte. Field was one of the principal mourners.

After this event, which must have brought back many memories, Field went on to Paris where the recently arrived Chopin heard him and was disappointed. The two men could never bring themselves to admire one another, and in later years Field dismissed his younger rival as 'un talent de chambre de malade' (a sickroom talent). Field may have heard Berlioz's remark 'il se mourait toute sa vie' (he spent his life dying). The Paris audiences were roused by Field to 'a veritable delirium', according to François Fétis, who, as a professor at the Conservatoire, and soon to be appointed director of the Brussels Conservatoire, may be presumed to represent informed opinion. And Joseph d'Ortique, another pundit, spoke of Field's playing as 'exquisitely spiritual, coupled with surprising aplomb and coquetry'. I quote from a translation, suspecting that the original French for spiritual was 'spirituel'—not quite the same thing. Coquetry is a word that Liszt would have understood. How difficult it is to persuade a student to play with coquetry!

Field went on to an extensive tour of France and neighbouring countries. In Italy he applied himself too much to the bottle and was taken to hospital in Naples where he remained a whole year, too poor and too ill to move. Fortunately a Russian noble family heard of his plight and rescued him. Their name was Rachmanoff. Knowing of the difficulties of transliteration from the Russian alphabet I have wondered whether . . . Probably not, since the biographies of Rachmaninoff make no mention of the incident though they do recall that Rachmaninoff's grandfather had lessons from Field. If he had rescued Field he would surely have boasted of it.

The Rachmanoffs put him on his feet and, in Vienna, he gave three concerts, staying with Czerny. He died in 1837 in Russia.

His music and his playing were enormously influential. We may recall the verdict of Glinka, the greatest of Field's pupils, the man who virtually created Russian opera. 'His fingers fell on the keys as large drops of rain that spread themselves like iridescent pearls.'

Mendelssohn, who delighted in Field's playing, was on the way
to having an enormous influence on pianists without aspiring to
'pianism'. While still quite young he preached the gospel
according to Bach. Bach, of course, was admired by musicians,
but Mendelssohn played Bach on the pianos of music-lovers;
he persuaded organists not to rush through the fugues, as many
then did; but, above all, he organized the first performance of
the *St. Matthew Passion* since the death of the composer. This
performance may seem marginal to the story of the piano, but it
set up a chain reaction that set the publishers, the professors
and the pianists scurrying to rediscover, re-edit, rethink the
great clavier music with which we are all now familiar.

Mendelssohn was only seventeen when he formed a small
select choir. They grew better, they grew more ambitious, they
campaigned for music that many experts thought unperform-
able. A choir of 300 or 400, the Singakademie, went to work.
The public were aroused and flocked even to the rehearsals.
Opera singers gave their services. On the great day a thousand
people were turned away from the doors. The triumph was
complete—though not all musicians were pleased by the
success of a boy of twenty who had had the determination to
spend several years at this task. In all this he was, of course,
supported by his family: also by an actor named Devrient.
When it was all over, Mendelssohn said 'it was an actor and a
Jew who restored this great Christian work to the people' and
he never mentioned his Jewishness again.

Well-to-do and a celebrity he went on his travels, and his
letters and sketches from Germany, France, England and Italy
reveal a young man who was handsome, charming, versatile—
and a bit of a prig. One quotation—nothing to do with the
piano (apparently)—helps to explain why his immensely popular *Songs without Words* now seem too 'ever so nice'. He is
speaking of French and Italian operas:

> One of the distinctive characteristics of them all is precisely of a
> nature that I should resolutely oppose, although the taste of the
> present day may demand it . . . I allude to that of immorality. In
> *Robert le Diable* the nuns come one after the other to seduce the
> hero, till at last the abbess succeeds. The same hero is conveyed
> by magic into the apartment of the one he loves and casts her from

him in an attitude which the public here applauds, and probably all Germany will do the same; she then implores his mercy in a grand aria. In another opera a young girl divests herself of her garments, and sings a song to the effect that next day at this time she will be married; all this produces effect, but I have no music for it. I consider it ignoble, and if the present epoch demands this style and considers it indispensable, then I shall write oratorios.

It has to be admitted that fashionable Paris in 1831 was a veritable sink of iniquity, and the Opéra backstage was a den of vice, but Mendelssohn's letter makes it clear that his music would never bring a blush to a maiden's cheek.

He was still in his early twenties when his first half dozen *Songs without Words* began to captivate thousands of pianists. These little pieces were played in public, they were played at home by serious amateurs, they were taught to every schoolgirl.

He delighted in the spread of musical knowledge and was patriotically proud that this was so noticeable in Germany. As for France, music was too concentrated in one city. He complained that though Paris had '1,800 piano teachers—and still not enough—there is practically no music at all in other cities'. He admits that the Conservatoire orchestra is the best in Europe but he despises the fashionable audiences who, to show how much they love Beethoven, 'speak of Haydn as an old wig and of Mozart as a good fellow'.

He was much happier in London. Here is his picture of a rehearsal, with Moscheles, of his own two-piano Concerto in E:

> Yesterday we had the first rehearsal at Clementi's piano factory. Mrs. Moscheles and Mr. Collard listened. I had no end of fun; for you cannot imagine how we coquetted; how the one constantly imitated the other and how sweet we were. Moscheles plays the last movement with remarkable brilliance; he shook the runs out of his sleeve. When it was over, they all said it was a pity that we had made no cadenza, so I immediately dug out a passage from the last tutti of the first part, where the orchestra has a pause, and Moscheles had to comply *nolens volens* and compose a big cadenza. We now discussed, constantly joking the while, whether the last little solo could remain where it was, since of course the people would applaud the cadenza. 'We must have a bit of tutti between the cadenza and the solo,' said I. 'How long are they to applaud?'

asked Moscheles. 'Ten minutes, I dare say,' said I. Moscheles
beat me down to five. I promised to supply a tutti, and so we took
the measurements, embroidered, turned and padded, set in
sleeves *à la Mameluke*; and at last, with our mutual tailoring, produced a brilliant concerto.

There's musicianship! But can one imagine Chopin behaving
like this?

He could be gay in London where the musical public hero-
worshipped him. He could also be serious in a city where many
people would have agreed with his father's belief that any room
in which Bach is played thereby becomes a church—a Protestant church of course; where there were 150 music shops; and
where the Royal Academy of Music had been opened in 1823.
The music shops sold and the Academy students practised
Mendelssohn's music. He was the golden boy.

The rehearsal in Clementi's factory took place when he was
twenty. Let us see him again in London at the age of thirty-
three.

> ... but the details of my last visit to Buckingham Palace I must
> write to you at once because they will amuse you so much, and
> me, too. As Grahl says—and it is true—the only friendly English
> house, one that is really comfortable and where one feels at ease, is
> Buckingham Palace. ... Joking apart, Prince Albert had asked
> me to go to him on Saturday at two o'clock, so that I might try
> his organ before I left England. I found him all alone; and as we
> were talking away, the Queen came in, also quite alone, in a
> house dress. She said she was obliged to leave for Claremont in an
> hour; 'But, goodness! how it looks here,' she added, when she saw
> that the wind had littered the whole room, and even the pedals
> of the organ (which, by the way, made a very pretty feature in the
> room), with leaves of music from a large portfolio that lay open.
> As she spoke she knelt down and began picking up the music;
> Prince Albert helped, and I too was not idle. Then Prince Albert
> proceeded to explain the stops to me, and while he was doing it,
> she said she would put things straight alone.
>
> But I begged that the Prince would first play something, so
> that, as I said, I might boast about it in Germany; and thereupon
> he played me a chorale by heart, with pedals, so charmingly and
> clearly and correctly that many an organist could have learned
> something.

After the prince and Mendelssohn had played the organ and the Queen had sung, the composer was given a beautiful ring in an inscribed case, and then they went through various corridors to the piano in the Queen's sitting-room. They were joined by the Prince of Gotha and the Duchess of Kent and the Queen then sang what she thought was one of Mendelssohn's songs. He accompanied her and gently corrected one or two mistakes.

> Then I was obliged to confess that Fanny [his sister] had written the song (which I found very hard, but pride must have a fall), and to beg her to sing one of my own, too. 'If I would give her plenty of help she would gladly try,' she said, and sang 'Lass dich nur nichts dauern' really without a mistake, and with charming feeling and expression. I thought to myself that one must not pay too many compliments on such an occasion, so I merely thanked her very much; but she said, 'Oh, if only I had not been so nervous; otherwise I really have a long breath.' Then I praised her heartily, and with the best conscience in the world; for just that part with the long C at the close she had done so well, taking it and the three notes next to it all in the same breath, as one seldom hears it done. . . .

I have always said that if only he had been an Englishman Mendelssohn would have become Sir Felix or even Lord Norwood—Norwood being the London suburb where, in a friend's garden, he composed the most popular of all his *Songs without Words*, the 'Spring Song'.

(I wonder what the Queen's piano was like. Once, when I was very young and they were very old, I played to two of her daughters. One of them asked my opinion of her piano. It was a poor instrument but, young and nervous, I said, 'A beautiful instrument, ma'am.' To which she replied, 'Yes, everyone says so.' I came away with the thought that royal persons will never know the truth about anything.)

Mendelssohn had an eye for the ridiculous and recounts how he rushed to remove a parrot when the Queen feared it would interrupt her singing; and he ends the letter to his Dear little Mother by swearing that he is a greater radical than ever. Maybe; but Kings and Queens always deferred to his judgement.

For example, the King of Saxony had been left a legacy with the request that His Majesty should devote the money to some worthy cause. Mendelssohn, who for some time had been conductor of the Gewandhaus Orchestra in Leipzig, persuaded the King to use the money to build a music school, and the Leipzig Conservatorium came into existence in 1843. Mendelssohn himself taught there for a while; so did his friend Schumann; and, three years after the opening, Moscheles left London to train the pianists of Germany.

What we pianists now owe to Mendelssohn lies not so much in the music that we play rather seldom as in his influence. He created enthusiasm, he attracted royal approval and his Conservatorium drew piano students from all over Europe.

The idea that Schumann should be trained as a lawyer now strikes us as laughable; but mothers of gifted sons fall into two categories—those who are sure that their darling boy must, of course, become great and famous, and those who are fearful of music as a profession and try to persuade a young genius to go in for something 'solid' while keeping music for 'one's own amusement'. Sure enough, Robert was soon neglecting law for music. He practised the piano for hours and hours—when he was not devouring the works of his favourite author, Jean Paul, a man who enchanted the young romantics with his mercurial alternations of laughter and tears. He composed in a vague, undisciplined way; he longed for a Stein piano and a fine teacher.

Then he met Friedrich Wieck, a piano teacher whose little girl, Clara, was a marvellous advertisement for his methods. Schumann began to take lessons, concentrating particularly on the *Forty-eight*, which were Wieck's musical 'bible'. But he was still restless and undecided, and he knew that his university life was costing his mother and brothers a great deal of money. He transferred himself to Heidelberg University, he went on a long and expensive holiday in Switzerland and Italy, he came back to endless discussions about music with congenial friends and hours of duet playing.

For him, too, Paganini opened new horizons.

At last Mrs. Schumann bowed to the inevitable, and her

Robert went back to Wieck with the intention of becoming a virtuoso. He was twenty and in a hurry. To make the fourth finger of his right hand independent he tied it in some sort of sling and went on exercising the other fingers. This invention damaged his hand so severely that, despite all sorts of remedies, allopathic and homeopathic, he had to abandon the idea of becoming a great pianist.

The great French aphorist, La Rochefoucauld, once pointed out that there are few defeats that a wise man cannot turn into a victory, and few victories that a fool will not turn into a defeat. With hindsight, we may say that Schumann was wise. We know what a great composer he became. But at that moment of his life he devoted a great deal of energy and time to being critic and editor. At the time when he wrote his historic article on Chopin's Op. 2 he fell into the habit of writing from more than one standpoint. He recognized two selves in his own nature, calling one Florestan and the other Eusebius, and imagined his outward self, accompanied by his two other selves, meeting to look at some music.

> . . . With the words 'Off with your hats, gentlemen—a genius,' Eusebius laid down a piece of music. . . . Here it seemed eyes, strange to me, were glancing up at me—flower eyes, basilisk eyes, peacock's eyes, maiden's eyes; in many places it looked yet brighter—I thought I saw Mozart's *Là ci darem la mano* wound through a hundred chords, Leperello seemed to wink at me, and Don Juan hurried past in his white mantle. 'Now play it,' said Florestan. Eusebius consented; and in the recess of a window we listened. Eusebius played as though he were inspired. . . .

This was written for the *Allgemeine Musikalische Zeitung*, but Schumann soon became disillusioned with the musical journals of his day. Some, put out by music publishers, merely 'puffed' the firms' wares.

At the age of twenty-three Schumann founded a journal of his own (he must have had very good and trusting friends to put up the money) and in its columns he waged war on music that attempted nothing more than the making of a quick and easy effect. Not being able to pay many contributors he wrote a good deal of the *Neue Leipziger Zeitschrift für Musik* (New

Leipzig Musical Times) himself, using various pen-names. He had peopled his imagination with fantastic figures—his friends and his own several selves—constituting a company of 'Davidites' out to slay the Philistines. These *Davidsbündler* were to appear in his compositions, but for the time being they were warriors in a literary war. The articles were rather particularly devoted to piano music and to demolishing those specimens that were 'noticed' elsewhere like this:

> It is short, it is only nine pages long, but it is beautiful. There is something extremely neat and highly piquant about it. It looks easy to play; indeed it is not difficult. But the staccato! The shadings! They demand something of the player. But the piece is surely worthwhile, and it will be especially welcome in sociable society.

That is how a Viennese musical journal reviewed Kalkbrenner's *Rondeau Fantastique*.

Curiously, Schumann was not an impatient writer: he would analyse mediocre pieces quite pedantically. When he encountered what he thought was great music he abandoned analysis as irrelevant and wrote in tones of rhapsody. He was, like any critic, often wrong. He turned against Chopin's music later on. About the B flat minor Sonata he wrote, 'He calls it a sonata. One might regard this as capricious, if not downright presumptuous, for he has simply tied together four of his most unruly children.'

He found the Funeral March largely repulsive:

> . . . And what we get in the last movement under the title *Finale* is more like mockery than any kind of music. Yet one has to admit that even from this unmelodious and joyless movement there breathes on us a singular and terrifying spirit which pins down with mailed fist whatever would resist it. So we listen, uncomplaining as if transfixed, to the end—but not to praise; for this is not music.

(Chopin, not in any spirit of retaliation, said of Schumann's *Carnaval*, 'It's not music at all.')

Like Mendelssohn, Schumann extolled the music of Bach. As a romantic composer he was always looking for more and

more heart-searching harmonies. And where did he find them?
In Bach.

For him Bach was the first and greatest romantic, and he saw
nothing wrong in highly expressive performances. In our own
day, when a dangerous littleness of learning evokes monotonous
and metronomic performances from pianos pretending to be
harpsichords, I confess to some sympathy for Schumann. He
declared that every fugue was a 'character piece' and every
prelude was an *étude*. Why not, when Bach himself used the
word *Clavierübung* as a general title for works as different as the
Partitas, the Italian Concerto, the Goldberg Variations?
Clavierübung literally means keyboard exercise.

Nothing in piano-writing interested Schumann more than
the *étude*, and it is interesting to find that when he became a
song-writer the piano parts of his *Lieder* often had the feel under
the fingers of an *étude*. As for his *Études Symphoniques*, they are
inescapably part of our repertoire.

However, the songs and the *études* lay in the future. He went
on with his work as writer and composer and was still deeply
attached to the Wiecks. There was more than a little feeling
between him and Clara, but at the age of twenty-four he fell in
love with one Ernestine von Fricken. This attachment lasted
only for a year but pianists cannot afford to ignore it since the
girl had some influence on two great works. One is *Carnaval*, a
succession of small pieces that 'describe' persons and events at
a masked ball. The persons are Schumann's Davidites and his
own two selves and such traditional figures are Pierrot, Harlequin, Pantaloon and Columbine. Also there are Ernestine
(called Estrella) and Clara (called Chiarina), not to mention
Chopin and Paganini, the whole thing ending with a march (in
three time) of the Davidites against the Philistines.

Ernestine's guardian, Captain von Fricken, fancied himself
as a composer and showed Schumann a set of variations. The
variations were mediocre, but Schumann took over the excellent
theme and on it wrote a set of variations that he called—one
does not quite know why—*Études Symphoniques*. We need not be
surprised to find that variations and *études* can have much in
common, and we are sometimes puzzled to know how to place
them in effective order since Schumann more than once

altered his mind about which to publish, with the result that in most editions one finds extra variations after the finale. Never mind: the music is one of the great sets of studies that raised piano-playing to new levels.

One curious eccentricity, more noticeable in *Carnaval* than in the *Études*, became more noticeable still in later works. He became very fond of off-beat accents, continuing them with such regularity and so insistently that the listener hears the off-beats as main beats. If the composer had placed these off-beats above an on-the-beat accompaniment, audiences would have been much the wiser. As it is, they often hear a rhythm that Schumann never wrote. In the last movement of the piano concerto there are long passages that pianist and orchestra play (with difficulty) in syncopated 3/4 time. The listeners, most of whom cannot read music, quite happily hear an unsyncopated 3/2 melody and enjoy it very much.

Unlike Chopin, who totally avoided picturesque titles, Schumann was always 'poetic'. He also enjoyed a little mystification. Remembering that Ernestine came from the little town of Asch, and noticing that A-S-C-H were letters in his own name, he made a 'motto' of the notes, using them as a basis for many of the melodies in *Carnaval*. Translating from the German, we find that S (Es) is E flat, and H is B natural. Furthermore, if we combine the first two letters—As—we have A flat.

Schumann was sometimes asked whether he thought of a title before or after composing a piece. In *Carnaval* he must have thought of the titles first, but he said of many of his pieces that the titles were there not to describe the music but to indicate, better than expression marks could, how the music should be played. He felt that a title helped the pianist to express something more varied and subtle than mere light and shade, joy and sorrow.

The Ernestine affair petered out, perhaps because Schumann discovered that the Captain was not really *von* Fricken and that his adopted daughter was really someone's illegitimate child. One could wish that Schumann had found better reasons for cooling off, but for musical reasons we may be glad that he turned from the unremarkable Ernestine to the highly gifted Clara.

To her father's consternation. Old Wieck had dreamed of a great career for his wonderful daughter, and he feared an alliance with Schumann, whom he regarded as altogether unpractical and dreamy and unreliable—not at all the husband for a woman pianist. This was very much a case of true love not running smooth, and the young couple had to obtain the permission of magistrates to marry against the wishes of the bride's father. In court, the father stormed and raged, to no avail, and was committed to prison for eighteen days.

In the long run, the father's ambitions were fulfilled. Clara Schumann became one of the acknowledged great pianists, and continued as such long after her husband's death. Even before the young couple were united, Chopin, visiting Wieck's house, had said that she was 'the only woman in Germany who can play my music'.

Marriage turned Schumann, quite suddenly, into a great song-writer. I have said that his accompaniments often have the feel of *études* under the fingers, but he was well aware of the danger of too much pianistic brilliance and kept away from the keyboard while writing a song. Like Schubert, whom he enormously admired, he found wonderful pianistic shapes that were, mysteriously, counterparts of the words without being crudely descriptive. Germany was full of poets, some, like Heine, truly great. Through Schumann's genius these poets were made, so to speak, to play the piano and to 'say' something that lay beyond words. Some of the poems were written almost as though the poets had a presentiment that there would be music. Despite the fact that the German language often seems to run to polysyllabic words and endless sentences, Heine created poems that seemed childlike in their simplicity while setting into vibration the deepest echoes in the mind. Since polysyllables and parenthetical clauses make a song unintelligible, Heine's poetry was Heaven's gift to composers—though Heine, the most cynical of the romantics, a Jew driven into exile by the bigotry of his fellow countrymen, would have smiled to hear that he was a gift from Heaven.

Schumann's outlook on music at the time when he was waiting to marry Clara can be understood from his letters. For example, in 1840 he met Liszt. Of course he was impressed, but he wrote to Clara '. . . his world is not mine, Clärchen. Art as we know it—you when you play, I when I compose—has an intimate charm that is worth more to me than all Liszt's splendour and tinsel.' As for song-writing, '[I] should like to sing myself to death, like a nightingale.' And, at another time, 'The only thing I can work for is a car made of roses, drawn by an army of butterflies, harnessed with gold and silver threads, and flying with it towards home.'

Nowadays we tend to dismiss all this as sentimental vapourings, or we regard the army of butterflies flying towards home as a scarcely disguised sexual image. But our piano-playing fingers know better than to be sophisticated, and we cannot live without 'fantastic' pieces entitled *Why?*, *Soaring*, *The Poet Speaks*, *Scenes of Childhood*, *The Prophet-Bird* and a hundred others.

Part of Schumann's appeal lies in his very attitude to composing. He wrote about the *Davidsbündlertänze*, 'If ever I was happy at the piano, it was when I was composing these.'

Happy *at the piano*. Every pianist—indeed everyone who thinks it must be nice to play the piano—has imagined himself roaming about on the keys in a state of happy inspiration—like the man in Sullivan's song who, with his fingers wandering idly 'over the noisy keys' discovers The Lost Chord . . . never to be found again. And, of all the great composers, Schumann is the one who seems to indulge his fancies in a state of inspiration. This impression is deceptive, but it is the impression he often sought to make. No one who plays the music can doubt the professional skill that produced the concerto, the sonatas, the Fantasy in C, the *Études Symphoniques* and many other works; but how often we seem to see the 'poet' who gazes at the stars or sits by the fireside, allowing joy and sorrow to flit across his expressive features; whose right hand seems not to know what the left is doing while the heart, with poetic syncopation, misses a beat; whose creative fancy produces something like a flower, the very symbol of perfection without apparent contrivance.

In a large output a few of these flowers are unremarkable and are strung together like a daisy chain, but one must agree with Liszt who said that Schumann appeals to 'meditative souls . . . who know how to plunge into the depths of the waters to seek the hidden pearl'.

13. 'Con Amore'

We left Chopin at the age of twenty on his way out of Poland
to a wider world. What happened to him can best be seen
through his eyes and his letters. And every pianist and piano-
lover seeing Chopin's Vienna, Chopin's Paris, must exclaim
'How strange! How familiar!'

He had been joined by Titus Woyciechowski in Kalisz and
they travelled by way of Breslau (where Chopin's music puzzled
the ladies) and Dresden (where the ladies displayed their
diamonds and plied their knitting needles), and they arrived in
Vienna to be cordially welcomed by the musicians. They took
an elegant apartment of three rooms. Graff immediately
promised to send a piano. There was talk of giving a concert.
Beethoven's friend Malfatti embraced Chopin promising every
kind of help. He went to the opera, he dined in great houses:

> Among the numerous pleasures of Vienna the hotel evenings
> are famous. During supper Strauss or Lanner play waltzes. . . .
> After every waltz they get huge applause; and if they play a
> *Quodlibet*, or jumble of opera, song and dance, the hearers are so
> overjoyed that they don't know what to do with themselves. It
> shows the corrupt taste of the Viennese public.
>
> I wanted to send you a waltz that I have composed, but it is
> late now; you shall have it afterwards. I don't send the mazurkas
> because they are not copied yet; they are not for dancing.

It is hard to believe that Chopin would have composed
waltzes if Strauss and Lanner had not infected the world with a
waltz epidemic from which few were immune. But, ever scornful of popular taste, Chopin made it clear that *his* dance music
was not for dancing. There is a paradox here. Among great
pianists the only ones who play Chopin's dance music really
well are those who, if they had cared to, could have made a
fortune in light music. Rubinstein for one.

Hotel evenings were one thing: the cathedral was another.

... I strolled along slowly alone, and at midnight went into St. Stephen's. When I entered there was no one there. Not to hear the mass, but just to look at the huge building at that hour, I got into the darkest corner at the foot of a Gothic pillar. I can't describe the greatness, the magnificence of those huge arches. It was quiet; now and then the footsteps of a sacristan lighting candles at the back of the sanctuary, would break in on my lethargy. A coffin behind me, a coffin under me;—only the coffin above me was lacking. . . .

His social life was active. He went with Czerny to visit the pianist-composer-publisher Diabelli. He again met Hummel whose son did a crayon portrait of the young Pole. He was angry when he heard Austrians speaking slightingly of Poles yet he himself always spoke slightingly of Jews, particularly when he was trying to get a good price out of a publisher.

As a Pole more Polish than the hundred-per-cent Poles, he was distraught when he heard that an insurrection had broken out in the country he had so recently left. Titus immediately left for home. Chopin, who could never have taken up arms, stayed in Vienna wondering despairingly about his family and the girl he still longed for. How well we understand him—those of us who can remember the time, not long ago, when we tried to comfort distinguished musicians who wept and shivered in London or New York and wondered what Hitler and Stalin were doing to Poland. A few sentences from various letters:

Write to me. You in the army! Is she in Radom? Have you dug trenches? Our poor parents. . . . Why can't I even beat a drum? . . . From the day when I learned of the events of November 29th,* until this moment, there has been nothing except distressing anxiety and grief. . . . Will there be any end to the bloodshed? . . .

Curiously, in the very letters that contain these outbursts, he includes professional gossip: how he found a bound copy of one of his manuscripts in the Imperial Library, how he played in a grand house at a party in honour of Malfatti.

The moon shone superbly, the fountains played, a delicious smell from the orangery they have put up filled the air; in a word,

* 1830.

a glorious night and a most gorgeous place. You can't imagine how beautifully designed is the salon in which they sang; huge windows, thrown wide, from which you can see all Vienna; plenty of mirrors and very few lights. . . . The genuine amiability of our host, the elegance and comfort, the merry company, the witty conversation that was the order of the day, and the excellent supper kept us sitting late; it was about midnight when we got into the carriages and dispersed for home.

As regards expenses, I manage. . . .

The character of Chopin and his music begins to emerge. He went to the cathedral, not to hear Mass but to sense the atmosphere and reflect on coffins; he wept and trembled to think of his loved ones in the midst of 'the events', but he could still enjoy a musical party amongst grand people. He was physically frail, he was almost neurotically sensitive, but he was tough. His music is sensitive. . . .

And much tougher than most people realize.

When it was time to move on he had passport trouble, he had to write home for more money. He was torn by inner conflict: 'I'm puzzled, I'm melancholy, I don't know what to do with myself; I wish I weren't alone.'

Why not? He was only twenty-one.

In Stuttgart the quelling of the Polish revolt became clearer.

Moscow rules the world! Oh, God, do You exist? You're there, and you don't avenge it—How many more Russian crimes do You want—or—are You a Russian too!!? My poor Father! The dear old man may be starving, my mother not able to buy bread? Perhaps my sisters have succumbed to the ferocity of Muscovite soldiery let loose! . . . Where is she [Constantia]?—Poor girl, perhaps in some Russian's hands—a Russian strangling her, killing, murdering! . . . Sometimes I can only groan, and suffer, and pour out my despair at the piano!—God, shake the earth, let it swallow up the men of this age, let the heaviest chastisement fall on France, that would not come to help us. . . .

Pouring out his despair at the piano he had been composing the Scherzo in B minor and the Ballade in G minor; and nobody has quite disproved the legend that it was on hearing of the fall of Warsaw that he composed the Étude in C minor (Op. 10, No. 12) that has ever since been called 'The Revolutionary Study', though Chopin himself never gave a picturesque title to anything.

What to do? Where to go? The answer was scarcely in doubt. France, as Mendelssohn had observed, was not an outstandingly musical country, but Paris was the city above all others in Europe where reputation was made. And French was Chopin's other language.

His first impressions of Paris are mixed:

> I have arrived here fairly comfortably (though expensively), and am glad I am remaining here; I have the first musicians in the world. I know Rossini, Cherubini, Paër, etc., etc.; and perhaps may stay longer than I intended. Not because I am getting on any too well here, but because, with time, I may get on well.... But I am writing you nothing about the impression produced on me by this big town after Stuttgart and Strasbourg. There is the utmost luxury, almost swinishness, the utmost virtue, the utmost ostentation; at every step advertisements of venereal disease [he shortens the word venereal as though unable to bring himself to write it]; shouting, racket, bustle, and more mud than it is possible to imagine: one can perish in this paradise, and it is convenient from this point of view, that nobody asks how anybody lives. . . . The memory of Teressa [who was Teressa?] forbids me to taste forbidden fruit. But I already know several lady vocalists, and lady vocalists here are even more anxious for duets than those of the Tyrol. Once on my fifth floor (I am at Boulevarde Poissonière, No. 27—you wouldn't believe what a delightful lodging; I have a little room beautifully furnished with mahogany from which I can see Mont Martre to the Panthéon and the whole length of the fashionable quarter; many persons envy me my view, but none my stairs). . . .
>
> I expect to stay here three years. I am in very close relations with Kalkbrenner, the 1st pianist of Europe, whom I think you would like. (He is one whose shoe-latchet I am not worthy to untie. Those Herzes, and so on,—I tell you they are just windbags and will never play any better.)

For a while he thought of taking lessons from Kalkbrenner, who said that the young Pole had Cramer's method and Field's touch, but he soon resumed his usual habit of playing and composing in his own way and without taking anybody's advice or instruction. Soon he was able to write home that he had a huge reputation among artists. He also wrote a little scornfully of the review that Schumann had written about the Op. 2 Variations.

> [He says] that they are not Variations in the usual sense, but some kind of fantastic tableaux. About the 2nd Variation he says that Don Juan is running with Leperello; that in the 3rd he is embracing Zerlina and Masetto raging in the left hand; that in the fifth measure of the Adagio Don Juan is kissing Zerlina in D flat major. . . . One can die of the imagination of this German.

He is astounded by the Opéra. The singers are such as he had never heard before, including Mme Malibran, who, in black-face, sang Othello. He has none of Mendelssohn's disdain for Meyerbeer: and writes enthusiastically of *Robert le Diable*.

> It is a masterpiece of the new school, in which devils (huge devils, huge choirs) sing through speaking-trumpets, and souls rise from graves . . . in which there is a diorama in the theatre, in which at the end you see the interior of a church . . . lighted up, with monks, and all the congregation on the benches, and censors:— even with the organ, the sound of which on the stage is enchanting and amazing, also it nearly drowns the orchestra; nothing of the sort could be put on anywhere else. Meyerbeer has immortalized himself! But he has spent three years in Paris to get it done; it is said he has paid 20,000 francs to the cast.

Amidst all these events he is glad to know that his family is well, and not too upset to know that Constantia has married. He writes to his old teacher, Elsner, to explain why he will not attempt to compose an opera. He writes to Titus about the pornographic books on sale 'sometimes very wittily written' and he is aware of the widespread poverty: 'you can often meet ragged folk with important faces'. He sees riots from his balcony, the fights with the police, the singing of the *Marseillaise*. His health is bad and 'inside something gnaws at me . . . desire for life, and the next instant, desire for death'. But he is on his way up:

> I have got into the highest society; I sit with ambassadors, princes, ministers; and even don't know how it came about, because I did not try for it. It is a most necessary thing for me, because good taste is supposed to depend on it. . . .

Though this is only my first year among the artists here, I have their friendship and respect . . . even people with huge reputations dedicate their compositions to me before I do so to them . . . finished artists take lessons from me and couple my name with that of Field.

But I am ashamed of all this bosh that I have written; I have been boasting like a child. . . .

I have five lessons to give today; you think I am making a fortune? Carriages and white gloves cost more, and without them one would not be in good taste.

I love the Carlists, I can't endure the Philippists, myself I am a revolutionist; also I care nothing for money, only for friendship, for which I beg and pray you.

This is a vivid Self-Portrait of the Artist as a Young Man. It is not a perfect likeness. He did care for money, he was only what we should now call an armchair revolutionist and, like most of us, he was a name-dropper.

As for not knowing how his success came about, we know very well how this happened. Prince Valentin Radziwill introduced him to the Rothschild family. The Baroness Rothschild was one of the few great ladies able to run a successful *salon* to which the rich and the famous were glad to be invited.

(If I had a time-machine I would instantly go back to one of her parties. 'Do come in, cher M. Harrison, and meet . . .' Chopin, Liszt, Rossini, Balzac, Berlioz, George Sand. . . .)

Soon he was the most expensive and fashionable piano-teacher in Paris. He had the *entrée*—by the front door—to great houses. His pupils came to his elegant apartment in the Chaussée d'Antin and were admitted by a manservant. A lady's maid discreetly placed twenty francs on the mantelpiece or the *escritoire* during a lesson—no lady came unchaperoned—and he could afford not to follow the life of a virtuoso. Indeed, as time went on, the very rarity of his public appearances guaranteed success; Liszt said, 'It was not so much a question of the School of Chopin as the Church of Chopin.'

The Baroness Rothschild does not appear in Chopin's letters. In later years he dedicated the C sharp minor Waltz and the F minor Ballade to her, but he writes nothing about her. Why? Is it possible that he disliked being beholden to her? At that time both French and Polish society were unfriendly to Jews and, from an aristocratic point of view, which Chopin shared, the Rothschilds were *nouveaux riches* and *parvenus*. All this is guesswork, but it is hard to think of any other explanation. It is only fair to say that his anti-Semitism was not of the virulent kind that the world was to see in Wagner. He admired Kalkbrenner (whose father, of Jewish extraction, was named Christian Kalkbrenner). And later in life he turned to Jewish doctors.

Chopin's pupils, alas, failed to leave any clear account of how he taught. We know that he anticipated later teachers in his use of the arms and argued that the way the arm behaves is analogous to the way a singer breathes. He liked his pupils to play 'easily' and he was scrupulous in pedalling, in a way that almost certainly does not exactly correspond with the marks in his manuscripts or first editions. (We shall return to this subject when we examine Liszt as a teacher.) But he founded no school of pianists.

His supreme gift to the piano is the *Études*. They are unique. They are not symphonic studies like Schumann's: they are not transcendental studies like Liszt's. Except for perhaps two that could have been called Nocturnes (E major Op. 10, and C sharp minor Op. 25) they are studies . . . like studies.

What is a study? The quick answer might be a glorified exercise, using the word 'glorified' colloquially. But a Chopin *étude* is a truly and wondrously glorified exercise. Taking some simple scale or arpeggio or broken chord such as every diligent student practises on the run-up to an examination he transforms it in a way that could never have been dreamed of by Clementi or Czerny or Cramer or Moscheles.

In Op. 10 the first study consists of wide spans of the C major arpeggio; the second combines the A minor scale with small chords to mark the beats; the fifth explores the possibilities of nothing but black keys for the right hand; the seventh alternates thirds and sixths. Op. 25 begins with arpeggiated chords in contrary motion (but they support a magical melody); the study in chromatic thirds (No. 6) really is just that. There is a study in sixths for the right hand, a study in octaves for both. Inevitably some *Études* have acquired names—the 'Harp', the

'Butterfly', the 'Winter Wind'—but Chopin himself would have despised such titles. He quite rigorously wrote studies, fulfilling all the requirements of a technical 'Method' and gave us one of the wonders of the pianistic world.

The music is made of a tough but springy steel, tempered in a fiery furnace.

Over the years writers have argued about the character of Chopin's music. Some have found it feminine, for no better reason than that it is often charming and elegant. Others have reacted as though any such suggestion is insulting and have assured their readers that Chopin was thoroughly manly, almost persuading us that he would have played rugger if only his health had been better. The argument is absurd. All men have a feminine *persona*. The balance between the two sides of the character varies. Bach was seldom feminine. Mozart, as an opera composer, knew the secrets of a woman's heart. Beethoven was quite sure that his sonatas were peopled with men and women. Schumann is often feminine in an almost maternal fashion. As for Liszt and Wagner with their 'eternal feminine'....

Chopin was frail and sensitive and elegant but he sometimes seems to me to be an unconquerable man with a rapier in his hand.

He envied Liszt's strong fingers, but his own playing had extraordinary intensity. One Ernest Legouvé wrote:

Once at the piano Chopin played until he was exhausted. In the grip of a disease that knows no mercy, dark rings appeared round his eyes, a feverish brightness lit up his face, his lips turned to a vivid red and his breath came in short gasps. He felt, we felt that something of his life was flowing away with the music; he would not stop, and we had not the strength to stop him. The fever which consumed him took possession of us all.

When Chopin went to Dresden in 1836 Schumann heard him play two studies from Op. 25: the A flat and the F minor.

Let one imagine that an Aeolian harp had all the scales and that an artist's hand had mingled them together in all kinds of fantastic decorations, but in such a way that you could always hear a deeper fundamental tone and a softly singing melody—there you have something of a picture of his playing. It is wrong to suppose that he brought out distinctly every one of the little notes; it was rather a billowing of the chord of A flat, swelled here and there by the pedal; but through the harmonies could be heard in sustained tones a wonderful melody, and only in the middle section did a tenor part once stand out more prominently from the chords and the principal theme. When the study has ended you feel as you do after a blissful vision, seen in a dream, which, already half-awake, you would fain recall . . . and then he played the second, in F minor . . . so charming, dreamy and soft, just as if a child were singing in its sleep.

Allowing for Schumann's rhapsodic style, it must be assumed that he knew what he was talking about. There was, of course, some resistance to Chopin's music at first. It did not reveal its quality to every easygoing pianist who tried it over to see what it was like, and even the experts were shocked by the chromatic harmonies and the curious mixture of volcanic violence and surface elegance. Schumann later described the *Polonaises* as guns buried in roses. But in a world where the piano was the instrument of instruments this music soon became internationally famous.

International fame occasioned Chopin some difficulty. There was no international copyright law, so negotiations had to be carried on that resulted in French, German and English editions, with the inevitable discrepancies that have bothered Chopinists ever since. These negotiations found the composer as a quite tough bargainer: he was never a man easy to persuade.

As for his social position, he was never snubbed. Nobody was grand enough to look down on Chopin.

In the year 1832, when Clementi died, Liszt heard Chopin play. He was greatly affected by Chopin's music; but then he was greatly affected by everybody's music; he Lisztified everything that took his fancy. This Lisztification occurred on two levels: on the superficial level it resulted in innumerable transcriptions (which consisted of a great deal more than merely transcribing other men's notes on to his own manuscript paper); on a deeper level it produced music that reminds us of the virtuosity of Paganini, the heart-searching intimacy of Chopin,

and all those ideas about heaven and hell and eternal woman-
hood and mystical aspiration that Liszt later shared with Wagner.

In 1833 Chopin gave a party and Liszt was there. Some say
he was brought by Berlioz. It was a very distinguished party:
Meyerbeer the great opera composer; George Sand the great
woman novelist; Eugène Delacroix the great painter (whose
portrait of Chopin now hangs in the Louvre); Mickiewicz the
great Polish poet; Nourrit the great singer; Heine the great
German poet. And a beautiful young married woman, the
Countess Marie d'Agoult, whom George Sand described as
'straight as a candle, white as a sanctified wafer'.

The Countess never forgot that first meeting with Liszt. 'He
seemed, with his air *distrait et inquiet*, like a phantom for whom
the hour when it must return to the darkness is about to sound.'

Soon they were in love, and in due course she eloped with him.

The love stories of pianists and composers are not our immediate concern, but the story of the piano cannot be told without
touching on the Great Pianist as Great Lover. And, furthermore, we cannot doubt that many of the pieces collected into
Liszt's *Années de Pèlerinage* (Years of Pilgrimage) relate to the
years of love-making. Still further, it is through reading what
Marie d'Agoult wrote about Liszt that we get our most vivid
picture of a handsome, idealistic young man who was also a
careerist on the make.

> Franz spoke with a vivacity, an abundance and an originality
> of impressions that awoke a whole world that had been slumbering
> in me; and when he left me I was sunk in reveries without end. . . .
> The voice of the young enchanter, his vibrant speech, opened out
> before me a whole infinity, now luminous, now sombre, for ever
> changing, into which my thoughts plunged and were lost. Nothing
> of coquetry or gallantry was blended with our intimacy, as so
> often happens between fashionable persons of opposite sexes.
> Between us there was something at once very young and very
> serious, at once very profound and very naive.

While all this was going on, one of Marie's children died, and
suddenly it seemed possible for him to write 'we will fly far
from the world; we will live, love, and die for each other alone'.
In 1835 they went to Geneva. For a titled married woman of

thirty to elope with a *parvenu* pianist of twenty-four required a deal of courage. She must have been very much in love.

Playing the first volume of the *Années* we wander with the lovers 'Au Bord d'une Source', we hear from distant towers 'Les Cloches de Genève', we sketch our impressions in 'Album d'un Voyageur'. But the Bells of Geneva are dedicated to their first baby, and babies must be housed and fed and clothed. It was all very well to welcome George Sand on a visit and for Liszt to sign a hotel register as 'Musician-philosopher, born in Parnassus, coming from Doubt, journeying towards Truth' but then there is the bill to pay. And there is also a social bill to pay.

Later, when three children had been born (the middle one grew up to become that formidable woman, Cosima Wagner), and Liszt's first great love affair had come to an end, Marie d'Agoult wrote a novel that revealed, under the thinnest of disguises, the predicament in which she found herself. The heroine, a beautiful and high-minded young aristocrat, married to a brute of a husband, elopes with a young man of genius— not a pianist but a painter. They go . . . where? . . . to Geneva. She seeks to redeem him from his lack of education, his vanity, his desire for easy fame. He goes into society in search of commissions, since he must earn a living for them both. Often the heroine is not invited to the best houses: respectable hostesses could never welcome a fallen woman, though they could flutter round a lady killer. If the heroine was invited, by a hostess more broad-minded than most, she was aware of covert glances and whispered comments.

The novel, *Nélida*, written under the pen-name of Daniel Stern, is a sentimental affair in which the painter leaves the lady, is himself left by another woman, falls on hard times, sends despairing messages to the heroine (seeking solace in 'good works'), and finally dies repentant in her arms. We can disregard a great deal of it, but it paints a picture that history has repainted again and again of the audience whispering, 'What a fabulous man! How *could* she?! Of course you know what artists are like! Any chance of tickets for his next concert? . . .'

Then and thereafter, Liszt could never resist a pianistic challenge. In Paris, society was wild about Sigismond Thalberg, illegitimate son of Count Moritz von Dietrichstein and the Baroness von Wetzlar, and there were some who asserted that he was the greatest. In such circumstances, how could Liszt stay at home or play the role of good husband and father?

In 1837 he and Thalberg both played at the *salon* of Princess Belgioioso. Neither pianist played anything so boring, as say, a sonata. They mounted their pianistic war-horses and charged along to the thunder of operatic transcriptions, and the victor of this tournament was Liszt.

A Liszt operatic transcription might begin with thundering octaves, or a few ejaculatory phrases from an aria, well separated by pregnant silences. Then, with affecting simplicity, the great tenor aria falls on our ears. Suddenly it is engulfed, but never silenced, by a torrent of arpeggios and passages and cadenzas. More octaves. The right hand is a woman, the left hand is a man, and all ten fingers are an orchestra. The piano is almost ready to sag at the knees. With a final flourish and a leonine glance heavenward, the great man compels an earthquake of applause.

Chopin was unimpressed.

> When I think of Liszt as a creative artist, he appears before my eyes rouged, on stilts, and blowing into Jericho trumpets for-tissimo and pianissimo—or I see him discoursing on art, on the nature of creativeness and how one should create. Yet as a creator he is an ass. . . . He wants to attain Parnassus on another man's Pegasus.

Well said, by a man who certainly admired Liszt as a pianist. Perhaps if Chopin had lived longer and known the Liszt who composed the Sonata and other serious works he might have modified his opinion, but at that time he was not the man to be bamboozled by blasts from Jericho trumpets. He would only say, on another occasion, 'I should like to steal from him the way to play my own *Études*.'

Other judges might also write a little mockingly, but they could not deny Liszt's extraordinary magic. Here is Heine:

> I forget what he played but I would swear it was variations upon themes from the Apocalypse. At first I could scarcely make them out, those four mystical beasts; I only heard their voices,

especially the roaring of the lion and the croaking of the eagle. But the ox with a book in his mouth was very plain to see. What he played best was the Valley of Jehosaphat. . . . First came Satan galloping in the lists, black-besaddled on a milk-white charger; and, riding slowly behind, Death on her pale horse. Last came Christ in golden armour, on a black steed. With his holy lance he first thrust Satan down, then Death—and the beholders rejoiced loudly. Stormy applause greeted Liszt's playing. He left the piano exhausted, and upon the lips of the beauties there was that melancholy-sweet smile.

How interesting that Chopin should speak of Jericho trumpets and Heine of variations on themes from the Apocalypse. Almost nobody could write quite soberly about him. Clara Wieck said, 'He arouses fright and astonishment. . . . His passion knows no limits.' Sir Charles Hallé wrote of an occasion when Berlioz conducted the March to the Scaffold from the *Symphonie Fantastique*. Liszt then came on to the platform and played his own transcription of the same piece 'with an effect even surpassing that of the full orchestra, and creating an indescribable furore'.

Obviously no piano version of Berlioz's music can surpass the orchestral original; but the fact that such a thing could be said by a musician of Hallé's eminence makes us realize that Liszt was positively hypnotic. A poet named Saphir spoke of 'an inexplicable apparition'.

The conquered pianos lie scattered around him, broken strings float like trophies, wounded instruments flee in all directions, the audience look at one another, dumb with surprise, as after a sudden storm in a serene sky. And he, the Prometheus, who with each note has forged a being, his head bent, smiles strangely before this crowd that applauds him madly.

He was a devil, and later in his life he was to compose several Mephisto pieces—notably the first Mephisto waltz.

Let us return to Marie. After the conquest of Thalberg and a visit to George Sand's country home, Liszt had had enough of Switzerland, and he and Marie went to the Italian lakes. It was there that he composed the second set of *Années de Pèlerinage*, six Paganini studies and twelve *Études d'Exécution Transcendante* (later to be rewritten). He also wrote a transcription of some Rossini songs, the *Serate Musicale* ('Soirées musicales'). This was the life that Marie wanted, but her Franz could not live long without applause. Hearing of floods in his native Hungary he dashed off to Vienna to give concerts in aid of the disaster fund. His phenomenal success and the way he wrote about it in his letters were sad intimations to the Countess that their life together would come to an end, even though not immediately; and when he returned home and she taxed him with his infidelities 'he reasoned about them like a philosopher'. Perhaps earlier she herself had reasoned like a philosopher about her unfaithfulness to her husband.

However, they were still a couple. They went to Rome, and there a child named Daniel was born to join Blandine and Cosima. Rome was then, and would be later, a key city in Liszt's life, but, despite Liszt's assertion in a letter to Berlioz that Raphael and Michelangelo made Mozart and Beethoven more easy for him to understand, the family were soon on the move again.

Another event gave him the chance to take wing. In Bonn there was a project to erect a Beethoven monument. Money came in slowly and Liszt, hearing of this, grew angry. He got an estimate from a Florentine sculptor, took the project into his own hands, and arranged for Marie and the children to stay with his mother in Paris. He was off to Vienna to make money.

His success in Austria and Hungary was such that, reading about it today, we can scarcely credit the facts. He played very box-office pieces, many of them his own transcriptions of melodies that the audience knew and loved, and the Bonn project was saved—though what Beethoven, in the Elysian Fields, thought of the programmes is a matter for delighted conjecture.

How could so famous an Hungarian play in Vienna and not visit Buda-Pesth? A deputation from Hungary besought him to revisit his native land and there he was received by crowds, bands, deputations. Remembering his boyhood on the estate at Raiding, Liszt must have relished the presence of Count Esterházy in *une caravane aristocratique*, and Esterházy must have smiled when he realized that Liszt had forgotten how to speak Hungarian and had to make his speeches in French. Once again there was a succession of triumphs followed by banquets and torchlight processions. And, of course, his transcription of the Rákóczi March sent patriotic blood coursing through Hungarian veins.

One tires at last of reading of the endless successes and the procession of ladies willing to jump into bed with him, but the visit to Hungary brought an important new influence into his life. Having no contact with the peasants he heard nothing of their folk music. What he did hear was gipsy music, and this deeply accorded with his own nature, as anyone can sense in playing the Hungarian Rhapsodies. His enthusiasm wells out in a book he wrote on gipsy music (or, as one translation has it, *The Gipsy in Music*). He describes an occasion when a gipsy band, sheltering in a large shed during a downpour, began a performance.

> But the brandy which circulated, and the wine which had already circulated since the day before, soon brought about a *rinforzando con rabbia*. In a few moments came the distant roll of thunder, sounding like a deep organ-point, whilst the timber work of the roof being very high, and the dilapidated walls of very thin wood, we had the full benefit of an echo which gave us every note again, producing the most chaotic confusion. The passionate passages, the ornamentations, the virtuosity and all feats of technique continued, however, unaffected; all being rolled together in one formidable *tutti*. The roar went on increasing; being varied occasionally by sounds more acute and piercing, as well as by the lightning which came at short intervals to enliven the scene. Sometimes the latter threw a pale greenish light and sometimes a transparent brilliancy of roseate tint, enveloping the performers in an apotheosis as Bengal fire shows up the demi-gods at a theatre.

This is the passage chosen for quotation by Walter Beckett in his *Liszt* (Master Musicians series). Sacheverell Sitwell's *Liszt* chooses another episode:

> The men resemble each other like sons of one mother. Some of them have profiles in which sarcasm seems to be actually sneering. Their tawny skins and faces are framed in locks of hair which fall like snakes of a bluish-black tint upon their necks, the colour of which is a lively orange. Their eyes shine like sparks which seem to be illuminated and extinguished by some interior contrivance.

They got up from the ground to look at some horse that had been given them in exchange that day. This pleased them and they put on quite a heavenly smile, showing off their teeth which were as white as snow. After this, they started imitating castanets by cracking the joints of their fingers, which are always long and charged with electricity. Still uncertain, they began throwing their caps into the air, and followed this by strutting about like peacocks. Then, they looked at the horse again, and as if suddenly given the power to express their pleasure in the bargain, they flew to their violins and cymbals, and began playing in a fury of excitement. The Frischka, or quick Gypsy dance, rose into a frenzy of delirium till the dancers were breathless and fell to the ground.

After Liszt had thrown them some money they played again and differently.

This time it was the gentle and melancholy Lassan, the slow measure of the Gypsies, but as it quickened they grew more excited and led forward the prettiest of the girls for me to dance with. The orgy went on far into the night, while the clearing was lit by a dozen barrels of pitch, the flames of which rose up into the air like cylinders of fire.

A sober historian would never accept these passages as evidence that Liszt had gipsy blood in his veins, but is he not describing his own nature?

While he was in Hungary there was talk of giving him letters of nobility and he asked Marie to design a coat of arms. Nothing came of this, and it all sounds idiotic, but it presaged the time when popular musicians would receive knighthoods, orders of the Légion d'Honneur, and honorary degrees. Liszt had to be content with a sword of honour set with precious stones, about which someone wrote

> Liszt alone, of all warriors, is without reproach
> For in spite of his big sword, we know that this
> Has vanquished only semiquavers
> And slain only pianos.

After Hungary, Germany seemed cool. They were too classical in outlook, those audiences in Leipzig.

He made friends with Mendelssohn and Schumann and

played the latter's *Carnaval*, without much success. However, the three men got on well together, and Mendelssohn's tact helped to smooth Liszt's feelings ruffled by a degree of failure.

Paris next. He did not stay very long. In 1840 he left for London where he was welcomed by lords and ladies. Lady Blessington looked at her fascinating visitor and said, 'What a pity to have put such a man to the piano!'

If she had never said or done anything else she would be worthy of a place in history.

'Such a man' never lacked vanity and he asked Marie to send him various robes and suits, plus a portrait and a statuette, that would enable him to cut a dash, and one wonders just how he was dressed when he went to Buckingham Palace to play to the Queen. As in the case of Mendelssohn, the Queen and her Consort were charming. He played three times at Philharmonic concerts and may have been a little irked to read in the *Morning Journal*, 'Liszt has been presented by the Royal Philharmonic Society with an elegant silver breakfast service for doing that which would cause every young student to receive a severe reprimand—viz., thumping and partially destroying two very fine pianofortes.'

Marie came to join him and complained, 'Yesterday, all the way from Ascot to Richmond, we drove along without your saying a single word to me that was not a wound or an insult.'

London brought them little happiness; and the English provinces brought poor audiences. Maybe the Victorians could not love Mendelssohn *and* Liszt. Liszt cancelled several concerts and made up the impresario's losses. All this cost him more than a thousand pounds. But he tried hard to fulfil what he had promised. He went to Ireland and in the little town of Clonmel played to an audience of twenty-five on a little square piano built by one Tomkinson. He was well received in Edinburgh, however.

After the long journeys and the mixed receptions Liszt left early in 1841 and did not revisit London for many a year. He and Marie rented a pretty little island in the Rhine as a summer retreat, but their life together was coming to an end.

It was about this time that he came near to going to Constantinople with Marie Duplessis—the real-life courtesan recognizable as *La Dame aux Camélias* in the play by Dumas *fils*; *La Traviata* in Verdi's opera. He travelled for a while with Lola Montez, the 'adventuress' (who later brought about the abdication of the King of Bavaria), and at last became tired of her displays of temperament. He locked her in a hotel room and, when paying the bill, added extra money to cover any damage she might do. After finally breaking with Marie d'Agoult he went to Spain and there met Caroline d'Artigaux, the now married and middle-aged version of that Caroline Saint-Cricq who had been his first love. It must have been a traumatic experience for them both.

On and on he went. In Berlin adoring women picked up his cigar ends, collected the water in which he had dipped his wonderful hands, wore brooches and cameos depicting him.

When he left, a cavalcade of carriages escorted him on his way. And when he arrived in St. Petersburg his first concert was before 3,000 people in the Salle de la Noblesse. Three thousand would be a large audience even today. It was almost unheard of in his day; and presumably they were all *de la noblesse*. Perhaps not all. Glinka was there. So were Stassov and Serov, students then but later famous as supporters of the Russian nationalist composers. Stassov did not find Liszt handsome, and Serov took exception to the orders that dangled on chains from the lapels of Liszt's coat.

> Liszt mounted the platform, and pulling his doeskin gloves from his shapely white hands, tossed them carelessly on the floor. Then, after acknowledging the thunderous applause, such as had not been heard in Russia for over a century, he seated himself at the piano. There was a silence as though the whole hall had been turned to stone, and Liszt, without any prelude, began the opening bars of the overture to *William Tell*. Curiosity, speculation, criticism, were all forgotten in the wonderful enchantment of his performance. His Fantasia on *Don Giovanni*, his arrangement of Beethoven's *Adélaïde*, the *Erl-King* of Schubert, and his own *Galop Chromatique* followed upon this. After the concert, Serov and I were like madmen. We scarcely exchanged a word, but hurried home, each to write down his impressions, dreams and raptures. But we both vowed to keep this anniversary sacred for ever, and never, whilst life lasted, to forget a single instant of it.

Nowadays we all play Liszt, our pupils play Liszt, and some pianists even disdain to play Liszt. We press buttons and turn knobs and are disposed to return a record to the music shop if we hear so much as one wrong note. There are some who say that 'Liszt wouldn't cut much ice nowadays' and that we would laugh at his mannerisms and his vanity. The opinion is useless and meaningless. He lived *then*; and mannerisms and vanity, though they may have impressed the sillier kind of women, cannot account for the impressions of Chopin and Clara Wieck and Stassov. As for vanity, yes, he was sometimes absurdly arrogant, but who, other than Liszt, would have rebuked the Tsar for talking during the music? Liszt simply took his hands off the keys.

'Why have you stopped?'

'Music, herself, should be silent when Nicholas speaks.'

I have dwelt on the Liszt stories and the liaison with Marie d'Agoult because, until the era of film stars and pop stars, there were no people more ardently worshipped than great pianists. Though the Liszt story is the most extraordinary of all it is, in a curious way, typical. Many great pianists would later travel the world and bewitch the women and make small fortunes, often outrivalling even great actors and opera stars. Not one of them would become such a legend as Liszt has always been. Amazingly, after the Russian tour, Liszt gave up being a professional pianist.

14. *Chopinski*

Chopin's love life is not part of the legend of the Great Pianist, yet if pianos could speak they would assuredly talk about it. Two of the women in his life seem to belong to the nature of his music, but George Sand, with whom he lived for years, seems oddly removed from it. We accept as natural that he should have fallen in love with the beautiful singer, Constantia

Gladkowska, and we are touched by the melodies that are, so to speak, theirs. And we feel sad for poor Chopin because of what happened to his love for Maria Wodzinska.

In 1835 (he was twenty-five) he went to Carlsbad to meet his parents and take the waters. He little knew that this would be their last meeting. However, he had a happy month with them. Then he went to Dresden and there met a family named Wodzinski whose three sons had lived at Nicholas Chopin's school. With the lads was their young sister, no longer a little girl but a young woman who played the piano well. She was beautiful in an Italianate way and had already attracted attention from a poet and the man who later became Napoleon III. Frédéric fell in love and first expressed it by writing the first few bars of his Nocturne in E flat on a card and adding the words 'Soyez heureuse'. Maria's mother, the Countess, smiled on all this and Chopin was happy.

Back in Paris he was ill. Influenza laid him so low that there were even rumours of his death.

In the following summer he joined his beloved in Marienbad and spent August in her company. The menfolk were away. The Countess was in Marienbad with her daughters only. Maria walked and talked with Chopin and painted his portrait. At last, early in September, Chopin made a formal proposal, and the Countess said a provisional 'yes', it being understood that she would have to persuade the Count to agree. She was concerned about his health: he must at all costs keep well.

He went back to Paris via Leipzig and spent a day with Schumann (we have already noticed Schumann's description of Chopin's playing). Alas, he was ill once more.

The Wodzinskis tried to be kind. They had visited the Chopins in Warsaw, and Maria had given them her portrait of Frédéric. But the Count remembered that Frédéric's sister had died of consumption, a terrible and prevalent scourge for which there was no cure. Maria wrote fewer letters and at last there was an embarrassed letter from her mother to which the girl added only a postscript.

After Chopin's death a packet was found amongst his papers. On the outside was written *Moja Bieda* (My Misery), and inside were Maria's letters.

Poor Chopin, poor Maria! She married another man but the marriage ended in divorce. She married again and her husband died of consumption. She herself lived on until 1896.

After the collapse of his hopes, Chopin paid a visit to London in the company of Camille Pleyel. A Polish friend wrote: 'He is here with Pleyel, famous for his pianos and for his wife's adventures.'

What Chopin thought of Pleyel pianos we know. He liked them best. What he thought of the lady who had jilted Berlioz to marry a rich piano manufacturer is not on record. We do not even know what he thought of her piano-playing, for which she was celebrated.

In London Chopin and Pleyel lived grandly and saw the sights. Chopin dined with James Broadwood in Bryanston Square, arriving incognito as Monsieur Fritz but being instantly recognized the moment he touched the piano.

The Maria Wodzinska episode was over, but pianists and music-lovers must remember her for two reasons. One is that, in her company, he composed the A flat major waltz that has ever since been known as the Farewell Waltz (Op. 69, No. 1 is a misleading number because publication was posthumous). The other reason is that it was she who wrote, 'We never cease to regret that you are not called Chopinski.'

Frédéric was most completely Chopinski when he composed mazurkas and *polonaises*, yet they scarcely seem to belong to the era of nationalist music. This is because he never wrote pictorially. He never slapped on 'local colour'. We listen to certain kinds of Russian music and we can see the dark forest, the broad Volga, the Tatars, the dances of the muzhiks. We go to Spain with Spanish or French composers and there, before our very eyes, is the land of the bullfight. Chopin's music is not like that.

It may be that Poles see their native land in Chopin's music, but there is something else that we must understand. The mazurka derives from the peasants: the *polonaise* from the nobility. A great many ballroom dances are refined versions of village hops, tavern music and so on, and the mazurka is 'folkloristic' in origin. The *polonaise*, on the other hand, is regal. There is a legend that it originated in a dancing procession of ladies presenting themselves to a new young king. When it evolved into a court dance, a gentleman and his lady were side by side, not face to face, and the procession of pairs always had some quality of military formation. I must quote Arthur Hedley:

> Only when he had left Poland did Chopin begin to see the polonaise in another light—as an epic form in which he might enshrine his country's glory, as Mickiewicz had enshrined it in the pages of *Pan Tadeusz*. We, in our prosaic age, can scarcely imagine the fantastic splendour with which the polonaise was danced by the Polish nobility, in full national costume, in the seventeenth and eighteenth centuries. It had lost most of its character by Chopin's time, but his vivid imagination was able to conjure up visions of the past.

Perhaps it is as well that Chopin lived in French exile. Away from the commonplaces of an actual Polish ballroom he could transmute a rhythm of three in a bar into something that seemed strangely like a march. Never himself able to wield a sword he could make every Pole feel like donning armour, jumping on a white steed and galloping into a battle that would free his unhappy country from all its oppressors.

The realities of battle—the blood, the mud, the stink—are totally absent. A *polonaise* is something like one of those battle pictures in which even the most gravely wounded warrior can still hold up his head and salute the banner of St. –. (Choose your own Saint: a romantic battle is a romantic battle.) Yet there is something more in a Chopin *polonaise*. It is something more than Schumann's 'guns buried in roses'. It is a celebration of the spirit of heroism. And who can doubt the heroism of the man who fought ever advancing tuberculosis to the last drop of his blood? His music never gave in.

While he was still engaged to Maria Wodzinska he went to a salon given by the Countess Marie d'Agoult. There he met the celebrated, notorious feminist and writer who called herself George Sand. He was not attracted. She was a few years older than he. She was a woman of personality, but she had never been beautiful. And her libertarian opinions were not, surely,

1. 'Piano e forte' by Bartolomeo Cristofori of Florence. This model, the improved type built about 1720, is in the Metropolitan Museum of Art, New York, and is the earliest known piano to survive

2. A square piano by Longman & Broderip of London, *c.* 1795

3. A transitional giraffe piano. The true giraffes have all their strings above the keyboard. Piano by Van der Hoef, Amsterdam, *c.* 1810

4. A Clementi piano. Inside the open cupboard one sees a barrel with pins. This is activated by clockwork. The piano, therefore, is also a musical box. This must have been a very rare specimen of Clementi's output

5 (a) and (b). A Robert Wornum piano in the Victoria and Albert Museum, made originally for the museum's first curator *c*. 1875—a very late example of a piano with down-striker action. It plays very well and feels normal.

The hammers return to the up position very readily, just as the lighter end of a seesaw jumps up after being depressed. One advantage of this layout was that the sound-board could be extended further towards the keyboard. On up-striking pianos the sound-board must be cut off to allow the hammers to jump up

6. A decorated Steinway belonging to the author. The piano was made for a stately home, almost never used, and then re-purchased by the makers, from whom the author later obtained it. Note the beautiful marquetry work. Some so-called 'art pianos' of this century were grotesque, but this is a handsome piece and a fine instrument

7. A Bösendorfer (Vienna) 'Imperial', one of the biggest and most splendid of concert grands

8. A Steinway-Welte reproducing vertical piano, *c.* 1910

9. The piano shown is a Kemble upright, typifying the sort of domestic upright that is to be found in households all round the world

10. A modern Yamaha piano for the drawing-room

those of a man who had always associated with ladies of wealth and rank and title.

She was herself of distinguished descent. Auguste II, King of Poland, was an ancestor. He was also an ancestor of the French kings Louis XIV, Louis XVIII and Charles X. She was certainly well connected. Nevertheless, as a girl named Aurore Dupin she had had a hard life. She had been the mascot of her father's regiment in the Peninsular War. She had tried, as a young woman, to earn a living doing fancy-work. Marriage made her the Baroness Dudevant and she had a son and daughter. But marriage was not for her. She had a number of well-publicized love affairs with distinguished men, including Alfred de Musset and Prosper Mérimée. She ardently believed in freedom and scandalized conventional women by wearing trousers, smoking cigars and campaigning for women's rights. If she were alive today she would be a left-wing member of Women's Lib. She could hardly have been more different from Constantia and Maria.

The attraction of opposites is a fact of life and Chopin soon began to frequent her company. It could be argued that a woman of some means, with a fine country house in Nohant (near Châteauroux), offered a refuge to a stricken and ailing man. This I do not believe. When she wrote a note—'I adore you. George'—he kept it in his pocket book for the rest of his life. A man does not keep a meal-ticket next to his heart.

Their friends were astonished. Some thought that she was his evil genius. Mickiewicz, the poet, took a different view. 'Chopin is her evil genius, her moral vampire, her cross; he tortures her and will probably end by killing her.' Nobody took the affair lightly.

What does all this mean to the spirit of the piano? We must take note of an incident in Majorca and then consider George Sand's country house as a place of work.

The couple decided to go to Majorca to escape gossip and the Parisian winter. The Majorca of those days was backward and primitive, but they arrived full of hope and settled in Palma only to be thrown out of their abode when Chopin fell ill and coughed up blood. George Sand, healthy, vigorous and optimistic, got her invalid to the French consul's, pulled him round,

F 161

and then removed him and her children to the monastery of Valdemosa, deserted since an anti-clerical government had driven out the monks. There they rented rooms and Chopin found the place congenial for work. He wrote to his friend Fontana.

> Between the cliffs and the sea, a huge deserted Carthusian monastery where, in a cell with doors larger than gates ever were in Paris, you can picture me, my hair uncurled, without white gloves, as pale as ever. The cell is shaped like a high coffin, the enormous vaulting covered with dust, the window small; outside the window are orange trees, palms, cypresses, opposite the window my bed on straps, under a Moorish filigree rosette. Close to the bed an old, square, grubby writing-desk which I can scarcely use; on it a leaden candlestick (a great luxury here) with a candle in it, Bach, my scrawls and someone else's old papers— silence—you can yell—still silence. In short, I'm writing to you from a queer place. . . .
>
> I can't send you the Preludes yet; they're not finished. I feel better now and I'll hurry up. . . . The moon is marvellous tonight; I've never seen it like this before. . . . Nature here is kind but the people are rogues. . . . But all that is a mere grain of sand compared with this sky, the poetry which everything breathes here and the colouring of this most wonderful scenery, still uncontaminated by the eyes of men. Few are those who have startled the eagles which daily soar over our heads.

Chopin wrote in this vein so seldom, and the titles of his pieces are so uncommunicative, that we can too easily assume that he was uninspired by moonlight and mountains. Perhaps, after all, he was not so different from Schumann and Liszt and Schubert. And an incident related by George Sand gives further cause for reflection.

The winter came, the weather turned wet and cold. One day George Sand returning from Palma with her son arrived very late. They had been deserted by their coachman and had struggled home through floods. When they got to the door Chopin cried out, 'I knew that you were dead.' He seemed to be in a kind of trance. He said something about drowning in a lake while icy drops of water fell on his breast. George Sand pointed out, reasonably enough, that the rain had induced a dream, but he was not in a mood to accept reasonable observations.

Naturally musicians and biographers have searched the Preludes for the one that might have been inspired by this incident, and it is No. 15 in D flat that is usually called the 'Raindrop' Prelude. Equally naturally the sterner sort of commentator refuses to believe the story, either because George Sand was, in every sense, a story-teller, or because a serious historian does not go in for that sort of nonsense. Indeed, in Arthur Hedley's *Chopin* we read, 'We shall not repeat here the too celebrated story of the composition of the "Raindrop" Prelude in melodramatic circumstances. If a prelude *was* written in anything like the circumstances described by George Sand many years later, it was probably No. 15, which best fits the novelist's highly coloured account.' This is very hard on a reader who happens not to know the story.

For my part I accept a not-often-quoted comment by George Sand: 'His soul was full of the mysterious harmonies of nature, which he translated into sublime equivalents, not into servile duplication of external sounds.'

Picturesque stories *can* be absurd; but equally absurd is the refusal to believe that Chopin could possibly have been influenced by a 'melodramatic' incident.

Be that as it may, Chopin was once again his highly professional self. He let his companion get on with the cooking and the housekeeping and worked at the little Pleyel that, after long delay, arrived in the island. In January 1840 he sent the completed Preludes to Paris: a little later the second Ballade and a couple of *polonaises*. Nevertheless everyone was longing to get away.

He had a haemorrhage of the lungs on the ship to Barcelona and later had to convalesce for several weeks in Marseilles, but once again Chopin became businesslike.

He wrote in the friendliest way to Pleyel. He apologizes for Fontana's troubling him with his affairs, explains that the piano in Palma has been sold 'or practically sold' for 1,200 francs and adds that if the deal falls through he will see that the piano is returned. He says that he is recovering and signs himself 'my dearest friend, yours devotedly'.

But the letter was sent to Fontana to be forwarded, and in a covering note Chopin is quite different.

> I did not count on such a Jewish way of doing business on Pleyel's part, but since it is so, please hand him this letter . . . don't let Schlesinger take you in like Pleyel. . . . Scoundrels! And this Pleyel, my God, who adores me so! Perhaps he thinks I shan't return to Paris? I'll return sure enough, and both he and Leo shall receive their thanks from me!

When he was well enough they went to Nohant, to the house which, for me, has so much more atmosphere and reality than the pretty Chopin museum that thousands of tourists go to see as part of a package trip to Majorca. The locals call it 'the château', but it is not a great stately home. However, it is the sort of place that has 'grounds', and stables for visitors' coaches and servants' quarters. A house party could be amused by amateur theatricals (there is a large cupboard full of costumes made by visitors for the puppet theatre). There are rooms for Chopin, rooms for the boy and girl, and an enviable air of prosperity. Here Chopin could work or could be ill in comfort knowing that he would be devotedly nursed. And from here Chopin could go to Paris where society learned to accept the ménage.

In 1842 a Russian with the German name of von Lenz was in Paris in the hope of having lessons from both Liszt and Chopin. His book, *Great Piano Virtuosos of Our Time*, is full of good things, but let us pick a few vivid sketches of Chopin.

> I gave Liszt's card to the servant in the anteroom; a man-servant is an article of luxury in Paris, a *rarissima avis* in the home of an artist.
>
> The servant said that M. Chopin was not in Paris. I did not allow myself to be put out, and repeated 'Deliver this card, I will attend to the rest.' Chopin soon came out to me, the card in his hand; a young man of middle height, slim, haggard, with a sad, though very expressive countenance, and elegant Parisian bearing stood before me. I have seldom, if ever, met with an apparition so entirely engaging. He did not press me to sit down: I stood before him as before a monarch. 'What do you wish? Are you a pupil of Liszt, an artist?' 'A friend of Liszt. I wish to have the privilege of studying with you your Mazurkas, which I regard as a literature;

164

I have already studied several of them with Liszt'—I felt that I had been incautious, but it was too late.

'So?' said Chopin deliberately, but in his most amiable tone. 'Why, then, do you need me? Play to me please, those you have played with Liszt; I have still a few minutes'—he drew an elegant little watch from his pocket; 'I was going out—I had forbidden my door to anyone, pardon me!' . . . I went without further ado to the piano, and opened it as though I were quite at home. It was a Pleyel: I had been told that Chopin never used any other instrument. The Pleyel has an easier action than that of any other Parisian manufacture. . . . I ventured only one glance towards him, and then boldly struck up the B flat major Mazurka, the typical one, to which Liszt had noted the variants for me.

I got through well; the *volata* through the octaves went better than ever before, the instrument ran even easier than my Érard.

Chopin whispered engagingly: 'That *trait* is not your own, is it? *He* showed you that! *He* must have his hand in everything; well! he may dare—he plays to thousands, I seldom to *one*! Very well, I will give you lessons—but only twice a week, that is the most I ever give; it will be difficult for me to find three-quarters of an hour.' He looked again at his watch. 'What are you reading? With what do you occupy yourself in general?' That was a question I was well prepared to answer: 'I prefer George Sand, and Jean-Jacques, to all other writers,' said I too quickly—he laughed: he was *beautiful* at that moment. 'Liszt told you to say that. . . .'

I always went to him long before my hour, and waited. One lady after another came out, each more beautiful than the others.

Von Lenz hated George Sand, described her as a poisonous plant and quoted the English judge who in every criminal case put the question, 'Where is the woman?'

(*We* think it was a French judge who first said *cherchez la femme.*)

Von Lenz went to musical parties in carriages that were sent to convey Chopin, who said, 'We shall drive *en princes.*' He heard Chopin play Beethoven's A flat Sonata, Op. 26, and felt that Chopin had little sympathy with Beethoven. At a lesson he himself played the same piece to Chopin.

I felt I owed Liszt something, and played the Beethoven theme so as to express an autumn landscape, with a dash of summer sunlight! with the three well-graduated, very intense crescendos in the five consecutive A flats . . . Chopin came at once from the cabinet, and sat down near me, still in his shirt-sleeves. I played well, and glowed like a coal. . . . At the Thema, I stopped, and looked him quietly in the eyes. He laid his hand on my shoulder, and said: 'I will tell Liszt. It never occurred to me to play it like that, but it is *fine*. But must one *always* speak with so much passion?'

Von Lenz's first encounter with George Sand did not give him a good impression.

George Sand said not a word when Chopin introduced me. That was uncivil. For that reason, I immediately sat down close to her. Chopin hovered round like a frightened bird in a cage, he saw that something was coming. Was there ever a time when he was without apprehension in her presence? At the first pause in the conversation, which was conducted by Sand's friend, Madame Viardot (I was to become well acquainted with this great singer, later, in St. Petersburg), Chopin took me by the arm and led me to the piano. Reader! If you play the piano, you can picture to yourself how sorely I stood in need of courage! It was a *Pleyel upright*, which, in Paris, passed for a pianoforte! I played 'The Invitation' fragmentarily; Chopin shook me by the hand; George Sand did not say a word. I sat down by her. . . .

'Will you not come to St. Petersburg sometime,' said I, in my politest manner, to George Sand, 'where you are read so much, and so highly respected?' 'I will never lower myself, by visiting a country where slavery exists,' she answered shortly.

This was indecent, after she had been discourteous.

'After all, you may be right, *not* to come,' I replied in the same tone: 'you might find the door closed against you! I just thought of Tsar Nicholas.' George Sand looked at me, astounded; I looked steadily back, into beautiful, big, brown, cow-eyes. Chopin did not seem displeased. I understood every motion of his head.

Instead of answering, George Sand rose, and strode like a man across the room to the glowing fire. I followed at her heels, and sat down, ready primed, next her—for the third time.

She had something to say at last.

She drew an enormously thick Trabucco cigar from her apron pocket, and called back, into the drawing-room: 'Frédéric, un *fidibus!*' . . .

I felt insulted in him—my great lord and master: I understood Liszt's remark: *Pauvre Frédéric!* in all its bearings.

Chopin obediently brought a *fidibus.**

After the first abominable whiff of smoke, George Sand favoured me with a question: 'I suppose I could not even smoke a cigar in a drawing-room in St. Petersburg?'

'In *no* drawing-room, Madame, have I ever seen a cigar smoked,' I answered, not without emphasis, with a bow!

It must be said that George Sand bore him no rancour. The next day she called with Chopin at von Lenz's hotel but, by mistake, and to his annoyance, was told he was not at home. And later, at a lesson, Chopin told him that he had pleased her very much.

We owe to von Lenz an account of Chopin's *rubato* that makes us wonder just how free it was.

Once Meyerbeer came in while I was taking my lesson with Chopin. Meyerbeer was not announced; he was a king. I was just playing the Mazurka in C, Op. 33—on only one page, which contains so many hundreds; I named it the 'Epitaph of the Idea' —so full of grief and sorrow is this composition—the weary flight of an eagle!

Meyerbeer had seated himself; Chopin let me play on.

'That is two-four time,' said Meyerbeer.

For reply, Chopin made me repeat, and kept time by tapping loudly upon the instrument with his pencil; his eyes glowed.

'Two-four,' Meyerbeer repeated quietly.

I never but once saw Chopin angry: it was at this time! A delicate flush coloured his pale cheeks, and he looked very handsome.

'It is three-four' he said *loudly*, he, who always spoke so softly!

'Give it me, for a ballet for my opera (*l'Africaine*, then kept a secret), I will show you, *then*!'

'It is *three*-four,' almost screamed Chopin, and played it himself. He played it several times, counted aloud, and stamped the time with his foot—he was beside himself! It was of no use, Meyerbeer insisted it was two-four, and they parted in ill-humour.

It is likely that Meyerbeer was teasing Chopin. Von Lenz

* A spill or cigar-lighter.

167

liked Meyerbeer—liked him better than the Parisians—but he tries to put us to rights about *rubato*.

'The left hand,' I often heard him say, 'is the conductor, it must not waver, or lose ground; do with the right hand what you will and can.' He taught: 'Supposing that a piece lasts a given number of minutes; it may take just so long to perform the whole, but in the details deviations may occur!'

But I heard Chopin's rubato better defined by Liszt, at Weimar in 1871—as I heard it from his distinguished pupil, the capital Russian pianist Neilissow. 'Do you see those trees?' Liszt said to Neilissow; 'The wind plays in the leaves, Life unfolds and develops beneath them, but the *tree remains the same*—that is Chopin's rubato.'

As in the case of Mozart's *rubato*, one wonders how a left hand or a conductor can keep strict time while a right hand or a singer is free to be wayward. Any modern writer who assures us that Chopin always did this or never did that is deceiving himself.

Von Lenz was, of course, biased.

How could a French nature understand Chopin? A Sand could never take a loftier flight than: '*Jouez-moi quelque chose Frédéric! un fidibus, Frédéric!*' etc. *L'Artiste* was caught in a web, to which the spider was not lacking!

This is absurd, and we do not have to share von Lenz's belief that Chopin died not from consumption but of a broken heart, but he gives us many fascinating details—as, for example, a reference to 'the easy-running, narrow-keyed Pleyel'. Are the *Études* harder for us than for Chopin? We see the confrontation between von Lenz, the German-Russian gentleman, and the libertarian woman, with blue blood in her veins but the revolution in her heart. We hear the accents of romantic enthusiasm and positively enjoy the exclamation marks and the underlinings.

The Frédéric–George relationship began to fail when the children grew up. The son and daughter fought and bickered and fell in and out of love. The boy looked to mother, the girl used her wiles on Chopin. The situation became impossible. Chopin bowed out.

In 1848 there was a French revolution—yet another. Indeed, there were revolutions all across Europe. A devoted pupil, a Miss Jane Stirling, removed Chopin to London where, ill though he was, he played to the Queen. He then went to stay in Scotland with the titled relatives of Miss Stirling and tried to conceal his boredom. When it was safe to return to Paris, it was money from the Stirling family (15,000 francs) that paid his debts and allowed him to die in comfort.

Friends and admirers came to see him, and his beautiful compatriot Countess Delphine Potocka held his hands and sang Polish songs in her beautiful voice, since when there has been a persistent legend, unsupported by documentary evidence, that at some time they were lovers. (She is the dedicatee of the so-called Minute Waltz.) He had a grand funeral to the sounds of Mozart's Requiem and his own Funeral March, and, from the day of his burial (1849) until now, there have nearly always been flowers on his tomb.

15. *The New Piano-Makers and Their Customers*

The 1848 revolutions that drove Chopin to London drove the Steinwegs to America. They were a family that had survived hardship. Heinrich Steinweg had lost parents, brothers, sisters in the privations of war or by Act of God (lightning). As an eighteen-year-old he was at the Battle of Waterloo and won a medal for bugling in the face of the enemy. When peace came he began to make such instruments as mandolins, zithers and dulcimers. He worked as a cabinet-maker in an organ factory. When he married he made a small piano for his wife, with two strings to a note. Thirteen years went by before he made a three-string piano. What decided him to become a piano-maker was the winning of a first prize at a state fair.

By the time he had ten children the revolution ruined the

business, and one of the sons, Charles, decided to try his luck in America. There is a suggestion that the young man was sympathetic to the aims of the revolution—it was an age of terrible exploitation of the poor—and that his ideals, and perhaps fear of the police, impelled him towards the Land of the Free.

The family followed soon after and, at first, worked in various factories. In 1853 they decided to start in business together. Heinrich Steinweg became Henry Steinway, and Steinway & Sons entered into competition with the American piano-makers. By 1855 they produced a square piano that combined an iron frame in one single casting with over-stringing, and they called this the Steinway System.

One Steinweg son, Theodore, remained in Germany. He continued to make pianos there and was joined some years later by a piano-maker named Friedrich Grotrian who had spent some years in Moscow. However, in 1865, Theodore Steinweg sold out to Friedrich Grotrian and went to join his brothers in New York. Continuing as a much-admired instrument, the Grotrian-Steinweg piano, preferred above all others by Clara Schumann, had what was called the 'homogeneous sound-board'. The firm claimed to test for acoustic properties each strip of wood that went into the sound-board and they also took out patents for various improvements in the placing of hammers in relation to length of string, in screwing a 'freely balanced static metal frame' only to the outside of the sound-board, and in various other devices to improve tone and action. The Grotrians in Germany and the Steinways in America have never had business connections.

It was an age of new names, mostly German, competing for ascendancy. In 1856 Carl Bechstein managed at last to make a piano that satisfied him and showed it to Hans von Bülow who declared that he was determined to show the world that the best pianos were made in Prussia. The piano was publicly inaugurated with a performance of Liszt's sonata, and the name Bechstein was on its way to fame. Piano-makers at this time showed their wares at exhibitions and mentioned their successes on the sound-boards. They also mentioned Royal Appointments. No maker collected such a resounding list of royal patrons as Bechstein; and to this day there are serviceable

Bechsteins with a long list to be seen on the sound-board in Gothic lettering, beginning with the German Kaiser and going on to the Austrian Emperor, the Russian Tsar, the King and Queen of England and many crowned heads of countries that are now mostly republics, continuing in smaller lettering with mere grand dukes and princesses.

Bechsteins were amongst the very best pianos, and I have sometimes wondered, against my own democratic principles, whether Bechstein designers and workers were devoted beyond the call of duty, because a piano might, for all they knew, be put in a queen's boudoir. Of course the tradition of excellence outlived the emperors and empresses, but *was* there something?

In 1864 Wagner wrote to Bechstein:

> When I returned from exile for the first time, with my friend Liszt in Weimar, I came one day by chance upon an instrument which by its delightful, crystal-clear tone so charmed and enthralled me that my dear friend, Hans von Bülow, wishing to console me on my unhappy departure, had the inspired idea of providing an identical instrument to gladden me in my new abode.

(Wagner later eloped with Bülow's wife, Liszt's daughter.)

About the time when Bechstein was opening in Berlin, Julius Blüthner started a piano factory in Leipzig. No better centre could have been chosen, and soon Blüthners were used exclusively at the great Conservatorium. In 1873, and for many years afterwards, Blüthner pianos had, besides the customary three strings per note, a fourth, placed out of reach of the hammer. This fourth string had to be tuned an octave higher, with the object of providing a greater resonance of overtones by means of sympathetic vibration. Some pianists were convinced: some were sceptical; but Blüthner tone had its own special charm. The so-called aliquot-scaling has been abandoned, but Blüthners remain among the top pianos.

In Vienna, in 1828, the Body of Magistrates granted to Ignaz Bösendorfer 'the right to trade as a piano maker together with the title of a Burgher and Master'. Like Bechstein who was lucky to meet von Bülow, Bösendorfer had earlier been lucky to meet Liszt. The young Liszt was liable to render most pianos unplayable, but the Bösendorfer responded to all his demands and emerged unscathed. The reputation of the firm was made and in due course it attracted the loyalty of some of the greatest pianists in the world (and I am not surprised) (*see Plate 7*).

The new German and Austrian firms had to face the competition of the older manufacturers in France and England, but it is interesting to note that Érard's name had been Erhardt and that the father of the Pleyel whom Chopin knew was born in Austria, the twenty-fourth child of a village schoolmaster who, in the course of two marriages, had thirty-eight children. Bechstein learned his trade with the firm of Pleyel not only in Paris but at their branch in Dresden and may well have had the feeling that piano-making was really a German trade.*

In London, Broadwood and Collard were as British as they come, but in due course they had to face a rising tide of competition from German pianos, not only the great makes but also the Schiedmayers and the Ibachs and other pianos of quality and thence right on down, though London could more than hold its own on the general domestic level. What no British maker was able to do was to say, along with the Bechsteins and Blüthners and Bösendorfers, 'We make only the best: if you want something cheaper don't come to us.' Nevertheless thousands of excellent, durable pianos were made, and names like Chappell, Challen, Brinsmead, Spencer and Rogers were well regarded all over the world.†

It cannot be doubted that the European makers were greatly influenced by the advance in American piano-making, but few American pianos crossed the Atlantic. Only those pianists who went to the States were able to know that Baldwin, and Mason & Hamlin, and Chickering were names to be reckoned with. However, Steinway—and we must glance ahead to 1880—opened a factory in Europe, in Hamburg to be precise, to supply Europe. This made them international in a way that no

---

* Less famous but very influential is Jean Schwander, born in Alsace in 1812, who started to make piano actions in Paris in 1844. In 1865 his daughter married Josef Herrburger, who helped to develop the business. Today, the American-owned British factory of Herrburger Brooks Ltd. makes Schwander actions for pianos in a number of countries including a Russian concert-grand, the action being the result of many improvements.

† A detailed account of the British makers can be found in *The Piano Makers* by David Wainwright (Hutchinson, 1975).

other firm was, and many a pianist was puzzled thereafter to know whether he could describe a Hamburg Steinway as a German piano or an American piano made in Germany.

What nobody in the nineteenth century foresaw was the rise of the Japanese piano.

When Chopin was in Scotland he had to laugh, ill though he was, at his hosts' friends. He wrote to Wojciech Grzymala from Hamilton Palace:

> Lady –, one of the first ladies here, in whose castle I spent a few days, is regarded here as a great musician. One day, after my piano, and after various songs by other Scottish ladies, they brought a kind of accordion, and she began with the utmost gravity to play on it the most atrocious tunes. What would you have? Every creature here seems to me to have a screw loose. Another lady, showing me her album, said to me 'The queen looked in it and I sat beside her.' A third that she is 'the thirteenth cousin of Mary Stuart'. Another sang, standing up for the sake of originality, and accompanying herself on the piano, a French-English romance. . . . The Princess of Parma told me that one lady whistled for her with guitar accompaniment. Those who know my compositions ask me 'Play your second Sigh—I greatly like the bells.' And every observation ends with 'like water', meaning that it flows like water. I have not yet played to any Englishwoman without her saying to me *like water*!!! They all look at their hands, and play the wrong notes with much feeling. Eccentric folk, God help them.

However, the piano marched on. At that very moment Czerny was publishing Opus 700-odd, so somebody must have been busy practising. And inventors—eccentric folk, God help them—went to the extent of combining a piano with a bed, cupboards, a writing desk and a wash-basin. More sensibly some pianos were built with pedal-boards so that an organist could practise at home before going to church. What, alas, never came to fruition was a viable device to turn pages.

Before Chopin died he heard an American pianist, a boy of sixteen, play his Concerto in E minor. The audience at the Salle Pleyel must have been as surprised as they were impressed. An

American virtuoso? Chopin embraced the lad, whose name was Louis Moreau Gottschalk.

The new phenomenon came from Louisiana—he was born in New Orleans in 1829. His father, born in England, came from a German Jewish family, his mother was a French gentle-woman, a refugee from a slave rebellion in Santo Domingo. (Her uncle was a Count Moreau de l'Islet.) The child, then, was an American of French culture, speaking English with a slight French inflexion. Some of his compatriots pronounced his name Gotts-chalk, but must have originally been Gott-schalk. (The word *schalk* meant servant in the olden days and later came to mean rascal.)

After studying in Paris and meeting the great artists of the time, Gottschalk returned to America and thereafter toured, as the greatest American pianist, not only in the States but in the Caribbean and South America. Wherever possible he travelled with a Chickering grand piano and a tuner, and seems to have become familiar with every railroad in existence. Not even the Civil War deterred him. After achieving great fame in the eastern States he sailed to Panama, crossed the isthmus by train, sailed to San Francisco, and saw the California of the gold rush. There he travelled by stage-coach and must have played on appalling pianos. Taking ship to Peru he witnessed the horrors of a revolution (in which, he says, only foreigners succoured the wounded) and, nothing daunted, penetrated into the interior and up into the Andes. Again he goes on, by sea, through the Straits of Magellan to the Atlantic seaboard.

Wherever he went he played, sometimes on his own, some-times in a concert for perhaps twenty pianists at once—thereby avoiding the antagonism of the local professionals. He also organized monster galas with hundreds of performers. He died in Rio de Janeiro at the age of forty, leaving for posterity some popular small pieces—'The Last Hope', 'The Dying Poet', 'The Banana Tree', 'The Banjo'—that became bestsellers and paved the way for a whole corpus of American music. He also left a journal, *Notes of a Pianist*,* that is such a compelling and vivid account of the Americas in his lifetime as to make one feel that he could easily have been a journalist, perhaps a war

* Republished by Alfred A. Knopf, New York, 1964.

correspondent. The bare facts of his career may give the impression of a brash promoter. In fact he was a sensitive and imaginative man. Though a Southerner he freed his few slaves and sided with the North. He hated religious bigotry, he hated the bogus revolutions of South America that always ended in dictatorship, and he writes unforgettably of seeing a lynching. The victim was proved to be innocent three days later.

He thought of Hell as a piano warehouse in which multitudes of pianists played for ever such pieces as 'The Maiden's Prayer'. He knew only too well what public taste was like even amongst people who thought of themselves as persons of taste.

We must not assume that this was a peculiarly American state of affairs.

16. *He That Should Come*

The greatest number of real pianists, serious students and enthusiastic amateurs were to be found in the German-speaking states. It seemed to them the greatest piano music had been given to them by Bach, by Haydn and Mozart, by Beethoven, by Schubert and Schumann. Yes, there were the two foreigners, the Pole and the Hungarian, but the Germans could be forgiven for feeling rather smug. Nevertheless, there were some who felt that what the world needed was another Beethoven. They knew well enough that there could never literally be another Beethoven any more than there could be another Goethe, but there were some who longed for a sort of second coming.

In 1853 an extraordinary article appeared in the *Neue Zeitschrift für Musik*. It was written by Schumann, now forty-three years old. It was ten years since he had contributed to the paper to which he had at one time given so much time and energy, but now there was something that simply had to be said.

It seemed to me, who had followed the progress of these chosen ones with the greatest interest, that . . . a musician would inevitably appear to whom it was vouchsafed to give the highest and most ideal expression to the tendencies of our time, one who would not show his mastery in a gradual development, but, like Athena, would spring fully armed from the head of Zeus. And he has come, a young man over whose cradle Graces and Heroes stood watch. His name is Johannes Brahms.

Brahms was twenty, and Schumann was perfectly right. After this, allowing for an occasional hostile audience or a bad newspaper review, Brahms was successful for the rest of his life. In relation to the piano he was destined to create an enormous body of passionate and romantic music, but one looks in vain for a passionate and romantic life. The early life is interesting enough, but in every biography there is a moment when the writer has to say something like 'from this point onwards the story of Brahms is largely a catalogue of works'.

He was a very little boy when he announced that he wanted to learn the piano. His father, a very humble player of the double bass, sat at a piano to teach the child his notes and was considerably surprised to find that little Hannes not only knew the notes but, turning his back on the piano, could recognize them. There were plenty of piano teachers in Hamburg, and it is fortunate that the child was placed with a good, honest musician named Cossel who, some while later, persuaded the father not to listen to the blandishments of an agent who wanted to send the clever youngster to America as an infant prodigy. Indeed this incident led Cossel to ask a teacher greater than himself to take the boy on, and the celebrated Eduard Marxsen was a powerful influence for the good in Brahms's life. Both teachers were gratefully remembered.

Bach and Beethoven were the main part of the young pianist's musical diet, and he soon became, if not a great virtuoso, a formidable pianist. Still, composition was Brahms's passion, and he began to write quantities of music.

However, his parents were poor and, at the age of thirteen, he began to earn some money playing the piano in waterside taverns where prostitutes plied their trade amongst the sailors off the ships. This experience affronted him so deeply as to affect his attitude to women for the rest of his life. He might well have had a breakdown but for the kindness of a patron of the Alster Pavilion, where his father played in the band. In the country house of Herr and Frau Giesemann, Johannes discovered the beauties of nature and learned the comforts of well-ordered domesticity.

By the time Brahms was eighteen he had composed the Scherzo in E flat minor (later published as Opus 4) and the Sonatas in C major and F sharp minor.

When he was twenty he fell in with a violinist who was to be a considerable influence. This was an Hungarian Jew named Eduard Reményi who played in the *zigeuner* (gipsy) style— even sometimes in classical music. This man had left Germany after the political storms of 1848 and had gone to America, but in 1852 he was back again, and in 1853 he and Brahms toured together. It was at Celle where they were confronted by a piano a semitone below acceptable pitch. Brahms solved the problem by transposing up. He simply played Beethoven's C minor Sonata as though it had been written in C sharp. This was a feat, no doubt of it; but the point must be made that our own internationally agreed pitch is something new, resulting from recording, broadcasting and the like. In my own youth every accompanist had to cope with domestic pitch, concert pitch, French pitch and any other pitch that might have satisfied the local tuner, and one was frequently asked by a singer to 'Put it up a bit old boy' (or down for a soprano suffering from a cold). Also one played for musicians of every degree, in theatre pits, beneath the silver screens of silent films, in seaside bandstands, to earn the living that is now provided by government grant. I do not recall any brothels, but was probably too innocent to recognize one if I had seen it.

Association with Reményi gave Brahms a feeling for gipsy style that later came out in the Hungarian Dances—those four-handed pieces that were the delight of every musical home. And it was Reményi who introduced Brahms to a very different sort of Jewish violinist, the young Joseph Joachim, already established as a very great violinist in the strictest classical tradition, and an acknowledged interpreter of Bach's Chaconne and Beethoven's Violin Concerto.

Brahms and Joachim struck up a friendship that would last for a lifetime, and it was Joachim who began to introduce the young newcomer to the great world.

Whom should they visit first? Obviously Liszt with his generous enthusiasm for new music—Liszt to whom Joachim had for a while been attached as part of the 'neo-German' school.

And so to Weimar.

Liszt's home in Weimar had set all the musical world buzzing with argument and gossip. He had fallen under the spell of Princess Carolyne Sayn-Wittgenstein, a Polish lady of enormous wealth (she owned 30,000 serfs) who had left her husband, and they were living in Weimar because the Grand Duke had asked Liszt to settle there and revive the glories of the town that had harboured Goethe.

Almost unbelievably, the greatest pianist in the world had given up the life of travelling virtuoso and had settled down to compose more seriously than ever before and to conduct the opera. The Princess may have been a somewhat absurd woman who always called Liszt The Great One, or The Master; and the ménage undoubtedly annoyed the Grand Duchess who, as a sister of the Tsar, felt that the Princess was bringing the nobility into disrepute; but the fact is that Princess Carolyne was more successful than Countess Marie had ever been in persuading Liszt that he had a higher destiny than giving dazzling concerts and bewitching the women. As for money, she had more than enough. She had her way. It was during the ten years of Weimar that Liszt composed some of his finest pieces—the Piano Sonata can serve as example—and developed his powers as a composer for orchestra. He completed the final version of his Transcendental Studies, he composed his 'Faust' Symphony, he produced Wagner's *Tannhäuser* and *Lohengrin*.

It was to the Altenburg, the Liszt home in Weimar, that Joachim brought Brahms. They were well received and introduced to a company of distinguished musicians. Seeing that Brahms was too shy to play to the greatest of pianists, Liszt took the manuscripts and played them at sight, marvellously. The young composer was astounded: the older man was cordial. The visit ought to have been a total success, but the story goes that when Liszt played his own sonata Brahms nodded off. It seems a rather unlikely story and may have been put around by Reményi in a fit of mischief, but it was in Brahms's very nature that he could never become a Lisztian; and it was in the very nature of German musical society that he would later come to be the darling of the anti-Wagner faction.

Who after Liszt? Schumann was one of Joachim's friends, so were a family named Deichmann who introduced Brahms to a great deal of Schumann music that he had not previously known. At last Brahms made up his mind, went to Düsseldorf, and called on Schumann.

Once again he was made welcome. Schumann asked him to play. In a few moments Schumann stopped him and called to Clara. 'Now, dear Clara, you will hear such music as you never heard before; and you, young man, play the piece from the beginning.' The effect of the C major Sonata was such that Brahms was asked to stay, and he remained with the Schumanns not just for a day or two but for weeks. Schumann called him 'the young eagle' and, in a letter to Joachim, wrote, 'This is he that should come.' It was then that the older composer wrote his article for the *Neue Zeitschrift*.

Schumann alerted Breitkopf & Härtel, and the C major Sonata was published as Opus 1, though chronologically it was written after the F sharp minor Sonata (Opus 2) and the E flat minor Scherzo (Opus 4). The young eagle was free to soar.

Opus 3, also published at this time, was a set of songs. Brahms was in the Schubert-Schumann line of great *Lieder* composers.

Every new composer confronts the pianists of his era with new problems, but the fact is that Brahms did not and could not create a new pianism. Anyone who could play Beethoven's Appassionata, or Liszt's Mephisto Waltz or Chopin's *Études* could play Brahms's music even though he would have to think new thoughts about interpretation. Indeed it would never again be possible for a composer to revolutionize piano playing —not until that moment in the twentieth century when composers began to throw ping-pong balls on the strings of a Steinway.

What pianists found in Brahms was some difference in the

179

arrangement of notes in chords. For example, it had been almost a dogma in the study of harmony that the notes of a chord could be close together in the treble but should be more widely separated in the bass. Close chords in the bass were 'muddy'. You could play a G and put B flat close above it and the effect would be agreeable from somewhere near the middle of the keyboard to the far right. But play these notes in the bass, or below the bass stave, and your harmony professor would shake his head and say, 'You need a little air between those notes, boy; better put them a tenth apart.'

Not Brahms. This is not to say that he always wrote close chords in the bass, but he did it often enough for people to recognize a 'finger-print' and to suggest that the darker sound arose from his north German background. There was a belief that a Mediterranean composer would never have written like that. Brahms in due course settled in Vienna and spent many holidays in Italy, but his composing nature remained unchanged.

Some of the music is very 'stretchy'. Brahms had big, powerful hands. The two piano concertos are cruelly taxing to all but the most powerful women. Just occasionally he is unpianistic. His notes do not always lie 'gratefully' under the hands. Even the best pianists have to grab at certain runs in the E flat concerto, and I can think of one that I can play only by using some highly unconventional fingering and omitting one note. The notes are so numerous and the pace so fast that I have never found a colleague able to spot which note it is that I omit.

Brahms was certainly interested in pianism. He composed few *études* as such, but his two books of variations on a theme by Paganini are, in effect, a sequence of titanic studies, and they demand what Liszt would have called transcendental technique.

The smaller pieces, the intermezzos and capriccios, are curiously different from anything by Chopin. It is, I think, no accident that in the story of Brahms there is very little mention of princesses and countesses. Chopin's music is aristocratic. Remember that his mazurkas were 'not for dancing'. Remember that only ballet-dancers attempt his waltzes. Remember that Tchaikovsky's *polonaise* in *Eugène Onegin* belongs to a ballroom scene in which a Chopin *polonaise* would never have served.

Brahms is nearer to ordinary people. When, as a famous composer, he settled in Vienna, who should be among his close friends but the Johann Strauss who wrote 'The Blue Danube', a piece enormously admired by Brahms. At the opera he liked nothing better than Bizet's *Carmen*. His popular duets, Hungarian Dances and several sets of waltzes (not to mention the Love-Song Waltzes for piano duet and a quartet of voices), belong to the same general category as the Slavonic Dances composed by his protégé and friend, Dvořák. I cannot disagree with those who feel that Brahms is more middle-class than Chopin. This consideration has no influence on our enjoyment at this distance of time: it influences only our reflections on the nature of the music. The most ardent Chopinist I ever taught was a young left-winger from a mining village.

The subject of Brahms as an influence in the story of pianism has taken us beyond the encounter with Schumann. We must return to Schumann in order to shed some light on the romantic character of Brahms's piano music and songs . . . or should I say to *fail* to shed light?

Schumann, always somewhat unstable, began to suffer from softening of the brain. His last few years of madness, with only moments of peace and lucidity, are painful to read about. During this period Brahms was a devoted friend. Clara worked unceasingly, teaching and concertizing to maintain her seven children. Indeed, for over two years she never saw her husband because the doctors found that her visits seemed to make him worse. After Schumann's death she and her young friend, twelve years her junior, were very close, to a degree that set tongues wagging.

Most biographers—and I agree with them—are inclined to believe Clara in her letter to her children: 'Believe what your mother tells you, and do not listen to petty and envious souls who grudge him my love and friendship, and therefore try to impugn him or even to cast aspersions on our relations, which they cannot, or will not, understand.'

Inevitably the time came when they went their separate ways, though they were always friends.

Brahms never married. There were a few occasions in his life when it looked as though he might, but he tended to be tactless and sarcastic to women and on at least one occasion offended his friends by a violent diatribe against women in general. When he needed sex he bought it. Liszt would have found such a life totally incomprehensible, and so do many who love Brahms's music. If all this seems to make him a rather unattractive figure I must hasten to add that in fact he was very much liked. He could be very genial and he had a great capacity for friendship. And he could take a great deal of admiration without getting swollen-headed. Underneath that big beard there was the face of a very sensitive man.

Unlike most composers he had a warm relationship with his principal publisher, Simrock. When the money began to roll in, Brahms scarcely knew what to do with it, so Simrock became his financial adviser and invested the money to Brahms's best advantage. It is almost a unique relationship in the history of composers.

---

17. *An American Girl Learns from Liszt*

If Liszt could never understand a way of life like Brahms's, it is equally certain that Brahms must have been puzzled by Liszt. Indeed, all musical Germany tended to be either Wagnerians, and therefore Lisztians, or law-and-order people who found Brahms's blend of classic form and romantic feeling wholly admirable.

Brahms lost his faith in God: Liszt renewed his. The Princess Sayn-Wittgenstein was constantly petitioning the Pope to annul her marriage to her distant husband on the grounds that she had been forced into it. She longed for a life of pious respectability. It seemed at last that the Vatican was favourably inclined, but then the blow fell. The answer was quite finally no. There was another blow. Liszt's production of the opera *The Barber of Baghdad* by his young friend Peter Cornelius was hissed, not because of the music but because there were dis-approving people who wanted to be rid of Liszt and his Princess.

The Weimar period was at an end after some ten years. And perhaps the picture of Franz and Carolyne as great lovers was beginning to seem a little ridiculous. Disappointed by the Pope they went to Rome, of all places, where the lady began her great work in twenty-four volumes on *The Inner Causes of the Outer Weaknesses of the Church*. They now had separate establishments, and when Liszt called he had to take care not to bring any fresh air into a room full of cigar smoke.

It is understandable that the Princess should write about the weaknesses of the Church. It is—to me, at any rate—totally incomprehensible that that same Church should have made Liszt an *abbé*. It is true that an *abbé* is given only a few of the holy orders that would be conferred on a priest. It is also true that the title is a *title* and allows its holder to be religious in a fashionable manner. But Liszt now wore an air of holiness—within reason. I once wrote of him, 'Wearing his clerical soutane, his hair white, his eagle face marked by warts, his eyes still flashing, he was a semidemiwolf in saint's clothing.'

It may be that my agnosticism disqualifies me from under-standing Liszt's Catholicism. It may be that I take too northern a view of a man who would seem quite comprehensible to Mediterranean society. I try hard to be fair. I think Liszt was acting a part.

I sometimes play the last of all the pieces in the *Années de Pèlerinage*, the one called 'Les Jeux d'Eaux à la Villa d'Este'. It is a long piece full of pianistic waterfalls. On page 8 there is a footnote: *Sed aqua quam ego dabo ei, fiet in eo fons aquae salientis in vitam aeternam* (But the water that I shall give him shall be in him a well of water springing up into everlasting life—St. John 4–14). The Villa d'Este was the home of Cardinal Hohenlohe, but I constantly fail to feel that the pianistic droplets are holy water. Liszt was no religious prophet, but he certainly was a pianistic one, and what I do discover in this piece is the same water as is sprinkled all over the keyboard in Ravel's *Jeux d'Eau* written so many years later.

Liszt was now a poorer man. He had long since ceased to

earn money as a concert artist. He was free of his entanglement with Carolyne. He was given hospitality by great people—for example at the Villa d'Este—but travelling by train he went second-class. He divided his time between Rome, Weimar and Budapest and gave lessons to talented young pianists without ever charging a penny. When he was praised for his generosity he amended the expression *noblesse oblige* to *génie oblige*. Yes indeed: the obligations of genius *are* greater than the obligations of rank.

He knew well enough that nobody would ever again establish totally new standards of piano-playing and he applied himself to sharing his genius. The market for pianists was growing, and there would be some demand for them well away from the homes of the nobility or the cities of *la haute bourgeoisie*. In the provinces of many countries some sort of concert hall would be part of a town hall; the piano-makers who had previously offered *a* piano to *a* pianist in *a* city would begin to think of organizing tours that would advertise a piano together with its player. There would be concert managers and artists' agents and more and more newspaper columns devoted to 'crits'.

Talented young pianists flocked to the Liszt classes and some of the young would-be geniuses blatantly sponged on their master. Those who survived and went on to make successful careers never forgot their days with someone who was not anything like a 'music teacher' nor even a conservatory professor. The students had already passed their examinations or had attracted some notice at concerts. What they came for was inspiration and magic and personality.

Nobody has left a more vivid record of lessons with Liszt than a young American girl named Amy Fay. Coming from a well-to-do family and brought up by her father, the Rev. Dr. Charles to have a proper respect for serious study she spent six years in Germany from 1869 onwards. Later she wrote a book, *Music-Study in Germany in the Nineteenth Century*, that very deservedly became a bestseller. It is available in paperback: I recommend it to every pianist I meet. It is a book from which several writers have quoted, sometimes in a condescending way for no better reason than that the language is sometimes artless and gushing—and why not in a student's letters to father and mother? The plain fact is that many serious observers have noticed far less than this intelligent and warm-hearted girl did.

Before meeting Liszt she had lessons from Tausig and Kullak and sometimes from assistant teachers. Those were the days of almost military drill at the piano.

> You have no idea how hard they make Cramer's Studies here. Ehlert makes me play them tremendously *forte*, and as fast as I can go. My hand gets so tired that it is ready to break, and then I say that I cannot go on. 'But you *must* go on,' he will say . . . and if you happen to strike a wrong note he looks so shocked that you feel ready to sink into the floor.

Like any student she compares the great pianists. She tells us that Tausig's

> conception is so very refined that sometimes it is a little too much so, while Rubinstein is occasionally too precipitate. I have not yet decided which I like best, but in my estimation Clara Schumann as a whole is superior to either, although she has not their unlimited technique.

She is susceptible to personality.

> Tausig has a charming face, full of expression and very sensitive. . . . He is far too small and too despotic, to be fascinating, however, though he has a sort of captivating way with him when he is in a good humour. . . .
>
> I was dreadfully sorry to hear of poor Gottschalk's death. He had a golden touch, and equal to any in the world, I think. But what a romantic way to die!—to fall senseless at his instrument, while he was playing *La Morte*. It was very strange. If anything more is in the papers about him you must send it to me, for the infatuation that I and 99,999 other American girls once felt for him, still lingers in my breast!

Prussians are not to her taste.

> The Prussian men are often semi-insolent in their street manners to women, and sometimes nearly knock you off the sidewalk, from simply not choosing to see you. I suppose this arrogance is one of the benefits of their military training! They *will* have the middle of the walk where the stone flag is laid, no matter what *you* have to step off into!

Though Tausig was the sort of teacher who liked nothing better than to make his girl pupils cry, Amy Fay was very upset when he decided to give up teaching. He simply left his pupils in the lurch, told Bechstein that he was off, gave no instructions to his assistant, Carl Beringer (later an admired teacher at the Royal Academy in London), and retained only two pupils, one a princess, the other a countess. 'I was so provoked at him that after the first week I ceased to grieve over his departure.'

She grieves over the departure of young men to fight in the Franco-Prussian war of 1870. Naturally she sees things from the German point of view and regards the French as 'possessed by a mad thirst for glory'. She is sure that the Prussian army is invincible and hopes that it will quickly be victorious. But she is not exalted by the sight of military processions. 'It makes one groan for the poor Frenchmen when one sees those terrible great cannon passing by. The largest-sized ones were ordered for the storming of Metz, and each one requires twenty-four horses to draw it.'

I must resist the temptation to quote more from her comments on the war, on the victory celebrations, on public and private attitudes, but they all increase my respect for her powers of observation.

Before her meeting with Liszt she is already a Wagnerian.

> The whole musical world is in a quarrel over Wagner. He is giving a new direction to music and is finding out new combinations of chords. Half the musical world upholds him, and declares that in the future he will stand on a par with Beethoven and Mozart. The other half are bitterly opposed to him, and say that he writes nothing but dissonances, and that he is on an entirely false track. I am on the Wagner side myself. He seems to me to be a great genius.—Pity he is such a moral outlaw!

Wagner hardly comes into the story of the piano, but as teachers are always telling their students not to concentrate wholly on piano music I must be forgiven one more reference to him, conducting his Faust overture.

> He controlled the orchestra as if it were a single instrument and he were playing on it. He didn't beat the time simply, as most conductors do, but he had all sorts of little ways to indicate what

he wished. It was very difficult for them to follow him, and they had to 'keep their little eye open' as B. used to say. He held them down during the first part, so as to give the uncertainty and speculativeness of Faust's character. Then as Mephistopheles came in, he gradually let them loose with a terrible crescendo, and made you feel as if hell suddenly gaped at your feet. Then where Gretchen appeared, all was delicious melody and sweetness. And so it went on, like a succession of pictures. The effect was tremendous.

No wonder Wagner and Liszt understood one another so well.

Amy Fay seems to have been unaware of Brahms, but she worshipped Joachim. She also spent an evening with Clara Schumann's sister and father and was impressed by the way the old man, though getting deaf, trained pupils to sing their notes as a means of understanding touch. Old Wieck recalled how a newspaper referred to Clara when she was young: 'This young girl seems to have much talent; it is only a pity that she is in the hands of a father whose head seems stuck full of queer, new-fangled notions.' The new-fangled notions were Chopin's pieces. Like all German musicians Wieck was unwilling to believe that an American might have talent, so Amy Fay demonstrated hers by playing the fugue of Beethoven's Op. 110, 'and the old master was good enough to commend me warmly'.

At last—Liszt. Her first glimpse is at the theatre.

> Liszt is the most interesting and striking looking man imaginable. Tall and slight, with deep-set eyes, shaggy eyebrows, and long iron-gray hair, which he wears parted in the middle. His mouth turns up at the corners, which gives him a most crafty and Mephistophelean expression when he smiles, and his whole appearance and manner have a sort of Jesuitical elegance and ease.

She notices that his hands are very narrow, with long and slender fingers. I find this strange. Most pianists have broad hands and muscular-looking fingers. Narrow hands and slender fingers usually belong to aesthetes not athletes.

When she met Liszt at a musical evening and watched other young pianists play to him she was so nervous that she slipped out of the room. He followed her.

. . . took both my hands in his, and said in the most winning way imaginable, 'Mademoiselle, vous jouerez quelque-chose, n'est-ce pas?' I can't give you any idea of his *persuasiveness*, when he chooses. It is enough to decoy you into anything. It was such a desperate moment that I became reckless, and without even telling him that I was out of practice and not prepared to play, I sat down and plunged into the A flat major Ballade of Chopin, as if I were possessed. The piano had a splendid touch, luckily. Liszt kept calling out 'Bravo' every minute or two to encourage me, and somehow, I got through. When I finished, he clapped his hands and said, 'Bravely played.' He asked me with whom I had studied and made one or two little criticisms.

Liszt is just like a monarch, and no one dares to speak to him unless he addresses one first, which I think no fun.

Lessons proved to be quite unlike what she had experienced with her somewhat dictatorial German teachers.

Nothing could exceed Liszt's amiability, or the trouble he gave himself, and instead of frightening me, he inspired me. Never was there such a delightful teacher! and he is the first sympathetic one I've had. You feel so *free* with him, and he develops the very spirit of music in you. He doesn't keep nagging at you all the time, but he leaves you your own conception. Now and then he will make a criticism, or play a passage, and with a few words give you enough to think of all the rest of your life. He doesn't tell you anything about technique. That you must work out for yourself.

'He doesn't tell you anything about technique.' Evidently the classes were only for very advanced players. Even so, this is surprising. One must assume that the brilliant Liszt pupils 'caught' some of Liszt's technical tricks just by watching. I well remember catching tricks at recitals—particularly an over-and-over arm movement from Cortot—and I even had the courage to show them to my teacher who, bless his heart, was always interested. ('Just a minute, boy; what did you do there?') It is worth making the point that pupils of Liszt always described themselves as such and forgot to mention the teachers who made it possible for them to *become* pupils of Liszt. Nowadays young recitalists behave better, perhaps because they find that attendance at a master-class is not an out-of-this-world revelation. When I am master in a master-class I never persuade myself that I possess the one and only secret of piano-playing; and when I encourage my Academy students to go to master-classes in their holidays I find they return with a curious mixture of exhilaration and disillusion. For example: (1) He said the same things as you do, only in a foreign accent; and (2) At the end of her class I said to my friend, 'This woman must surely be Sidney Harrison's sister.'

This situation could not have existed in Liszt's day: he was so far above everyone else. And he had—and nothing is more important in teaching—the power to transport his pupils, to carry them up the mountain and give them a wider vision.

There is such a vividness about everything he plays that it does not seem as if it were mere music you were listening to, but it is as if he had called up a real, living *form,* and you saw it breathing before your face and eyes. Oh, he is a perfect wizard! It is as interesting to see him as it is to hear him, for his face changes with every modulation of the piece, and he looks exactly as he is playing. He has one element that is most captivating, and that is, a sort of delicate and fitful mirth that keeps peering out at you here and there! It is most peculiar, and when he plays that way, the most bewitching little expression comes over his face. It seems as if a little spirit of joy were playing hide and go seek with you.

Just how far a pianist should be seen to be living the music is something that can never be finally decided. Rachmaninoff was able to play passionately without there being any signs of emotion on his granite face, but he was one of those great exceptions that test all of our pet rules. Little though I like demonstrative playing from pianists who are always showing off, I have to say that there must be something in your demeanour that corresponds to what the music is 'saying'. The point can be easily tested. Try smiling while playing Chopin's Funeral March: try scowling while playing Debussy's 'Golliwog's Cake-walk'. It is reasonably true (nothing is totally true) that a pianist's hand is a conductor's hand and must explain to the piano what the instrument is expected to utter. (Of which, more later.)

Amy Fay was astounded by Liszt's powers of sight-reading and found it hard to turn pages for him because 'he takes in fully five bars at a glance'. Like any woman she has an eye for furnishings.

The walls are pale gray, with a gilded border running round the room, or rather two rooms, which are divided, but not separated, by crimson curtains. The furniture is *comfortable*—such a contrast to German bareness and stiffness generally. A splendid grand piano stands in one window (he receives a new one every year). The other window is always wide open and looks out on the park. There is a dove-cote just opposite the window, and the doves promenade up and down on the roof of it, and sometimes whirr down on the sill itself. That pleases Liszt. His writing table is beautifully fitted up with things that all match. Everything is in bronze—ink-stand, paper-weight, match-box, etc., and there is always a lighted candle on it by which he and the gentlemen can light their cigars. There is a carpet on the floor, a rarity in Germany, and Liszt generally walks about and smokes, and mutters (he can never be said to *talk*), and calls upon one or other of us to play. From time to time he will sit down and play himself where a passage does not suit him. . . . You cannot conceive, without hearing him, how poetic he is, or the thousand *nuances* that he can throw into the simplest thing, and he is equally great on all sides. From the zephyr to the tempest, the whole scale is equally at his command.

To a feeble student Liszt said, 'When *I* play, I always play for the people in the gallery . . . so that those persons who pay only five groschen for their seat also hear something', and, to Amy Fay, when she was wriggling her way through a passage, he said, 'Keep your hand still, Fräulein; don't make omelette!'

The young musicians were fired not only by Liszt's example but by Bülow's when they heard that in a few months he had given one hundred and twenty concerts. Evidently concert promoters were busy.

As time goes on, Amy Fay becomes more and more aware of the sheer calculation in Liszt's poetic performances.

But I doubt if he feels any particular emotion himself when he is piercing you through with his rendering. He is simply hearing every tone, knowing exactly what effect he wishes to produce and how to do it. In fact, he is practically two persons in one—the listener and the performer. But what immense self-command that implies! No matter how fast he plays you always feel that there is 'plenty of time'—no need to be anxious! . . .

Liszt does such bewitching little things! The other day, for instance, Fräulein Gaul was playing something to him, and in it were two runs, and after each run two staccato chords. She did them most beautifully, and struck the chords immediately after. 'No, no,' said Liszt, 'after you make a run you must wait a minute before you strike the chords, as if in admiration of your own performance. You must pause as if to say "How nicely I did that."' Then he sat down and made a run himself, waited a second, saying as he did so 'Bra-*vo*', and then he played again, struck the other chord, and said again 'Bra-*vo*', and positively, it was as if the piano had softly applauded! That is the way he plays everything. It seems as if the piano were speaking with a *human* tongue. . . .

Liszt sometimes strikes wrong notes when he plays, but it does not trouble him in the least. . . . An accident of this kind happened to him in one of his Sunday matinees, when the room was full of distinguished people and of his pupils. He was rolling up the piano in arpeggios in a very grand manner indeed, when he struck a semi-tone short of the high note upon which he had intended to end. I caught my breath and wondered whether he was going to leave us like that, in mid-air, as it were, and the harmony un-resolved, or whether he would be reduced to the humiliation of correcting himself like ordinary mortals, and taking the right chord. A half smile came over his face, as much as to say—'Don't fancy that *this* little thing disturbs me'—and he instantly went meandering down the piano in harmony with the false note he had struck, and then rolled deliberately up in a second grand sweep, *this* time striking true.

By the time her classes with Liszt were finished, Amy Fay felt qualified to summarize some of her ideas about piano study. She loathes Czerny ('tedious to the last degree') but the exercises compel you to play in strict time to the end of a passage. She takes to the discipline of daily Bach. She admires Clementi's *Gradus* ('not only good for finger technique—it trains the arm and wrist also'). When she has some lessons from the discouraging Kullak she still loves to talk of Liszt and tells us that in the days when he was living with his princess at the Altenburg he had nine grand pianos.

Before we say good-bye to Amy Fay we must take a glance

at her final teacher, Deppe, since he was a pioneer of modern piano teaching. He brought her down from the clouds and helped her with problems that the great Liszt ignored. He was against excessively high lift of the finger.

> Don't you remember my saying that Liszt had such an extraordinary way of playing a melody? That it did not seem to be so loud and clear-cut as most artists make it, and yet it was so penetrating? Well, dear, *there* was the secret of it! '*Spielen Sie mit dem Gewicht* (Play with weight)', Deppe will say. 'Don't strike, but let the fingers *fall*. At first the tone will be nearly inaudible, but with practice it will gain every day in power.'

Teacher and pupil were pretty unscientific in this. She thought 'the hammer falls back more slowly from the string, and that this makes the tone *sing* longer'. It doesn't take a mechanical genius to look at what goes on inside a piano to know that this is nonsense; and it proved to be a long-lived nonsense. But the idea that one could learn to use the weight of one's limbs was very fruitful, even though, in cold fact, a finger is not weighty enough to produce tone without muscular help.

Deppe realized the importance of weight; also the twists and turns of the arm and what is often inaccurately called a 'perfectly loose' wrist. He explained how a finger may turn on its tip ('screwing it round, as it were, on a pivot') and was adept in using his hand to guide the pupil's. ('Go on,' said Deppe. 'I can't when you keep your hand right in the way,' said I. 'My hand isn't in the way,' said he, 'but *your* hand is out of position.'). He had a multitude of phrases that may not be strictly in accordance with the laws of anatomy or of mechanics but impart the sensations of playing: 'Your elbow must be *lead* and your wrist a *feather*.' Even a pianist who disagrees with this recognizes that Deppe was a *teacher*.

And, surprise-surprise, 'Unless Deppe wishes the chord to be very brilliant, he takes the pedal *after* the chord instead of simultaneously with it.' Can it be true that neither Tausig nor Liszt explained the 'syncopated' pedalling in which the foot remains down until the hand actually sounds the next chord, at which point the foot comes up to wipe out the chord that has come to the end of its time. Having brought the foot up at the very beginning of a new sound you must put it down to sustain the one you have just sounded. In simple terms, the foot comes up on the beat, down just after the beat.

Poor Amy literally cried to think that she had met the man she ought to have gone to four years earlier. No wonder! What could be better than this:

> But Deppe, instead of saying, 'Oh, you'll get this after years of practice', shows me how to conquer the difficulty *now*. He takes a piece, and while he plays it with the most wonderful *fineness* of conception, he cold-bloodedly dissects the mechanical elements of it, separates them, and tells you how to use your hand so as to grasp them one after the other. In short, he makes the technique and the conception *identical*, as of course they ought to be, but I never had any other master who trained his pupils to attempt it.

The pianists who were Liszt's rivals, though never his equals, are now seldom remembered, but one name continues to be mentioned. This is Alkan, who grew up as Charles-Valentin Morhange but then took his father's first name. He was an infant prodigy and then a virtuoso taken seriously by Liszt and Chopin. Indeed, when Chopin died many of his pupils went to Alkan. Very curiously, in his early forties, he grew misanthropic and disappeared from view. After the age of sixty he began to give infrequent concerts and died in 1888 at the age of seventy-four. The end was dramatic. A pious Jew, he was reaching up to a high shelf for a religious book and brought the whole book-case down.* A romantic painter should have depicted it—the old man, his sightless eyes turned towards heaven, surrounded by books, his right hand clutching the Talmud.

His music is neglected but refuses to die. He wrote with a sense of grandeur. His twelve *études* in minor keys are not just twelve studies. Nos. 4–7 constitute a *symphonie* for piano alone; the next three are a concerto for piano alone; then there is an overture for piano alone, followed by No. 12, 'Le Festin d'Esope' (Aesop's Feast), which is itself a set of twenty-three variations. This music has never lacked powerful friends, even if its public is small, and every now and then there are new recordings.

*Not all authorities accept this story, alas!

18. *How to Make a Pianist*

In one of her letters Amy Fay mentions a splendid new Steinway that had been presented to Liszt. The Steinways were
certainly enterprising men. So were the Chickerings. They vied
with one another at the great Paris Exhibition of 1867. Steinways received the first gold medal, but C. Frank Chickering
was made a *chevalier* of the Légion d'Honneur. Berlioz described
the Steinway as magnificent, though he was generally credited
with hating pianos and was the one composer who never used
a keyboard. Rossini said it was a nightingale cooing in a
thunderstorm—but he always was a bit of a joker. And Liszt
graciously agreed to accept a Chickering for his Roman apartment and described the piano as lordly. The perfect diplomat,
he managed to praise the Steinway with equal enthusiasm.

Steinway would not build their Hamburg factory until
1880, but they had a Steinway Hall in New York by 1866, and
in 1872 they went into concert promotion, making an agreement in Vienna for Anton Rubinstein to tour America, promising him 200 concerts at $200 each. In the event he played 215
concerts in 239 days always, of course, on a Steinway. This was
the shape of things to come. (*See Plate 6*).

A Chickering tour for Bülow ran into trouble because he was
a decidedly awkward customer. When he saw the maker's
name in large lettering hung on his piano he took it off, threw
it on the floor, and said, 'I am not a travelling advertisement.'
Few other pianists were so high-minded: they remembered
their high fees.

Steinways were unique in one respect: they made *all* of a
piano, unlike other makers who were willing to buy parts from
specialist suppliers. They also, undoubtedly, set the pace for
the great European makers who had a healthy respect for
American inventiveness and business acumen. The 1880 Steinway factory in Hamburg brought Steinway competition back
to the country that the family had left more than thirty years

earlier, but the market was big enough for several great makers. As for Bechstein, about half the output was sold to England—as I always recall when I hear the Noël Coward record of 'The Stately Homes of England' ('We've sold the Bechstein grand').

Promotion took curious forms. In America there was, for a while, a *Musical and Sewing Machine Gazette*. And why not? Pianos and sewing machines can easily be sold in the same shop. The *Gazette* was renamed *Courier*, and its descendant, the *Musical Courier*, is influential to this day.

The Boston *Musical Herald*, appealing to the family at home, displayed advertisements for music, patent medicines, knitting patterns and corsets. It all sounds preposterous but it reflects an attitude. In the days before recording and radio and suchlike, the piano was almost as important as the family hearth as a source of warmth and pleasure. Arthur Loesser, in his *Men, Women, and Pianos** tells us that on 'every working day of 1870 eighty persons bought a new piano; in 1910 twelve hundred persons did so, fifteen times as many, whereas the population had multiplied itself by no more than two and one half in the meantime'. He also tells us of one Alfred Dolge who invented a machine for covering sets of hammers with felt in one operation. He was able to turn out six full sheets of felt in one operation, enough for a hundred sets of hammers. After which he bought timber-lands and sawmills and invented new sawing and gluing processes so that two men could plane three hundred sound-boards in a ten-hour day. His monument is a town called Dolgeville.

Some manufacturers produced so-called transfer or stencil pianos which could be called by any name that suited the dealer who bought them. Sometimes the dealer proudly displayed his own name, sometimes he invented one that had a vaguely German sound. I once met a dealer in Canada who claimed to have sold Japanese pianos as Steigermann. What he did was to take the syllable Stein from both Steinway and Bechstein, remove the final letter, and put it at the end of the word German. That's what the man said. I do not vouch for his story.

While the commerce of piano-making was going on apace,

* Published by Victor Gollancz Ltd., London, 1955.

the teaching profession grew *pro rata*. In the days when there was a music shop in every high street there was a piano-teacher in every side street. Well, perhaps not every side street, but a common sight was a brass plate announcing that Miss X or Mrs. Y or Madam Z taught piano and theory. And for good measure some taught harmonium and singing. The men usually reckoned to be superior. They were organists: they had more letters after their names. All of them looked up to conservatory professors. And even conservatory professors had to acknowledge that it was Leschetizky in Vienna who turned out the greatest number of virtuosi.

His pupils are a fantastic list, and he had the breadth to be able to cope with a Paderewski on the one hand and a Schnabel on the other, and no two pianists could have been less alike.

There are not many of his pupils left now, but my old friend Frank Merrick remembers lessons with the great man. Like other products of Leschetizky's 'stable' he is satisfied that there was no Leschetizky method, with the result that an audience could never say of a new pianist, 'Obviously a Leschetizky pupil.'

I once interviewed Merrick in a radio programme and asked him if he now ever thought of his teacher. 'Yes, often.' 'What do you remember?' 'The look on his face.' He then went on to tell me of an occasion when Leschetizky described a performance by Anton Rubinstein of a Beethoven concerto. Leschetizky spoke with a sort of rapture about the way Rubinstein began the slow movement. He did not attempt to imitate Rubinstein: he just talked; and Merrick insisted that he remembered the performance that he never heard better than any he had heard since. This is the inspirational aspect of all good teaching.

Leschetizky may well have been unscientific in some of his remarks. Like most teachers he would talk about a pianissimo that carries to the last row of the topmost gallery in a concert hall. It is certain that an effective pianissimo must include notes that are loud enough to be heard at a distance and also loud enough to be effective for their whole length. A concert pianist's pianissimo is no more a pianissimo than an actor's stage-whisper is a whisper. But pianists are not made purely by a succession of scientifically verifiable statements.

The attempt to establish a truth that would satisfy engineers came in the time of Matthay—*despite* Matthay—and few things interest me more than why he was so successful while saying things that could not be true. (We shall come to that.)

Leschetizky was not an out-and-out relaxationist but he did recommend relaxing (he said devitalizing) all muscles not needed at a given moment. If this seems obvious and simple, try playing a scale in which, while one finger is holding a note, all the other fingers are so relaxed as to have their tips lying on the ivories. It is a good illustration of how to combine relaxation with exact effort in exactly the right place.

Leschetizky, born in Poland, studied with Czerny in Vienna, had a short career as a concert artist, and then became the magnet for every aspiring prodigy and artist in Europe. He married four wives, three of them pupils.

He was lucky in having Paderewski, whom he at first was reluctant to teach. Paderewski went on to become not the greatest pianist in the world but the greatest name amongst pianists. This in itself was guaranteed to send many bright pupils to Leschetizky. It was fortunate for them that he was as good as they expected.

Paderewski was not a Jew, but a surprisingly large number of his fellow students were; and Leschetizky's eyes always brightened if he heard that a newcomer was a Jew or a Slav or preferably both. This is a mystery, and we must probe it a little.

The Jews have produced a remarkably large number of virtuoso pianists and violinists. It became almost an assumption that a great pianist would be a Jew. As for violinists, a stream of infant prodigies came out of Russia and Poland all called Jascha or Mischa or Sasha or Toscha. And nowadays there are still quite a few from Israel.

The explanations come thick and fast. The Jews are so musical. Really? Ask any Jewish artist if he regards a totally Jewish audience at, say, a Jewish charity concert as conspicuously musical.

It is something to do with their religious music. Can this be true? Since, in orthodox synagogues, the music is totally vocal, no instruments being permitted, why are there not multitudes of Jewish singers?

What about persecution? The persecuted Jew is so sensitive.
The persecuted Jew is so tough. The lofty Jew understands all
mankind. The 'pop' Jew understands the hoi-polloi. It's a
divine gift. It's a conspiracy.

For my own part I began as a sensitive little boy of four. I
climbed on to a piano stool, knowing nothing of gifts or con-
spiracies or history or religion and having little example from
parents who were only very mildly musical. I took to piano like
a duck to water. As far as I was concerned there was a tall,
black, brass-candlesticked plaything, and if only I could find
the right black and white notes I could find all the music in the
world.

I am as mystified as anyone else and am very dubious about
the usual theories. One point, however; the Jewish religion is
the only one that asks its adherents to be literate. A Barmitzvah
boy must not just recite the Law, he must read it. And his
mother, even if *she* should be illiterate, must see to it. Furthermore a rabbi is not a priest but a teacher. The religion equates
goodness not with innocence but with wisdom. Add all those
considerations to the ancient tradition of studying a text, and
studying it again, and studying the commentaries on it, and
studying possible further interpretations, and even an agnostic
like me may wonder. . . .

On second thoughts, perhaps not. Nobody knows.

Many great pianists began as infant prodigies, but not all
prodigies ended as great pianists. What goes wrong? In the
first place he may not be as prodigious as his friends believe. A
musical child, much encouraged and taught with great skill
and patience, may make rapid progress, causing loving parents
to think that their little one is to be a star performer. But your
true prodigy is not produced by parents and teachers: he or she
surprises them; they 'can't make it out'. How does the child
know?

A prodigy is usually not a 'normal, happy child'. This is not
to say that all prodigies are neurotic monsters but only to point
out that a Mozart does not go fishing for tiddlers or kick a football up and down the street until he smashes a window. What
does sometimes make a prodigy neurotic is his parents' realization that he is special. The mothers of little pianists, like the

mothers of little ballet girls, can become absurdly possessive and protective. Fathers, too, in some cases. I remember one child, decidedly less than prodigious, whose mother was convinced that he ought to play to the Queen, regardless of the fact that Her Majesty is unmusical and that if she listened to one little pianist she would have to listen to dozens.

Nevertheless, sensible parents have to realize that a genius child is a special case. What about general education, and how can time be found for music? Before education became universal and compulsory this was no problem. Leopold Mozart did not have to argue with a Ministry of Education or a headmaster intent on sending boys to university. Did little Wolfgang *ever* go to school?

Interestingly, the great prodigies seem to have suffered very little from lack of formal education. They learned languages and geography by travelling. They learned arithmetic by listening to arguments about fees and expenses. They learned mythology at the opera house. Their very gifts disciplined them in a way that a cadet corps never would.

In our modern world schooling is a problem. A musical child needs plenty of time off for practice, and there are still headmasters who find this something that they don't want to encourage. It upsets the time-table.

What about special schools? This is one answer and it can be a good one, but there is much to be said for a conventional school if it is governed by a headmaster who is willing to say: 'A pianist is an athlete, a keyboard is a running track, this boy is excused games. And let us cut out one or two subjects if he is never going to be any good at them.'

The problem used not to arise. We read of amazing children who were taken on long tours without interference from education authorities. We are inclined to think that such exploitation was cruelty to children, but some of these youngsters became successful concert artists and continued to tour until an advanced age. And at least a few of them became healthy, wealthy and wise.

The pupils of Liszt and Leschetizky are to be found in abundance in Harold Schonberg's *The Great Pianists* and I shall not attempt to retell his stories. Great pianists have their day and are quickly forgotten. Reprocessed old records revive memories, so do reproducing player-pianos, but I find that my students scarcely know, or want to know, the names of pianists who brought their parents and grandparents flocking to the box office.

The ones who concern us are those who made piano-playing what it is today. And the composers who concern us are those who have had a hand in moulding hands.

It would be a mistake to concentrate only on the greatest works and the greatest pianists. Schumann knew what he was about when he composed his *Album for the Young*. Mendelssohn's *Christmas Pieces* and his *Songs without Words* were almost a sign of middle-class respectability. These created a musical climate. So did the piano music of Grieg.

Grieg was lucky. An early work came to the notice of Liszt, and Liszt wrote a note of appreciation to the unknown Norwegian and hoped they might meet. In due course Grieg arrived in Weimar and brought, in manuscript, his new piano concerto.

Reading manuscript is always twice as hard as reading print, but Liszt, in the presence of various guests, played the solo part and the orchestral tuttis in one great demonstration of pianistic prowess and then said something about 'going banco'—an expression that may be freely translated as 'a trump card'.

And so the concerto proved to be—with the possible exception of Tchaikovsky's No. 1—the most popular concerto in the world. It is a brilliant display piece—and the only thing of its kind in Grieg's output. Why he never again deployed his gift for virtuoso writing is a mystery.

Not only Liszt but Brahms was kind to Grieg. Brahms felt the same sympathy with the Norwegian as he did with the Czech. Dvořák's *Slavonic Dances*, Grieg's *Norwegian Dances*, Brahms's *Hungarian Dances* vied with one another in delighting the amateur pianist. The publishing firm of Peters found a little gold-mine in Grieg and published volume after volume of his *Lyric Pieces*, not to mention piano versions of the *Peer Gynt* suite.

It can be argued that Grieg had little gift for writing big works and that his concerto is really a set of lyric pieces strung together; but the argument seems scarcely convincing when one remembers how one melody succeeds another and how effectively the concerto fills the biggest hall. The music is not pretentious and there is little padding, but the work has a certain grandeur and plenty of panache.

The *Lyric Pieces are* padded. In six pages of print the last two are mere repetition of the first two, and the amount of genuine invention in the whole piece may amount to only a few bars at the beginning of section I and of section II. Fortunately some of them have gained a new lease of life in light orchestral arrangements. Repeats become acceptable if a violin melody later becomes a flute melody.

One odd fact about Grieg is now unknown to most music-lovers. He composed second-piano parts to some of Mozart's piano sonatas. He thought his versions were improvements. They were not, of course, improvements, but they should not be denounced unheard.

In America a somewhat Griegish music was composed by Edward Macdowell. His *Sea Pieces* became very popular, and his two piano concertos had a vogue.

All this happened, so to speak, yesterday. Liszt lived till 1886, Brahms till 1897, Grieg till 1907. The old masters are recent masters.

Turning from composers to pianists there are some that demand attention. The one who was most of a legend in his own lifetime was Paderewski. He had a positively Lisztian effect on women. They lined the waterfront when he arrived or departed by ship. They crowded the railroad platform when he travelled by train. They adored him from the seats in the concert halls. An American reporter at a recital described him as 'girled in' and surrounded by a 'gynarchy'. He was grandly handsome: his golden-brown hair was a halo. He was eloquent in several languages.

He was astutely managed by one Hugo Görlitz who, in Paderewski's earlier days, would give free tickets to those students who would stampede through the hall and crowd the front of the platform.

He did not arrive at this success easily. He was not well trained as a child, he was an unsuccessful concert artist as a youth. When he presented himself to Leschetizky the great man thought he was probably too old to be worth teaching.

Will-power and persistence won the day, he made his début in Vienna in 1887, and then in the following year became the rage in Paris. By 1891 he was playing 107 concerts for Steinway in America. Critics might prefer other pianists: for the general public Paderewski was the greatest. It was not only a matter of personality: there was an intensity that magnetized his listeners. He was something of a composer, but the only piece that became a bestseller was his Minuet in G. It was much in demand as an encore piece and must have made a lot of money as sheet music and, later, as a record.

Money flowed into the Paderewski coffers. He travelled in a private railway coach with chef, masseur, doctor, piano tuner. He and his wife were a kind of royal couple and were treated as such. Anyone listening now to Paderewski records may wonder what the fuss was about, but he was not intended by nature to be the invisible pianist. A Paderewski performance had to be seen to be done. Other pianists could only wonder and be envious.

A much greater master of piano-playing was Josef Hofmann who, in 1887, at the age of ten, astounded an audience at the Metropolitan Opera House by playing Beethoven's C major concerto and a number of difficult solos. The result was fifty-two concerts in ten weeks. The New York Society for the Prevention of Cruelty to Children became concerned, and there were letters of protest in the press. Fortunately a philanthropist named Alfred Corning Clark gave $50,000 (the sum seems unbelievable) to allow the boy to retire from concert-giving and to study until the age of eighteen, and young Josef became the one and only pupil of Anton Rubinstein, a teacher who would say one thing one day and another the next, demanding strictness from his pupil while himself playing with great liberty.

As a mature artist Hofmann was reckoned by Rachmaninoff to be the best in the world, and who will dare to argue with Rachmaninoff, to whom some of us would give that very title?

One must also mention Godowsky, a technician so formidable as to find Chopin's *Études* too easy. He wrote variants, changing single notes into thirds and sixths, combining one study in the right hand with another in the left—not so much playing the studies as playing with them. In 1900 a Berlin audience that included some very famous pianists stood and shouted and clapped like mad, the artist's room after the concert was pandemonium, the newspapers next day were full of rave notices. Godowsky comes into our story because, by all accounts, his was the greatest technique of all in that era.

Meanwhile there was in Russia a young man who had no special ambitions to be a travelling virtuoso. He was the composer Rachmaninoff, who in 1893 wrote a set of piano pieces that included a Prelude in C sharp minor. This was destined to be one of the most popular piano pieces of all time. It did not directly make Rachmaninoff's fortune. Inadvisedly he sold it outright and never enjoyed the royalties on its enormous sale. But it did help to make him famous around the world, and in later years he must have made a small fortune out of his recordings of this piece. (We shall return to him.)

Rather earlier than these but, in some ways, a modern pianist is Ferruccio Busoni. He disdained to play nothing but box-office programmes, he was something of a musical philosopher, he composed (for me he is a would-be composer), and he gave a great deal of attention to music that other pianists neglected. While they were playing transcriptions of Strauss waltzes he was sternly offering Beethoven's Hammerklavier and Bach's Goldberg Variations. When he composed a piano concerto it had to be an endless work with a choral last movement.

The pianist of today is principally aware of music apparently composed by somebody named Bach-Busoni. (There is the story of a musician being introduced to Mme Busoni and exclaiming 'Not Mme *Bach*-Busoni!') The Busoni versions of Bach are now frowned upon by the stricter scholars, but they are very compelling and stimulate us to think seriously about what to do with music's music on a piano.

In passing, we should remember that the Steinway of Busoni's era had three pedals. The middle one could sustain selected notes, leaving the remainder of the keys to be pedalled or not pedalled according to taste. The pianist played perhaps a bass octave and depressed the middle pedal. A long horizontal rod, inside the piano, slid into a position that prevented those notes, and those only, from being damped. In this way one could, to some extent, imitate an organ pedal-note, sustaining the bass while being free to play upper harmonies cleanly.

It is a device that one uses only occasionally, but it could be very effective and is now found on nearly all very big, very expensive pianos. It calls for action in Busoni's transcriptions of Bach organ fugues.

19. *A Thousand Kinds of Bach*

Let us ignore 'received opinion' and think over the Bach problem from the beginning.

Bach, more often than not, wrote a musical design without indicating anything about speeds or intensities. How are we to choose a speed? One way is simple trial and error. You play a piece at this speed and that until you light on one that seems to make the whole thing 'work'.

Or perhaps you ask yourself the simple question: is minor music likely to be slower and sadder than major music? How naive! But there is no harm in asking.

A more brainy approach is to learn some of Bach's choral music. If you then come across a keyboard piece that reminds you of Crucifixion music you will know better than to play it *allegro giocoso*.

Then there is the question of phrasing which can be simply expressed as: How long is a bit of Bach? If this keyboard fugue were being sung, where would the choir breathe? If it were played on an organ, where would you move your hands to a different manual (keyboard)? How much of the fugue-subject is *legato*, how much *staccato*?

What about rhythm, as distinct from mere counting of time? In the days of harpsichords and organs—instruments almost without accent—the players were up to all sorts of tricks to suggest accent, either by means of ornaments or by playing one *staccato* note immediately before an important held note.

Why not take full advantage of grand pianos and great pianism and re-create the music as Bach would 'undoubtedly' have done if only he could have been resurrected?

Boldly Busoni did just that, and here is a description of his playing of the first Prelude and Fugue in the *Forty-eight*. The writer is his admiring biographer Professor Edward Dent:

> He played the first Prelude of the Forty-Eight, and it became a wash of shifting colours, a rainbow over the fountains of the Villa d'Este; he played the Fugue, and each voice sang out above the rest like the entries of an Italian chorus, until at the last stretto the subject entered like the trumpets of the *Dona Nobis* in the Mass in B minor, though in the middle of the keyboard, across a haze of pedal-held sound that was not confusion but blinding clearness.

Today's professors shrink in horror, but, after all, Bach did compose the *Dona Nobis* and it does have trumpets. . . .

The fact is that Bach's music shares a certain quality with Shakespeare's plays. This is not—repeat not—to say that Bach is the Shakespeare of music. Bach was never a theatre man. No: the point about Shakespeare is that he can be presented in a thousand ways. I have seen Shakespeare in the theatre sumptuously mounted and produced; I have heard him on the radio and seen nothing but what is in my imagination; I have seen *Julius Caesar* in modern dress presented as the story of a fascist *coup d'état*; I have heard *Othello* transformed into *Otello* by Verdi and seen *Romeo and Juliet*, all words abandoned, danced to Prokofiev's music. And how will they do Shakespeare next?

I have heard Bach played on harpsichord, clavichord and organ. I have heard the keyboard music sung with *dooba-dooba* syllables by a small choir. I have heard it played on a computer. I remember when the organ Fantasia and Fugue in D minor was orchestrated by Stokowski for the Philadelphia Orchestra, becoming one of the best-selling records of all time. I have attended many a lecture and read a number of learned tomes. And still I am sure that there are new ways of playing Bach. The breath-taking impudence and ignorance of celebrated men (and women) who are sure that their way is right never ceases to amaze me. As for Busoni's re-creations I obstinately continue to admire the one that, on the face of it, seems most absurd—the outsize piano transcription of the Chaconne that Bach wrote for unaccompanied violin.

Returning for a moment to the *Forty-eight*, I once heard the first Fugue played by a string quartet at a teachers' conference in Canada. The leader of the quartet of the University of Edmonton, Thomas Rolston, explained that after hearing his wife play this four-voice fugue on the piano he could not help wondering what it would sound like on four instruments.

The quartet began and, with proper respect for baroque style, played up-bow for the first note and down-bow for the next, and so on. The result was unpalatable.

'Come to think of it, this music may have been played on a harpsichord, and harpsichords have plucked strings. Why don't we try playing *pizzicato*?'

The result was hilarious.

'The heck with it. Why don't we play it as though it were Schubert.' The result was so beautiful that nobody knew what to say. No doubt vibrato was unstylistic and long bowings were anachronistic but the music was wonderful.

I am reminded of an occasion when, as a student, I was working at home at the E flat minor Prelude in the first book of the *Forty-eight*. When I stopped for a meal my mother said, 'What was that beautiful piece you were playing?' 'A prelude by Bach.' 'No, I don't mean Bach: what was that *beautiful* piece you were playing?'

I shall never be sure of how Bach should be played. I am sure only of how he should not be played, which is in a totally inexpressive, unaccented, undifferentiated way calculated to prevent the hearer from knowing what is going on in the music. This kind of playing throws away all the qualities of a piano without acquiring the character of a harpsichord. What the future holds in Bach interpretation is anybody's guess. Not, I think, the first Prelude masquerading as a rainbow over the fountains of the Villa d'Este—the prevalence of harpsichords will prevent that—but perhaps with more flexibility of beat. 'Sewing-machine Bach' has always been a blight, and I have never understood why so many people assume that Bach should be played as though to a metronome (the metronome was not invented in Bach's day) right through a piece until the last bar but one.

The argument continues.

20. *No More Rules of Harmony*

Busoni, with all his profundity and intellectuality, never provided pianists with a quantity of music that audiences would wish to hear. Indeed, though he was a pianist of enormous renown, he was not everybody's idol. There was a conflict between his Italian background and his German culture, between his love for Liszt and his rather cold attitude to Chopin, between his tendency to rewrite other people's music and his profound respect for Beethoven.

Very different was Rachmaninoff, and he stands above most of the pianists of his era because of his compositions. Who else could write such music and play it so marvellously? Certainly he tended to write the same sort of music over and over again: he did not alter the course of musical history; but no composer has ever spoken in a more heart-to-heart manner or made a more magic compound of melancholy and brilliance.

Two of his most famous pieces were early works—the already mentioned Prelude in C sharp minor and the second Piano Concerto in C minor. They have one extraordinary feature in common. The Prelude ends and the Concerto begins with a procession of slow chords—very similar chords—in fact chords that dominated Rachmaninoff's harmonies throughout his life. They were his obsession. In simple terms the formula is: play a chord, alter one note, alter one note, alter one note, each alteration being a shift of a semitone. More specifically put your thumb on middle C and play up through F, A flat and C. Play it again with the addition of D flat. Play it again, changing D flat into D natural. Play it again, changing D into E flat. Now give your attention to the A flat. Change it into A natural. And so on.

At the beginning of the C minor Concerto this is all plain to see and hear, but again and again in concertos, in preludes, in *études-tableaux* the harmonic formula produces its effect however much it is submerged in cascades of brilliant notes.

The other Rachmaninoff 'finger-print' is the extraordinary length of his melodies. Other men's melodies may seem to go in phrases of two, four or eight bars, but his go flowing on in what seems to be an unending succession of nostalgic sighs. In cold fact, against a stop watch, such a melody may last only a minute and a half, but it has a long, lingering, last glance, farewell character that only the stony-hearted can resist. And, as anyone can discover by experiment with other men's music, a minute and a half is a long time for one continuous melody.

The C minor Concerto is dedicated to the doctor who, with the aid of hypnotism, got Rachmaninoff past a bout of despondency and melancholia, and no doubt the composing of the concerto clinched the cure. I am reminded of the statement that an artist is a neurotic who knows how to use his neurosis; and since we are all at least a bit neurotic Rachmaninoff is our friend who understands us so well. ('Do you feel like that too?' he seems to say.)

Like Chopin's, Rachmaninoff's music is extremely 'grateful' to play. It invites the hand, it pleases the piano. And, like the title of the old song, it is 'For You Alone' even when it is being played to 5,000 people.

As a young man in Russia Rachmaninoff was primarily composer and conductor. He conducted symphony concerts, he conducted opera. Of course, when it was a question of introducing a concerto, he could play the solo in a succession of concerts and play as well as anybody in the world, but he was not the typical travelling virtuoso, and when he first went to America, in 1909, he hated the emphasis on business and felt driven by the promoters. One odd feature of that tour was that he dedicated his new D minor Concerto (No. 3) to Josef Hofmann, but Hofmann never played it. Even the offer of the conductorship of the Boston Symphony Orchestra could not make Rachmaninoff like America—at that time. Wherever he went he had, of course, to play *the* Prelude (he was to write a couple of dozen more preludes) and to endure the popular beliefs that the music represented bells tolling at the burning of Moscow or even a man in his coffin *hearing* the bells of Moscow tolling during the great conflagration.

The great turning point in Rachmaninoff's life was the Russian revolution. He was invited to play in Stockholm. Once away from Russia he never went back. He and his family went to America, a land he came to admire, and the great pianistic career began, as a matter of economic necessity. To that career we shall return.

Meanwhile, Russia was featuring more and more in recital and concert programmes. Tchaikovsky's concerto (No. 1 was never challenged by the others) was a never-fail smash hit on pianos that could now withstand any amount of smashing and hitting. And the music of Scriabin, with its many echoes of Chopin, charmed many. Scriabin was fortunate in being helped by Belaief, a rich timber merchant who subsidized the publishing of new music, and by the conductor Koussevitzky who, like Rachmaninoff, later made a great career in America. However, Scriabin was not content to write a kind of imitation Chopin and in due course developed a new style. This was influenced by his ever-growing interest in mysticism. In his orchestral *Poem of Fire* he included a colour keyboard that could control the throwing of a succession of colours on a screen. This was all part of his new aesthetic theories.

His piano pieces took on a new character, and he made great use of a 'mystic' chord consisting of C, F sharp, B flat, E, A, D. With the aid of this he wrote a more and more frenetic music. His fifth Sonata (there were ten all told) begins with a quotation from the *Poem of Ecstasy* (there is an orchestral *Poem of Ecstasy*) that may be translated as: 'I call you to life, O mysterious forces, submerged in the profound obscurity of the creative spirit. To you, shadows fearful of life, I bring audacity.' One is then invited to play *Allegro, Impetuoso, Con Stravaganza*. As the piece continues, the composer calls for exaltation, intoxication and imperiousness, punctuated by moments of sweetness and languor; and so much of the music is written on three staves as to make one wonder if it should not have been written for two pianos.

Much more than the 'reactionary' Rachmaninoff, Scriabin

heralded the future, and it was in something like Scriabin's late style that Alban Berg composed his Op. 1 Sonata.

Scriabin did not write music that was Russian in a picturesque sense. For that sort of music one turns to Mussorgsky's *Pictures from an Exhibition*, but Mussorgsky was not by nature a writer of piano music, and some people prefer to hear the *Pictures* in Ravel's orchestral version. Rimsky-Korsakov also had little feeling for the piano. His concerto never had much success. Medtner was much more the pianist-composer but he seems overshadowed by Rachmaninoff.

For composers who compelled pianists to play in a new way we must go further south to the Paris of Debussy and Ravel, and I have a personal recollection that illustrates just how puzzling their music was at first. When I was a boy at school, perhaps eleven or twelve, I was having lessons with a remarkable man named Francesco Berger, who had recently retired from twenty-seven years' work as secretary of the Royal Philharmonic Society. He was an old man whose memories included taking Tchaikovsky home to dinner and taking Dvořák out to lunch. He thought Wagner was modern enough for anyone. By the time I was his pupil Debussy was a world-famous composer, but England was ever cautious of new-fangled, foreign ideas, and Berger was decidedly Victorian in his outlook.

One day I arrived for lesson and found him attempting to play Debussy's *La Cathédrale Engloutie*. What did he find? A succession of 'consecutive fifths' sternly forbidden by all harmony professors, and a mark of expression that said *sans nuances* (how can one play *without* expression?). He automatically changed the pedal at every new chord, not realizing that there was a long, tied-over bass note that had to be held by the foot through all the conflicting harmonies to create a new, mysterious sound that would seem to well up from the bottom of the sea. Debussy asked him to make the music 'emerge gradually from the mist'. It was all outrageous. And what did one find at the end? At the bottom of the last page, not at the top of the first, one saw the title, printed small, in parentheses, after three dots: (. . . *La Cathédrale Engloutie*). It was all too ridiculous.

I have no wish to make my distinguished and much-loved

teacher seem ridiculous. I merely tell people familiar with Debussy's music how strange it seemed at first.

Even younger, more enterprising pianists could be puzzled by Debussy's unresolved discords—one beautiful sound after another with no attempt to resolve, say, a dominant ninth into a tonic chord. They wondered how some of the pieces, full of stops and starts and silences, could be made to hang together. They did not immediately realize that a piece seeming to have almost no rhythm might need to have its time-values scrupulously counted to make Debussy's magic work.

And Debussy was, in some respects, a magician. A magician is emotionally uninvolved: he is a calculator. He places everything just so and then says *See*! I am not very fond of using the vocabulary of other arts to describe music, but it is not hard to understand how Debussy's music is described as Impressionist art.

The music is often shudderingly beautiful, but it is inhuman. It is peopled with caricatures (Mr. Pickwick) and puppets (the Golliwog) and ancient marbles (*Danseuses de Delphe*). There are sails on the sea but no sailors. The Girl with Flaxen Hair is taken not from the life but from a painting; and even one of his most wonderful Spanish pieces is inspired not by the country, which he never visited, but by a picture postcard, which he glorified.

He was no great pianist, but he played with intensity of hearing rather than 'with heart'. The great pianist Cortot once played a piece of Debussy's to the composer's schoolgirl daughter expecting to be complimented, but the child said, 'Daddy listened better.' Such music as his could not have been composed earlier. It needed the modern piano in all its glory, even though Debussy at work was often content to use an upright. In a quite unaccustomed way pianists had to learn to search for sounds without searching for passion or heroism or sweetness or for any kind of 'argument', and he still puzzles the sort of intellectual musicians who are never happy except when they are demonstrating how a theme is developed.

Debussy must inevitably be paired with Ravel. They undoubtedly were similar in many ways, and one can find pages of music that might have been composed by either. But Ravel is more extrovert than Debussy—at times. He owes something to Liszt. I have already said that his *Jeux d'Eau* seems to derive from Liszt's fountains at the Villa d'Este; and if one compares Ravel's Toccata from *Le Tombeau de Couperin* with Debussy's from *Pour le Piano* one has to say that Ravel's is the more exciting and sensational. Also it consists of one of the longest crescendos in history and, in that way if in no other, resembles the later orchestral *Bolero*. It starts not gently, but with a very distant *forte*, and goes on hammering away, getting nearer all the time, in a way that would have been foreign to Debussy.

His highly effective Spanish-style *Alborada del gracioso* also takes technique to the limit. Like Debussy he composed marvellously for orchestra, so much so that it is sometimes hard to persuade concert-goers that the 'Pavan for a Dead Infanta' and the *Valses Nobles et Sentimentales* were originally written and published as piano works.

What did these two composers think of one another? I once asked this question of Debussy's stepdaughter when she came to lecture in London. She replied, 'I never once heard Debussy mention Ravel's name.'

Neither composer was much to the taste of Saint-Saëns, but we have only to listen to two pianists playing Sant-Saëns's *Carnival of Animals* to realize that the Spirit of the Age casts a spell over all composers at a given time, so that this piece, like many by Debussy and Ravel, leads us to the amusing music of Poulenc.

Saint-Saëns did not, however, change the course of piano history, but he certainly knew how to provide very effective music on traditional lines, and his concertos, particularly the G minor, are popular, no matter what the critics say. Other pieces 'crop up', and I have played his 'Bourrée for the Left Hand Only', many a time, as an encore that is almost guaranteed to evoke a second encore.

If Debussy and Ravel seem like (non-identical) twins, so do the Spaniards Albéniz and Granados. Both composed with, at times, too many notes, and one feels a little like the conjuror who juggles with an unbelievable number of spinning plates and keeps half a dozen balls in the air. The problems are more pianistic than stylistic. Pianists already familiar with Bizet's

Carmen—and who was not—had no difficulty in grasping the feel of the music. In the case of Albéniz we need not be surprised at his grasp of virtuosity: he was a Liszt pupil. His *Iberia* suite shows the influence. Oddly enough, his little Tango is quite simple. It remained for Godowsky to transcribe it with great skill and elegance and make it suitable for a grand recital.

Granados resembles Ravel in being able to take his own piano music and present it in new colours. His opera *Goyescas* is largely made out of piano music, and it is a strange experience for a pianist to hear 'The Maja and the Nightingale' sung by an operatic soprano—and very enlightening as to how the piano solo might be played. The word Maja is often translated as Maiden, but literally it means Woman. A Spaniard who once tried to explain to me that Maja meant an ordinary sort of woman, not an educated lady, proposed that the English title might be The Wench and the Nightingale.

In 1916 Granados died in a ship that was torpedoed on its way home from New York.

There were more shocks in store for pianists. Little did most of them know about Bartók or Stravinsky or Schoenberg. Meanwhile, just when they were deploying ever-increasing pianistic skills, there were people who wondered whether piano music might be made easier to perform.

21. *Strange Pianos and Argumentative Teachers*

For piano enthusiasts looking ahead, there were three possibilities: to redesign the piano, to rethink piano teaching and to make an automatic, self-playing piano.

One amendment to piano design was to build a curved keyboard. This idea goes back to 1780 and an inventor named Neuhaus in Vienna; it was revived in 1824 by Staufer & Haudinger and in 1910 by Clutsam. They all argued that the extreme ends of the keyboard could be brought more comfortably within reach if the keyboard partially surrounded the player, but the problems of making a satisfactory piano action put that idea out of court.

Then there were various attempts to rearrange tones and semitones to get rid of the highly illogical pattern of white and black keys with which we are all familiar. There is no need to discuss all the cranky ideas that had their brief vogue, but we must take notice of a Viennese singer and opera composer named Vincent (originally Heinrich Winzenhörlein) whose theories were developed by the Hungarian Paul von Janko. He constructed a keyboard in six tiers of keys rather like the banks of letters on a typewriter. They were so arranged that any note was playable from three of the tiers. Each had its notes arranged at the interval of a tone. To play from a natural to a sharp you had to change tier. One tier would have tone-intervals starting from C, the next would also have tone-intervals but starting from C sharp, and so on. The keys were narrow, and the pianist played not only along the keyboard but across it. Stretches and arpeggios became much more comfortable, and a leap of the arm became a mere turn of the wrist.

The piano firm of Ibach in Barmen took it up, and there was much talk of this being the piano of the future.

Another Hungarian, Emmanuel Moór (and here we come well into our own century), brought out a piano in 1921 with two keyboards rather in the manner of a harpsichord and borrowing the harpsichord device of octave coupling. The two keyboards, however, were not tuned at the same pitch. Moving straight forward from the lower to the slightly higher keyboard the pianist played a note an octave higher than the one just quitted. Here again we find the notion of wide leaps transformed into much narrower forward or diagonal movements. The back part of the white keys was raised to the height of the black keys to facilitate *glissando*, and many distinguished musicians were impressed by the way they could 'get about the keys' with new facility, while continuing to be able to use the lower keyboard in the traditional way if they preferred.

The piano made a considerable stir. Moór's wife, Winifred Christie, played it with great skill, various famous manufacturers decided to make a few specimens and, at various stages

214

in his career, Moór was in collaboration with Pleyel, Bechstein, Aeolian and Bösendorfer. Backhaus, Gieseking and Godowsky were great pianists who took an interest. That formidable pundit, Donald Tovey, gave public demonstrations. Bruno Walter was impressed when he conducted for Winifred Christie's performances in Berlin of Beethoven's Emperor and Chopin's F minor concertos.

The Duplex-Coupler piano, as it was called, had obvious advantages. What were its disadvantages? The worst was that when one key was made to produce an octave by means of the coupler, the finger needed twice as much energy—the touch became twice as heavy. A similar change can be noticed in a coupled two-manual harpsichord, but a harpsichord is an altogether lighter instrument than a concert grand. Then again, in coupling, one cannot make a difference in tone between the lower and upper note, whereas in playing conventional octaves one may decide to 'bring out' the thumb or bring out the little finger.

The Duplex-Coupler failed to conquer the world. My Royal Academy of Music colleague Max Pirani, friend and biographer of Moór, possesses a fine specimen. It is a beautiful example of those inventions that, it seems, must succeed yet don't.*

On an altogether lower level one must mention the transposing piano. This is a very simple device. Imagine that the block of wood at each end of a keyboard is the roof of a little tunnel. Hidden in those tunnels are extra notes. You turn a handle and the whole keyboard begins to slide. Top notes disappear into the top tunnel. New bottom notes emerge from the bass tunnel. The whole action has gone along with the keyboard so that when you play the keys of a C major scale the hammers will hit a different set of strings and produce, if you like, E major.

In the days when pitch varied from place to place, when in

---

* In 1812 Érard had brought out a piano with two actions and two sound-boards. One set of strings was tuned an octave higher than the other, and both sets could be coupled. There was also the possibility of producing accent by energizing not three strings to a note but six. Another inventor built a piano with a keyboard at each end to play two-piano music on one instrument.

one and the same city the conservatory might use one pitch and the opera house another, a transposing piano may have been a boon to accompanists. I am told that a transposing piano was used by Irving Berlin who with its aid could compose at the piano in simple keys and then discover what his tunes sounded like when put up or down. I do not despise this. The man is a genius and must be allowed to work in his own way.

There were various kinds of transposing pianos: I have described the one I have actually played.

Inventors not only redesigned the piano to make playing easier or more effective: they redesigned notation. The most successful of these inventions brings us a little ahead of our story but it may be convenient in the context of reformed pianos to mention Klavarskribo. (The word is Esperanto.) In 1935 a Dutch engineer named Cornelius Pot published a number of pieces in the new style. Instead of drawing five lines across the page, he drew five *down* the page, spaced out like the five black notes on a keyboard—first a pair and then three. Reading down the page, the pianist simply inspects the keyboard position of each note—on a line for a black note, beside a line for a white one.

I have described the system in bare outline, but that is the gist of it. It has many advantages. No ledger lines, no accidentals, no key signatures, no feeling that C major is normal and all other keys are 'harder'. It does seem very much tied to keyboards, but the Klavar Institute has published a pocket score of *Till Eulenspiegel* (though in this case the lines do have to travel across the page).

The Dutch Klavarskribo Institute publishes a very comprehensive library of standard works, and it is in Holland that the greatest number of Klavar players and teachers are to be found. There is a branch in London and several other capital cities, but the great weight of tradition makes dissemination very uphill work. From the point of view of the advanced student and the professional performer too, there is the disadvantage that the Klavar-reader cannot look at a facsimile of a manuscript or buy an Urtext and see what the composer actually wrote.

Many of the adherents of Klavarskribo are self-taught amateurs who can, as the phrase goes, sit down and play the piano for their own amusement. The qualified musician tends to be snooty. But I honestly think that the music of Schoenberg and Stockhausen could more sensibly be printed in Klavar than in 'Old Notation'.

If reformed keyboards and a location-notation are not to your taste, is there some means of making technique and touch feel easier? Can one use weight and deploy relaxation so as to make piano hammers behave in some hitherto unsuspected fashion, so that tone quality can be changed without altering tone quantity?

Deppe thought so. Amy Fay thought so. And more and more teachers and pianists were persuaded. But inevitably there were stony-hearted people who looked inside a piano and could see nothing but a hammer flying towards a string at a speed that controlled the loudness. As a schoolboy, and not at all stony-hearted, I looked inside our piano and saw just that, and I still think that, taking a single note by itself, without any musical context, you can push a key down in almost any way you like and the quality of the tone will be what you paid for in the piano shop. Only quantity and duration can be controlled.

However, music does not consist of a note without context, and as soon as you have chords and phrases, melodies and accompaniments, loudness and softness, and all those varieties of touch that are called *staccato*, and *mezzo-staccato*, and *legato*, and *legatissimo*, it is possible for a fine player to make a mediocre piano sound better than it deserves.

Also there is a personal context. For example, while your arm is in the air above the keyboard you are not apparently affecting the piano in any way. But on the way down towards the keys you need great subtlety of judgement. You must be able to play fortissimo with subtle judgement: you must be able to exert the will-power that produces the most delicate pianissimo.

None of this can be done by just giving a shove—not even by a careful shove. You have only to play a ball-game to know that mere hitting will not make you a star in tennis or golf or cricket or football or billiards. There is the swing, and the timed impact; there is putting your weight behind it; there is follow-through. Yet with all this, the moment of impact is the moment of truth, and you do hit the ball. And the hammer must always hit a string. It cannot invite the string to sound, or stroke the string, or plead with the string.

Being made as we are, we are governed by notions: we play *as if*. . . . A games-coach may say 'Don't aim at the ball: swing right through it'. Literally, objectively, nobody can swing *through* a ball, but the notion may be just what the player needs.

Pianists are often helped not only by physical notions but by emotional ones. ('Play as though you *loved* the chord.') These notions, if they have the effect of truth, can come to be regarded *as* truth, with the result that some quite absurd arguments can start up between artists and scientists. The artists' attitudes are of two kinds: (a) we are right and you are wrong; and (b) your apparatus is too crude and you will find later on that we are right.

In his *Oxford Companion to Music*, Percy Scholes tried hard to put the second of these views.

> But when the manufacturer has done the best he can (for the particular sum paid him) there remains something for the player to do in the matter of tone-quality, as can be proved by the following experiment: With right pedal down repeat a chord many times, beginning very softly and working up gradually to very loudly; do this first with the utmost rigidity of arm and fingers and then with the utmost suppleness of all these parts; in the first instance the tone will be found to be hard and harsh, and in the second to be round and pleasant. The reason why this difference occurs is a subtle question, probably involving a great many factors and still open to discussion, but there seems no question of the existence of the difference, which is the basis of the demand for muscular relaxation in pianoforte playing. . . .
>
> There *is* surely such a thing as 'bad' and 'good' touch producing a 'bad' and 'good' tone in piano playing, though how it comes to exist may continue to be a matter of earnest, friendly dispute for some time yet. And beyond 'good' and 'bad' there are varieties of 'colour', though the way in which these are brought about may be still more debatable.

Nobody laboured more long or earnestly to investigate all these questions of touch than Tobias Matthay, with such success that in the first quarter of this century, the Matthay

Method became *the* method. And there are still many teachers who think that to question even one of his ideas is like saying 'I believe in seven or eight of the Ten Commandments'. There were Matthay schools and Matthay societies in Britain and America, and prodigies flocked to 'Uncle Tobs' as earlier prodigies flocked to Leschetizky. His greatest product, the one who achieved world renown, was Dame Myra Hess, but nearly all his pupils played very well and those still around revere his memory.

Nevertheless, it must be said that even Dame Myra was not a stunning virtuoso. Transcendental studies and Prokofiev concertos were not for her. What, then, had Matthay to offer?

A great deal. He examined the pianist's playing-apparatus limb by limb and asked himself exactly what does each bit of oneself do—what can it contribute to tone? He also thought about what a limb should not do and became deeply interested in the importance of relaxation. He realized that one's arm is a weighty object and that its weight can be used for playing purposes.

Another very important insight was the realization that technique is not always seen to be done. Besides the visible movement there is invisible condition.

Let us take a very simple example. Play a note with the right thumb. Unconsciously your arm is invisibly exerting itself in an unscrewing direction, as though about to use a door-handle anti-clockwise. Contrariwise, play a note with your little finger (right hand), and your arm must invisibly exert itself clockwise. A good pianist must understand the condition of arm or finger, what one might almost call its state of mind.

Then again he was very much aware of how we are a bundle of bits and pieces that are never independent. There is no such thing as *pure* finger technique. The arm has to be in the right place, in the right condition: the hand at the correct angle. Similarly there is no pure arm-touch. When the arm descends, the finger must exert itself to take the weight, otherwise the weight will be ineffectively dispersed in a collapse at the point of impact.

Although the weight of the arm could be allowed to fall *plomp*, it is in general lowered under control but—and this is important—with an accelerating impulse, even towards a soft note. In *pianissimo* the acceleration will be very subtle.

Matthay hated what he called key-bedding. This consisted of thrusting keys down even after a sound had begun—what I sometimes call pushing the piano through the floor, which is something beyond a firm arrival on the key-bed. So anxious was he to avoid this that he advocated a slight rise of the arm, immediately after a note sounds, in order to hold the note with minimum pressure for the remainder of its duration.

In fairness to a very remarkable teacher, I must quote verbatim from his *An Epitome of the Laws of Pianoforte Technique*. Here are a few important sentences.

> You must *time* the movement of the key itself towards Sound.
> The louder you wish the sound to be, the quicker must you move the key down. To obtain the best result from this tone-producing motion you must never hit or jerk a key down. Instead, you must always produce the down-speed *gradually*—by acceleration. This acceleration during descent must be not only 'gradual', it must be at an *increasing* rate of increase as the finger goes down with the key—it must be at 'increasing ratio'. It does not matter whether you call the result a better *quality* of tone, or merely a better *controlled* tone.

That last sentence was a concession on Matthay's part. Before he came to write his *Epitome* he had asserted for years that the result was a better quality of tone. No argument.

The business of releasing the whole of the arm's weight or only part of it; the possibility of using the weight of only the forearm; the addition of forearm exertion to upper-arm weight —all this was liable to interfere with simple direct action. But there was also the question of how to prevent the weight of the arm from bearing down on rapidly moving fingers in a way that would hamper them. For this Matthay recommended the 'poised' arm.

It must be said that expressions like 'poised' or 'balanced' are very imprecise; what else can one say? For myself I sometimes say 'Hold the arm as though it were resting on an imaginary table' and I justify the absurdity of this by reference to experience. Much depends on 'as though'. One says, 'Before the next phrase, rest your arm on the air, think, and then . . .'

Despite the imprecision of some of Matthay's instructions many teachers were able to persuade their pupils to produce more beautiful performances than ever before. A great deal of insensitive strumming was got rid of. For my part I am convinced that while people were releasing weight they were also releasing emotion, and the improved frame of mind was just as important as the improved condition of the limbs.

Quite objectively it does not matter whether a key is pushed down by finger exertion or arm weight or by laying on it a pebble from the beach. But the complex business of pre-judging a sound and relating it to all the notes that precede it and support it and are about to follow it cannot be done by a human being in a quite cold and calculating manner. It can be done by other means that we shall come to presently, but men and women must feel when they think about music.

Coldly and objectively one could say 'Play E flat at medium strength on the first beat and release it on the fourth.' But compare this with 'This is a crucial note in the piece and you must sink into it, sensing the sound as the arm goes down, and then you must feel yourself immersed in the note and listen to it all the time other notes are accompanying it; and when you feel the approach of the fourth beat you must begin to emerge from the note in such a way as to allow the end of the note to disappear into the beginning of the next note.'

Thinking in terms of sinking into a note, feeling its presence, and so on, a pianist is almost certain to judge his sounds with more subtlety, and the over-all effect is of good tone and a more expensive instrument.

It is not surprising that the Matthay method became a kind of holy writ. But like all holy writ it gave rise to heresy. What went wrong?

Matthay's book is difficult to read, partly because of over-eagerness. Matthay must have been a trial to his printers. Some sentences are in ordinary type, some are underlined, some are in italics. Whole paragraphs are in capitals, some in especially black capitals. There are asides in tiny type and also footnotes referring the reader to other books. The time came when his followers wrote books to explain what he meant, and one colleague of Matthay's said, 'I hear, Toby, that your books have been translated into every language except English.'

People unwilling to study the matter in depth were content to think that Matthay was keen on arm weight, rotary motion and relaxation, and they went on from there. One saw children laboriously hoisting their arms from place to place, tilting their hands from side to side to give aid to every finger, imparting an undulation to their wrists, and flinching away from the key-bed so that every downward action was immediately followed by not just a slight rise of the arm but a slight rise of the body from the chair. The result was very like the sort of old-fashioned elocution that was taught to genteel 'gels' ('How now, brown cow') so that a student's recital, like a 'poytry' reading, was nothing but *myoosical* refinement.

This was hard on a great teacher, but to some degree he brought it on himself. Let me quote the first sentences of his *Epitome*.

> The sole purpose of Technique should be to express Music. It is useless therefore to practise Technique as such. While trying to gain this technical equipment to express music you must un-remittingly give close attention to Music itself. Not to do this is self-defeating and harmful. To try to acquire Technique (as in the past) without constant reference to Music itself is just as stupid as trying to learn the use of the cricket-bat, tennis-racket or golf-club without reference to the ball!

Yes, yes; but champion games players must go to a gym and have a work-out; football teams go for a cross-country run to strengthen their legs and improve their wind; and ballet dancers limber up at the *barre* without reference to choreography or music.

One supposes that Matthay's own teachers had trained him in the old-fashioned way and that exercises had given his fingers a strength that he took for granted. Far too often his more distant followers ignored finger strength. They also forgot that music is not invariably refined and 'beautiful'. Assault and battery have at least some part to play. The man in love with a piano must occasionally be a wife-beater.

Among the conspicuous opponents of Matthay was a former

pupil named James Ching. In order to make himself more able to speak scientifically he took courses in anatomy and physiology. He read Otto Ortmann's *Physiological Mechanics of Piano Technique*, an account of painstaking research that showed beyond doubt that one cannot play a note in a beautiful way and then in an ugly way at the same loudness. Recognizing that psychology has a part to play in teaching he had himself psycho-analysed. He engaged in public debate with Matthayites. I once saw one of them and Ching go behind a screen to play selected passages of music to an audience that would not be told the order of events. The listeners were then asked to guess who played what. Ching easily deceived them. By playing slowly he persuaded the audience that his performances were done by arm weight and relaxation. Hearing the delayed notes they imagined the weighted descent into each sound.

However, a mystery remained. Ching once said to me, 'Everyone, surely, must agree that the faster the descent of the key, the louder the sound.'

My reply was 'In that case, how do you play *pianissimo prestissimo*?' After years of pontificating about touch he was momentarily flummoxed. He asked me what my explanation was. I went to the piano, turned my hand over, laid a light finger on the bottom note, and played a fast and soft *glissando* along the whole length of the keyboard.

I then played a fast, soft scale in the normal way and suggested that, in such a case, one doesn't follow each key down to its bed. The key is given a slight push and is abandoned by a finger that is being carried along by the flight of the hand. The key continues to descend, but, having no finger on it, slows down as it goes down. So we have the curious situation that the notes succeed one another very quickly but that each key arrives on the bed at a slow velocity.

'But could you control it, if your finger doesn't follow the key?'

'I like to think that that was what I have just done. But I also think that at *prestissimo* tempo there could be slight variations of loudness that wouldn't show up.'

Ching's response was typical. He fetched his special ciné-camera and asked me to repeat the experiment so that he could analyse it in slow motion.

Another heretic was the American pianist and teacher E. Robert Schmitz. He wrote a book called *The Capture of Inspiration* and followed it by some remarkable editions of music. I have his Chopin *Études*. This is full of symbols and letters and en-circled notes, and each piece has a preceding Explanatory Text. Quotation:

> The rhythm sequence is every three notes. For example, in the first six notes:
> On the first, drop forearm pronated.
> On the second, distribute without rotating.
> On the third, abduct upper arm, pivoting on thumb.
> On the fourth, adduct upper arm, well distributed.
> On the fifth, distribute without rotation.
> On the sixth, supinate on fifth finger (FrmR) while preparing the thumb distribution by pronation.

FrmR means forearm rotation. Abduction means arm away from body. Adduction is arm close to body. The student must learn that supination is a twisting movement in the direction of turning the hand over on its back. Pronation is the opposite. He must be aware of the Medial phalanx and the Proximal phalanx and inner humeral rotation. And lots more.

It would be easy to deride all this, but it has a serious purpose. Too many young players have no idea what is happening in their hands and arms at any given moment, and they can benefit from a course of Schmitzification. It would be absurd to take all the instructions as the only means of playing Chopin's music, but the arm should be able to say, in the words of the old song, 'I know where I'm going.'

A totally different approach to the Chopin problem is to be found in the edition of the *Études* published by the great pianist Alfred Cortot. Before each *étude* he offers a few pages of pre-liminary exercises. Every Chopin shape is rearranged in re-peated notes or altered rhythms or alternative fingerings. Chords are spread out as arpeggios: arpeggios are consolidated into chords. Each exercise seems to cry out, 'You're not ready yet: don't dare to begin the piece.' Cortot's attitude to technical exercises was positively sado-masochistic . . . as is made clear in his *Rational Principles of Pianoforte Technique*. This prescribes a preparatory period of six months' work.

During this first period of study, the anticipation of any chapter by a succeeding one must be absolutely avoided, all modification in the established plan being in radical opposition to the essential object of this work, which is the complete assimilation of each difficulty taken separately.

There is nothing arbitrary in the division of the work of each chapter into periods of thirty-six days. This is determined by adopting a different key as the starting point for the work of each day, and since the chromatic scale is composed of twelve sounds, there will be three divisions of twelve days each.

Cortot persuaded himself that all technical difficulties could be pigeon-holed into five categories: (1) Equality, independence and mobility of fingers; (2) Passing under of the thumb (scales–arpeggios); (3) Double notes and polyphonic playing; (4) Extensions; and (5) Wrist technique, execution of chords.

'Wrist technique' is a strange term. Since the wrist is a hinge, he might as well have talked of knuckle technique or elbow technique. Certainly one must study the behaviour of one's wrists, but it is curious to find nothing about arms in *Rational Principles of Pianoforte Technique*.

Following the preliminary warnings there are a hundred pages of exercises. Never is Cortot willing to suggest a few possibilities of refingering. He prints *all* possibilities. And at the end of the book he assumes that the serious student will wish to play studies by Clementi and Czerny. In the *Principles* one finds a chromatic scale in thirds (for one hand) fingered in something like thirty different ways. And in the Chopin *Études* there are many exercises that are the musical equivalents of tongue-twisters, as for example holding C with the second finger of the left hand while practising a trill on two notes below it—A and B flat played with the thumb and third finger. This is supposed to help us to play the 'Revolutionary' *Étude*.

This approach to total command of technique can easily produce total anxiety. Anyone old enough to have heard Cortot will remember that he was an unreliable pianist, though heavenly on his good days.

However, as with Schmitz, there is something of importance to be extracted from Cortot's self-torture.

Almost all the great pundits tend to be too learned. I am re-minded of the little girl who, given a book for Christmas, said, 'It tells me more about ponies than I want to know.' James Ching once confessed to me that he lacked the power of simple explanation, and his *Amateur Pianist's Companion* is tough going even for the experienced professional. Every possible playing activity is analysed and put into its numbered category, but I can think of few amateurs who will suddenly, or even in due course, find themselves playing Schumann's *Träumerei* more dreamily than ever before after reading Ching's instructions. Here are a few odd sentences.

> Thus, for example, for passages in Category I, and which demand Principal Movement I, the Joints of Movement are the elbow and shoulder joints. This makes the joint of forearm rotation (radio-ulnar joint), together with wrist, knuckle and finger joints assume the function of Joints of Transmission, and makes the hips become Joints of Stabilisation.
> . . . Tables I–IV give a detailed analysis of necessary tensions and their variations in respect of varying speeds and tones within the scope of the Four Categories of passages. . . . A control of the five degrees of tension for which directions are given will, more-over, be adequate for all practical purposes, although the ability to control as many as forty or even fifty appreciably different degrees at many of the joints of the body separately and indepen-dently is by no means unusual, even among amateurs with severe limitations of time for practice.

The great difficulty in writing books on piano-playing lies in the fact that a pianist is an athlete who thinks non-verbally. University graduates like James Ching, M.A., B.Mus. Oxon, were apt to think that all knowledge could be put into words. I seriously doubt this. Furthermore, academic language addressed to educated readers leaves children out of the picture, and real piano-playing is learned in childhood. It could be argued that a child's teacher could read a Ching treatise and translate the knowledge into teaching practice; but if Ching could not make himself clear why should we assume that a children's teacher will do so?

However, something of all this knowledge does in due course affect the way people teach. For myself I have learned at least something worth knowing from a number of treatises and also what not to do. I have become almost incapable of writing mandarin English, and my own *Young Person's Guide to Playing the Piano*—not exhaustive, not scientifically profound—consists of familiar words, short sentences and simple examples.

For those who want not a young person's but a mature pianist's guide there is a book that commands considerable respect: *The Technique of Piano Playing* by Jósef Gát.* It is not easy to read, it had better be studied a little at a time, but it is worth the trouble. The illustrations include strips of photo-frames taken from slow-motion film so that the reader can study the exact behaviour of fingers, inch by inch. There are also diagrams of the pianist's anatomy, including X-ray pictures of hands and arms, not to mention advice on useful gymnastics to be done away from the keyboard.

He warns against mere technical practice and says of the diligently drilled student: 'His fingers will not execute exactly what he wants because their movements were not automatized to the music but only to each other.'

He is oddly insistent that one ought not to look at the keys but should direct one's gaze towards the hidden hammers and strings, disregarding the fact that some of us use our eyes on the keyboard as an aid to memory, remembering not the look of notes on the page (photographic memory) but the look of keyboard patterns. We choreograph the dance of the ivories. He also neglects the possibility, in very tender music, of allowing a sound to happen and disappear in the course of a sliding contact with the key (a caressing touch). And, surprisingly, he devotes less than one page to the sustaining pedal.

He is penetrating on slow practice, realizing that it may not tell us much about fast playing, just as walking may not tell us how to run. It is surprising that he does not suggest the fast practice of a very few notes at a time. However, there is value in the idea that, when practising fast music slowly, one should expand and exaggerate each action. And while being as scientific as possible he knows that, although a reproducing pianola

* Published by Corvina in Budapest and, in English, by Collet's in London.

can imitate a virtuoso, a virtuoso cannot behave like a player-piano. As he says, 'And this is the truth, for after all, the piano is to be taught to reproduce the composition according to our musical conception. Our task is only to find the movements by which the piano can be compelled to do so.'

And here we come to a point worth making: when we talk of a piano-teacher we mean, of course, a pianist-teacher. It is the student who must become a teacher of pianos.

22. *Pianos Play Themselves*

If there was one thing that seemed to make the case for a scientific attitude to touch and tone it was the automatic piano. The 'reproducing piano' operated by a paper roll was brought to such a pitch of refinement as to persuade very great pianists to say 'This is *my* performance'. Quite evidently it was possible to produce any required tone by making sure that a hammer reached its strings at the right speed. And at the right moment.

However, the reproducing piano came at the end of a long process of development and we must begin with earlier attempts to produce music mechanically.

We have already seen that Clementi's firm made an instrument that was both piano and musical box. When wound up it sprang into action by rotating a barrel studded with projecting pins. This principle was later applied to the street-pianos of my childhood, often wrongly called barrel-organs or hurdy-gurdies. The operator wheeled his instrument on to his pitch and turned a cranked handle. What the passer-by heard was undeniably some kind of a piano, even though not played by a hand on a keyboard.

Meanwhile it had been discovered that certain kinds of industrial machines could be operated by feeding punched cards into the mechanism. There was a French maker of straw hats in Lyons who thought about the problem of making weaving machines produce patterns in different colours. This Joseph

Marie Jacquard brought the machine controls to a row of keys and then controlled the keys by means of punched and slotted strips of cardboard. He was awarded a medal at the Paris Exhibition of 1801, was interviewed by Napoleon himself and was set to work at the Conservatoire des Arts et Métiers in Paris. In later years he was hated by silk weavers fearing unemployment, but a new technology had been born.

The next great step towards the pianola was made by another Frenchman, C. F. Seytre, who in 1842 produced his Autophon worked by air pressure. Air passed through a hole or slot in perforated cards and operated a piston that in turn pushed at the tail of the hammer.

Yet another Frenchman, J. Carpentier, in 1880 exhibited a means of recording a performance by using electrical contacts to make ink-marks on a moving spool of paper.* When these had been used as a guide to the cutting of slots there was a mechanism full of rocking levers that allowed the machine to play back what it had recorded.

However, it was in America that the pneumatic, paper-roll machine was brought to fruition, and perhaps the true pioneer was Elias Parkman Needham, who invented an upright player action for reed organs. Many other inventors followed suit until at last there was an effective player.

The early players were separate from the piano. The machine had to be wheeled up to the keyboard and adjusted for height so that its projecting 'fingers' could lie on the correct keys. It was only later that the player-piano had its mechanism concealed inside.

Player-pianos of every make and kind are popularly called pianolas, but the name pianola properly belongs to the products of the Aeolian Company. The word caught on and was applied indiscriminately. The nearest modern parallel is the word Hoover. A housewife may say, to the annoyance of Hoover's, 'I do my hoovering with an Electrolux.'

What is the principle on which the automatic piano works? Most people have seen what they call a pianola (*see Plate 8*).

---

* There was a flurry of interest amongst inventors who tried to produce what were called stenographical pianofortes. Several patents were taken out in France and Germany.

The operator folds away the music-desk, opens a small door or hatch and reveals a horizontal bar with a line of small holes punched in it. Each hole is the visible end of a tube leading to the mechanism of a note.

Below the bar you place a roll of paper with its spindle parallel with the bar. You then begin to tug at the leading edge so that some of the paper begins to slide upwards across the bar until it can be attached to an upper spindle.

You then switch on. As the paper unwinds from the lower spindle and slides across the bar, slots begin to appear. And when a slot uncovers one of the holes in the bar, air rushes into the piano and plays a note.

Air rushes in? Whatever makes it do that? The operator is busy pedalling away at a pair of bellows. Surely bellows will increase the pressure in a piano so that air rushes *out*. Not necessarily. Bellows and pumps must take in air before they can push it out, and it does not require much ingenuity to devise bellows or pumps that pump air *out* of a piano thereby creating a partial vacuum. As soon as this vacuum (only a slight degree of vacuum is needed) has established itself you can work on the well-established principle that Nature abhors a vacuum and will do her best to get inside and restore normal pressure. So outside air is eager and ready to rush through the holes and play the piano for you.

Exactly how every detail of this machine operates is not a matter that concerns us here. Fortunately there are enthusiasts who restore old player-pianos with great devotion, much as other people restore the cars that Mr. Royce built for Mr. Rolls, and they are catered for in a number of books, of which one of the most splendid is *Player-Piano* by Arthur W. G. Ord-Hume—a history, a picture-book and a restorer's manual.

The early pianolas were plainly mechanical pianos. They made an obviously mechanical sound. There was only one kind of loudness (and no kind of softness) and rhythm consisted of no more than strict time. To put the matter in its simplest terms, a one-inch slot might hold the damper off the strings for a whole beat; a half-inch slot would account for a half-beat; and so on. There was no difference between melody and accompaniment or between accented and unaccented notes.

The roll-cutter measured everything up according to the text and set to work with a ruler and a sharp knife. And once a master roll had been made it could serve as a pattern for thousands of others.

One remarkable quality can be noticed—the extraordinary toughness of the paper. Rolls fifty years old are still usable, showing almost no signs of wear.

As time went on, inventors began to realize that the mechanical piano could become expressive. It seems obvious that if one can reduce the intake of air by means of a valve, the notes will be played more softly. What about expression-levers in the hands of the piano owner? Then again, piano rolls must be kept at constant speed to work in a consistent way, but what about something to govern the speed-governor? Why not other levers to produce *accelerando* and *rallentando*? Why not extra holes in the bar and the rolls that would operate the sustaining pedal at the right moments?

Now there was a new era. The owner of an expression pianola was like the conductor of an orchestra. *He* didn't have to play notes. All that was done for him. His job was to concentrate on interpretation.

On many of the rolls the manufacturers provided a wavy line. On the piano itself was a pointer. You moved the pointer to follow the wavy line as it swung right and left and the composer's expression-marks were obeyed. If you preferred an interpretation of your own you were free.

At this point enthusiastic owners began to practise. The frustrations of a would-be pianist melted away and the delighted pianolist yearned over his instrument and with infinite subtlety conjured out of it such nuances as the average pianist could not match.

For the less devoted owner there were popular song rolls that not only played accompaniments but printed the words so that they appeared syllable by syllable at the right moment and disappeared on to the upper roll.

At this stage of the game most players were inexpensive up-rights, and they sold in fantastic quantities. America was the great market, but there were plenty of players in Great Britain and in western Europe—also in colonies, settlements, dominions, etc., governed by the Great Powers who in those days possessed empires. The automatic piano was found in homes, schools, bars, brothels, theatres, churches. By this time the foot-operated bellows was largely replaced by the electric pump and the piano could be relied upon to go on playing untiringly for hours at a stretch. All that was necessary was that someone would remove a roll and replace it with another.

The busy inventors raised their sights. They began to think of designing pianos that would faithfully reproduce the performances of great artists. And this they succeeded in doing. There were a number of designs, but the three great makers were the AMerican PIano COmpany (Ampico), the British Aeolian Company and the German Welte, producing the Welte-Mignon pianos. Their designs were not 'compatible'—Aeolian rolls could not be used on the other people's pianos and so on—but we can understand broad principles of how the magic was achieved.

It is not difficult to imagine a set-up of electrical contacts that would mark a moving roll of paper every time a hammer hit its strings. This would give us the beginning of a sound. A similar arrangement could mark the moment when a damper descended on to strings. This would give the end of the sound. Other contacts would record pedal actions. In this way we would have all the great pianist's notes at their proper durations and speeds.

What is more difficult to understand is the recording of every subtlety of intensity. Let me quote from *Re-enacting the Artist* by Larry Givens, a small book devoted to the Ampico:

> An attachment was made for the action frame of the piano in such a manner that the silver contactor on each [hammer] shank would successively touch two small silver wires as the hammer passed through its final travel toward the strings. The distance between the two wires was precisely adjusted with a micrometer. By measuring the time interval between the silver bar's contact with the first wire and its succeeding contact with the second wire, the speed of the hammer could be precisely determined.
>
> The time interval under study was extremely short, and to make the system function properly the measuring device had to be keenly accurate. A spark chronograph was used for this purpose.

In its usual form, a spark chronograph is an electrical instrument in which a strip of paper passes between a spark gap at high speed. At the beginning of the time interval being measured, a high-voltage spark is shot between two electrodes, piercing the paper and thus marking it. At the end of the interval a second spark occurs and leaves a similar mark. By measuring the distance between the two marks and relating it to the speed of paper travel, the time interval can be determined.

Obviously each note was recorded as two marks very close together, and Dr. Clarence N. Hickman, Ampico's chief designer, had to design a very special spark chronograph to make each pair of marks identifiable as a particular degree of intensity between *ppp* and *fff*.

There remained the problem of taking the information provided by the spark chronograph and transforming it into mechanical control of the touch. In the Ampico there were two systems of control, working together in subtle interplay. One produced general *crescendo* or *diminuendo* by means of the opening or constriction of air passages, and there were, of course, fast and slow *crescendo* and *diminuendo*. The other provided seven definite steps of loudness. As Mr. Ord-Hume explains it in *Player-Piano*,

By means of side perforations in the music-roll, the intensity of the playing can be set to any of these seven steps and remains so set until a subsequent perforation, or combination of perforations, sets it to another step. The change in intensity takes place practically instantaneously. By quick changes in intensity settings, melody notes or accented notes can be brought out without affecting the loudness of the surrounding notes. The effect of using the steps and *crescendo* at the same time, made it possible for perfectly smooth *crescendos* to be played at the same time as clearly defined accents being given.

I quote only a small part of the description of the Ampico system. Mr. Ord-Hume is exhaustive about this and about the principal—and different—other systems. But perhaps one has glimpsed how the inventors' minds worked to produce what, to the casual onlooker, seems an inexplicable miracle.

When a pianist had played his performance, the technicians carefully studied all the information provided by the recording apparatus, and the master roll was cut accordingly. Then the artist was recalled to the studio and asked for his opinion. If he wanted some slight correction or alteration his commands were obeyed. Was this cheating? No more so than when an artist of today retapes a passage that is not up to his usual standard. The fact remains that if we compare a Rachmaninoff roll and a Rachmaninoff record of one particular piece made at about the same time, the performances seem identical.

Playing rolls today one must make sure that the speed indicator is in perfect condition and that the piano is of a type and quality similar to the one on which the roll was first made. Under ideal conditions the effect of verisimilitude is uncanny. H. G. Wells's 'Invisible Man' is playing, and one looks on astounded to see the keys moving as under the fingers of a very great pianist. Indeed, a number of records have now been made from these machines, and these played on hi-fi record-players are very convincing. Anyone old enough to remember some of the old pianists is startled to hear their patent characteristics.

The individual owner of a reproducing piano is nearly always convinced that the system employed on his instrument is the best, but I have listened to all three systems at the museum created by my old friend Frank Holland and I hesitate to make any pronouncements on this score.

Catalogues of rolls reveal a great deal about the taste that was prevalent during the pianola era. There is a great preponderance of popular works—not only the popular classics like the Moonlight Sonata but hundreds of arrangements of orchestral and operatic works. Some of these arrangements were made and played by the composers, and it is strange to hear Richard Strauss playing his orchestral pieces on the piano. My general impression is that most composers played their own works not very well, the great exception being Rachmaninoff. I cannot bring myself to admire Grieg and Debussy playing Grieg and Debussy.

When the industry was big and prosperous the advertising industry enjoyed itself. Sometimes an advertisement appealed to snobbery. For example a piano had been supplied, to the Dowager Empress of China, to Mussolini, to the President of France, to the crew of u.s.s. *Delaware*. The prospective customer was told that a reproducing piano made it no longer *necessary* for him to employ his own private orchestra. There were public demonstrations in which Godowsky played to half-way through a piece and then left the piano roll to complete the performance. Godowsky went further. He produced Master and Pupil Rolls. 'The child who is following the instructions plays treble to accompany the bass which is played by Godowsky.'

Some customers liked to be 'blinded by science'. They were told about the spark-chronograph and assured that 416/100,000ths of a second were required to produce the softest note and 51/100,000ths for the loudest. About sixty times more energy was expended for the latter.

Self-playing pianos acquired fancy names. One of the most popular was the Angelus. Angelus pianos were placed in movie studios. 'Many a star has, inspired by the Angelus, given a brand of acting otherwise unobtainable without the instrument's influence.'

The reproducing piano was very expensive. However, the simpler and older types went on being sold. There were coin-operated Coinolas and a multitude of other curious instruments that the interested reader can find described and illustrated in Harvey Roehl's *Player Piano Treasury*. Ford 'Tin Lizzies' were specially adapted so that dealers could deliver pianos without delay.

The player principle—the paper-roll technology—was adapted to automatic violins and orchestrions and 'grand' organs, but it was the piano that captured most people.*

Suddenly there was a collapse. The gramophone or phonograph outgrew the acoustic horn and the wind-up motor. Hi-fi lay still in the future, but now there was electric recording. There was the 'mellow'-toned radiogram ('listen to the bass') and it was no longer necessary to hear everything arranged for piano. All music could be recorded with at least some claim to fidelity, from a mouth-organ solo to a complete opera. To make things worse for the automatic-piano industry there was a

---

* As far back as 1730 a Moravian preacher named Procopius Diviss, or Divisch, constructed a keyboard instrument with 790 strings and 130 changes of registration. He also provided a means of giving the performer an electric shock, an admirable device for galvanizing a torpid student.

depression. Records were cheaper and handier than piano rolls.

What happened to tens of thousands of instruments is any-one's guess since a piano is, in fact, quite difficult to destroy. Fortunately some were saved and a great variety of automatic pianos can be seen at the British Piano Museum in Brentford in England, at Utrecht in Holland, at Disneyland in California, at Troy, Ohio, and at the Gay Nineties Village, Sikestown, Missouri. And, no doubt, elsewhere.

The great era of reproducing pianos lay between the early 1900s and the 1930s. The German Welte-Mignon, originally produced without keyboard, came into the world in 1901. Later the firm wisely produced their system in two forms, either incorporated into a normal hand-played piano or else built into a separate player that could be wheeled up to the piano or stood in a corner to look like a sideboard.

Inevitably Welte had an American offshoot, and it was in America that rivalry was keenest. The British Aeolian Company was also in America and in 1913 introduced the Steinway Duo-Art, buying Steinway pianos with specially designed cases and then fitting Duo-Art mechanisms in them.

Ampico came relatively late to the field. Their inventor, Charles Stoddard, had produced instruments in 1913, but the public début was in 1916 on the occasion, already mentioned, when Godowsky compared his live playing with his recordings.

All of these systems were fitted to a great variety of pianos, so that one might find a Welte-Mignon-Baldwin Reperforming Piano, or an Ampico-Grotrian-Steinweg Re-enacting Piano, not to mention a Duo-Art-Steinway Reproducing Piano. And the American trade was largely unaffected by the Great War of 1914–18. The great collapse took place in the thirties.

The preservation of a considerable number of rolls and the cutting of new copies allows us to recall the great pianists of a great era and to make comparisons, but all the writing in the world cannot conjure up the quality of the performances and I shall not attempt descriptions. I can only say: go to a museum of reproducing instruments or to the house or an enthusiastic owner and hear for yourself; or buy some of the discs made from rolls.

As for the personalities and careers of the recording artists, they are well depicted in Schonberg's *The Great Pianists*. It is strange, however, that a great pianist can never be brought to life as vividly as a great composer. The great pianist lives in the memory of people growing older and older; the young don't want to know—as I observe when I grow reminiscent in conversation with my students.

Anyone who collects music rolls finds amusement in accompaniment rolls. In these, well-known accompanists provided piano parts for the benefit of amateurs singing at home. They were never very successful. They prevented the singer from following his own inclination in the matter of rhythm—which may have been a good thing in some cases—and they created considerable anxiety whenever the singer had an unaccompanied phrase. At the moment when the piano fell silent, the singer never knew quite how fast to sing. If he arrived at the end of the phrase too early, he had to wait until the piano decided to resume. If he was too late, he found the last notes of his phrase accompanied by the first notes of the next piano-phrase.

These strange rolls remind us that a great deal of singing was done at home. Where there was only an ordinary, hand-played piano somebody had to be found to manage the accompaniment, and vocal music in the home ranged from a sing-song in the front parlour, 'rahnd the ol' joanna', to *Winterreise* in the drawing-room accompanied on the Bechstein by Cressida, just down from Cambridge, for Lancelot, recently home from Vienna. Between those two extremes there was a great deal of singing of drawing-room ballads.

These are now spoken of with indulgent smiles as something good for a giggle, but many were very expertly written and were sung with considerable effect in public by the most distinguished singers, some of whom, now elderly, swear that these songs were created by people who really understood the voice (not like some songs we could mention). It is not unlikely that the best of them will once more be taken up, much as the best of Victorian and Edwardian furniture and pictures are now part of the trend.

What made them unacceptable for a long time was the breakdown between their world and the modern world. With the end of British India, who could sing 'Pale hands I loved beside the Shalimar' or (thinking of places further east) 'The Road to Mandalay'? Whatever happened to the red sails of the fishermen of Devon after the diesel-driven trawlers went out from Hull towards Iceland to make profits for the manufacturers of Fish Fingers or Crispy Cod Fries? And what did the property developers do to 'The Little Grey Home in the West' but add mod.cons. and a thatched garage for two cars?

In America what white family would now sing Stephen Foster's plantation songs, and where are those polished performances of spirituals accompanied by academic harmonies on the piano?

These songs were sung when they were new, making a small fortune for their lucky composers. They were dropped when changes in society made them seem absurd. They may well be revived when they are as period as Nellie Dean's 'Old Mill by the Stream'.

One sees the beginning of this process at the last night of the Promenade Concerts at the Royal Albert Hall in London. Eight thousand youngsters sing 'Rule Britannia, Britannia rule the waves' without a thought of gunboat diplomacy.

Perhaps in a high-rise apartment, with double glazing, an amateur singer will switch off the telly, and his girl-friend will sit at the piano, and one will hear, 'Oh it's quiet down here.'

23. *The Final Romantics*

Even the young can be persuaded to take notice of Paderewski and Rachmaninoff. They belong to history in a quite special way.

During the 1914–18 Great War, Paderewski championed the cause of Poland. In the world at large he was the most famous of all Poles, he spoke several languages eloquently, he was an outsize personality. When the peace conference was convened at Versailles he was there, and when Poland was re-established as an independent country he became its Prime Minister.

Can a musician be a politician? Liszt liked to think that he could have been an ambassador. Mr. Edward Heath had a degree in music before he changed course and went in for politics. Indeed, Mr. Heath, in office as Prime Minister, conducted a symphony orchestra in public with very fair credit and thereby made a useful contribution to charity. But the melancholy fact must be recorded that Paderewski soon discovered the difference between eloquence and administration. Furthermore, he was the rich and famous exile who had travelled the world. What could *he* know of the feelings of the Polish man in the street? The tough Marshal Pilsudsky came to power and Paderewski, having lasted ten months, was back in the musical world.

When I heard him for the first time he was probably in his sixties—no great age—but he struck me as a stiff-fingered, over-rated old man. Until I heard him again. Then I began to understand something of his power.

He belonged to a former age. He belonged to an era that admired Caruso and Melba in the opera house, Sir Henry Irving and Sarah Bernhardt in the theatre, and Edward VII on the throne, an era that knew nothing of the microphone, the close-up, the throw-away line. It was the era of the larger-than-life. When he played the left hand before the right in the Moonlight Sonata it was like changing the word *moon* into *mahoon*, and when he lingered on a discord, delaying the resolution, he was commanding a rapt audience to wait for it.

I once tried to imitate his playing to show a gifted student how style changes through the years. I thought she might laugh, but she said 'I wish *I* could play like that' and seemed to imply that her teacher might do well to play more like that more often.

A colleague of mine tells of going to a railway station and noticing a crowd gathered round a compartment at the far end of the train. Obviously someone important was being seen off. My friend walked along the platform and was overtaken by a young man running. The young man broke through the crowd, knelt and presented flowers to Paderewski. And this was when

Paderewski was a really old man and generally regarded as a has-been.

Rachmaninoff belongs to history in a quite different fashion. First he was a great composer—not one of the greatest but certainly more than an interesting minor character. His music has a limited range, it seems to say the same things over and over again, but he belongs to that category of composers whom, like Tchaikovsky and Chopin, it is easy but futile to criticize. He wrote four concertos. Of them all I like the most popular one best—the second—but I understand the view of those who prefer the third even though it seems to me to be overdecorated with cascades of notes. The fourth was a failure and, towards the end of his life, Rachmaninoff partly rewrote it. To no avail. I believe I was the first pianist to play the revised version in England and gave it several performances. This was just after the war. I had been to New York, bought one of the first available copies (published after Rachmaninoff's death) and done my homework. Audiences were not very enthusiastic. My fault? Other pianists since then have tried. Records have been put on the market. It still fails to attract.

Besides the concertos there is the Rhapsody on a Theme of Paganini for piano and orchestra—a set of variations on the Paganini theme that Brahms borrowed for *his* variations.

I heard Rachmaninoff play this at his first London performance in the middle thirties. Nobody could have been less like Paderewski. His great stature, his granite-carved face, his close-cropped hair, his disdain for any kind of demonstrative gesture seemed totally at variance with the character of the music. This was very strange. It is generally true that a pianist's behaviour has some sort of tie-up with the sound he makes, but Rachmaninoff's art was of the kind that conceals art. One saw nothing and heard everything. The music was melancholy, gay, passionate, sardonic, moody, brilliant. Where did it come from? Rachmaninoff never revealed his feelings on his face.

The response of the audience was well worth watching because this happened at a time when anything labelled 'first performance in London' was guaranteed to keep the great British public at home. However, Rachmaninoff was always a crowd-puller and they were reasonably sure that they would be safe with him. *He* didn't write that awful modern music. With every page their pleasure grew, and when he played the eighteenth variation they did not notice that its opening notes were Paganini's little minor cluster of notes turned upside down and put into the major, they only knew that this was the great tune they would wait for for the rest of their lives.

An old lady once assured me that Rachmaninoff's music was a nightingale singing in the snow outside a lighted ballroom.

'But', I said, 'nightingales don't sing in the snow: they wait for the spring.'

'That's no way for an artist to argue.'

As a pianist—some say the greatest of his time—Rachmaninoff was most influenced by his memories of Anton Rubinstein and would talk at length about the way Rubinstein played Beethoven's Appassionata or Chopin's B minor Sonata or a small piece such as Schumann's *Bird as Prophet*. 'It was not so much his magnificent technique that held one spell-bound, as the profound, spiritually refined musicianship, which spoke from every note and every bar he played, and singled him out as the most original, the unequalled pianist of the world.' I quote from Rachmaninoff's *Recollections*.

The pianist who could amaze both Rachmaninoff and Leschetizky must indeed have been a giant.

It is astounding that a man who had not intended to be a travelling virtuoso should have been able, once he had left Russia, to conquer America and then other countries as a great pianist. He had a wife and family to support and he was soon able to give them something more than modest comfort. He was, however, a very private man off the platform.

Like Chopin's feeling for Poland, Rachmaninoff's for the country of his birth never abated. During the war and despite his detestation for Stalin he played for Russian charities and would not go along with some of his exile friends who argued that a Nazi victory would destroy Bolshevism.

There was a time in the thirties when Rachmaninoff's music had been banned in Russia. The collective representing the musicians of the Leningrad and Moscow Conservatoires declared—no doubt to their private grief—that Rachmaninoff's music portrayed 'the decay of the petty bourgeois spirit particularly harmful to conditions in the acute struggle on the music front'.

Nowadays, in his native land, the most reactionary of all countries on the musical map, Rachmaninoff is a favourite son.

It has to be said that Rachmaninoff did become the odd man out in the world of composition. He went on as though anything later than Debussy did not exist. He ignored the challenges of new sorts of music.

Those who accepted them needed a certain courage.

24. *Treat it Rough*

I begin with a rather jokey example—the piece called 'Ragtime' from *1922 Suite für Klavier* by the then young Paul Hindemith. Underneath the title (in English) we read (in French and English) *Mode d'emploi—Direction for Use!!* The Directions (there are actually four directions) are in German but I translate them as:

> Take no notice of what you learned in your piano lessons.
> Don't waste time worrying whether you play D sharp with the fourth or the sixth finger.
> Play this piece very wildly yet strictly in rhythm, like a machine.
> Regard the piano as an interesting kind of percussion instrument and treat it accordingly.

Little did we foresee the comparatively traditional and academic Hindemith who was to compose *Ludus Tonalis* as a sort of twentieth-century *Well-tempered Clavier*. Little did Hindemith guess that his country would become mentally deranged and force him into exile. In 1922 his *Direction for Use!!* was a straw in the wind.

Other composers were inclined to treat the piano in a way that would have scandalized Tobias Matthay. In 1912 Sergey Prokofiev had composed a Toccata that, in places, seemed designed to wreck all but the strongest pianos. Whether a Prokofiev *fortissimo* is literally more forceful than anything known previously is open to doubt, but there are plenty of pages in his later works, in his sonatas and concertos, where the piano seems to take a knock.

Audiences took a knock. They were startled to hear music where the pianist's right hand played in one key and the left in another. In 1918 Béla Bartók (Bartók Béla in Hungarian) published a piece called Allegro Barbaro (note the title) with just such a clash of tonalities. Take the right-hand melody— the one written in octaves—and give it to a student to harmonize and the chords will appear in the key of A minor, especially if you are cunning enough to write C where Bartók writes B sharp (the same note on the keyboard). The harmonies in the copy, however, definitely belong to F sharp minor.

Like other young men in other countries Bartók went to the peasants not to teach but to learn. Unlike Liszt, who was a cosmopolitan onlooker at a gipsy encampment, Bartók listened to Hungarians and Rumanians and the southern Slavs whom we now called Yugoslavs and found that their melodies were neither major nor minor, their rhythms were not manifestly in duple, triple or quadruple time.

It is very easy as a conservatory student to think that major and minor are normal and that anything else is exotic. It is equally easy to believe that playing in time and playing in rhythm are much the same thing.

The fact is that European musicians had delightedly accepted settled tonalities and time-schemes because these solved so many problems of composition and performance. For generations it had seemed obvious that you could not have an orchestral work in which half of the players were in one key and the other half in another: you could not expect clean playing and a good ensemble if the rhythm defied notation. Of course every good interpreter knew that there was more in rhythm than could be provided by a metronome, and every student knew that you could never modulate from one key to another without the help of notes and chords that are like stepping-stones: you can step out into the river and back, or you can step out and cross over. Even so, genuine peasant rhythms and melodies were different.

(I had a late glimpse of this when I went to Trinidad to

adjudicate a steel-band contest. Rhythm for those who cannot read music is not the same as the time-keeping that we hear in an English examination-room, but rhythm it certainly is.)

As often happens, Bartók's 'quite impossible' music became possible and, in some cases, popular. Today child-pianists are taught the simpler pieces from his *Mikrokosmos* and find nothing strange in a little piece, hardly more than a simple five-finger exercise, that has F sharps in one hand and F naturals in the other. But it took the world thirty or forty years to come round to the idea. And in the meanwhile Bartók, like Rachmaninoff and Hindemith, had to go into exile in hospitable America. Communists and Fascists alike had become so doctrinaire, so dogmatic and therefore so deaf as to be incapable of learning—as most of us had to learn after early lack of understanding. I have always said that the only safe composer in the lunatic countries would have been someone who could write a tune like 'Onward, Christian Soldiers' and change the word Christian to Soviet or Nazi.

More difficult than Bartók was Arnold Schoenberg—also destined to go to America. He did not write in two keys at once: he wrote in no key at all.

His early music belonged to the world of Richard Strauss and Mahler and he was quite gifted enough to vie with them. But he was a man of immense rigour of thought and he pondered over a long period about the possibility of a new harmony. When his atonal piano music began to appear it seemed to many people to *avoid* tonality. Just when a phrase might naturally have ended on a recognizable cadence in a key it ended on what seemed to many listeners to be plainly wrong notes. The musical world as a whole disliked his works and only a few devoted pianists played them. He went further and produced a music described as serial. A serial piece is based on the twelve notes of a chromatic scale placed in an order decided on by the composer—an order that must be maintained, or, if altered, must appear as in a mirror—a mirror flat on the table, the music vertical, so that where the note-row goes up on the page it will go down in the mirror version.

The basic version and the mirror version can also be played backwards.

The note-row is without rhythm itself and can be played in rhythms to be decided. And notes that follow one another in the note-row can be played simultaneously as chords. In Five Pieces, Op. 23 (1923) there is a waltz, apparently the first of Schoenberg's truly serial pieces. (See Example 9 where I have added note numberings to the opening line.)

Ex. 9

Pianists were very puzzled. For one thing, nowhere in this waltz is there the familiar *omm-cha-cha* of waltz rhythm. More puzzling was the fact that the marks of expression were very numerous and *had* to be numerous. Why was this? In earlier kinds of music it was often easy to guess an appropriate tempo or to know by the look of the thing where there might be accent or a hurrying of speed or a fade-away. One knew that, as a rule, discords tended to be stronger than their resolutions. It was like saying *angry*. Of course *ang* is louder than *ry*. In a piece that was quite without concords almost every note had to have its expression-mark. In fact Schoenberg was compelled to invent new marks. I quote from the Preface, which is printed in English as well as German:

At · it must be light and elastic; but at ▼ the staccato must be expressed in a hard, heavy manner. — means that the note should be lengthened. Often when the signs ▼ to ⸗ appear, it means that the notes should be accented and made longer (*tenuto* and *portato*). When the *staccato* point is placed above (‐) it means that the note must be well held on but separated from the next one by a slight pause.

There are other directions, but these will serve as examples. One thing was sure. Every note 'told' since there were no 'runs' and almost no pedalling. There were no picturesque effects, no demonstrations of virtuosity. Because every note belonged to its note-row there was some affinity with a very learned kind of fugal composition, but because almost every note was nuanced in some way there was also an air of almost neurotic sensibility.

This historic waltz proved to be immensely influential. It is seldom played, but serialism was adopted whole-heartedly by many composers and half-heartedly by some.

The most complete reaction against virtuosity came in the music of Schoenberg's friend and pupil Anton von Webern. His Variations Op. 27 (1937) proceed almost entirely in single notes or pairs. Just occasionally there is a run of three notes or a chord of three, but ones and twos and plenty of silences are characteristic. This is certainly not for the sort of person who likes music to 'wash over you'. Although it is notated with bar-lines and time-signatures there is almost no suggestion of so many beats in a bar.

After this there could only be John Cage's piano piece that consists of no notes at all. The pianist sits on the piano stool, does nothing and in due course gets up and walks out, presumably to no applause.

Another puzzle. We pianists practise a piece to get it right. It is true that, on impulse, we may vary our performance from day to day, but, in effect, we say to the composer 'Make your intentions as clear as possible and we shall try to present it to our audiences to the best advantage'. Inevitably this leads to standardized performances.

Karlheinz Stockhausen makes sure that no such standardization of performance is possible. His Klavierstück XI is packaged in a cardboard cylinder. Inside is a large sheet of paper 36 inches by 21 (92 cm. by 53), and this can be pinned on to a folding music-desk thoughtfully enclosed by the publishers. On this are printed nineteen separate fragments of music of varying lengths. All are very difficult to play because of the many wide leaps and the complex time values. At the end of each fragment is a pair of signs. One is conventional—*ff* or *pp* maybe. The other consists of T° (short for tempo) followed by a figure. The Tempo signs range from T°1 (very fast) to T°6 (very slow). These tempo signs govern notes printed in normal type. Notes in small type have to be played as fast as possible.

Why is a tempo sign printed at the end of a fragment? When you see this speed indication you choose another fragment at random and play it at that tempo. Let me quote the composer himself:

> The performer looks at random at the sheet of music and begins with any group, the first that catches his eye; this he plays, choosing for himself tempo (small notes always excepted), dynamic level and type of attack. At the end of the first group, he reads the tempo, dynamic and attack indications that follow, and looks at random to any other group, which he then plays in accordance with the latter indications.
>
> 'Looking at random to any other group' implies that the performer will never link up expressly chosen groups or intentionally leave out others.
>
> Each group can be joined to any of the other eighteen: each can thus be played at any of the six tempi and dynamic levels and with any of the six types of attack.

It is hard to believe that, before an audience, a pianist will genuinely play at random and never know in advance how fast he intends to play what Stockhausen calls a group. The music is very difficult even at a tempo practised over a period of time. To be able to play each item at six tempi is asking more than a great deal. When the music was recorded, how random was the performance?

Working along a different line is the French composer Olivier Messiaen. His is the music of Heaven and Nature and Ecstasy, the music of Roman Catholicism, and the music of bird-song. It seems to owe something to Liszt—the Abbé Liszt —to Debussy and Ravel, to oriental music, to religious paintings and 'objects of piety' and to mystical meditation. This music does require virtuosity. Although—I confess it—it is little to my taste it is not pianistically in opposition to what my hands have taken a lifetime to learn, and every pianist can obtain a clue to performance style from such titles as *Visions de l'Amen*, *Vingt regards sur l'Enfant Jésus* and *Catalogue d'Oiseaux*.

Pianists do not have to relearn their art for this music. Manufacturers are not challenged by it. And the same is true for most Soviet music—or what the West knows of Soviet music. In this respect the Catholics and the Marxists can agree, and maybe the time will come when Moscow students, trained to play Scriabin, will give convincing performances of the *Twenty Glances at the Child Jesus*. And no doubt there are pious pianists in Paris who, having studied César Franck's *Prélude, Chorale et Fugue*, will not need to confess that they are practising Shostakovitch's *Preludes and Fugues*.

In considering not modern music but what modern music has done to pianos and pianists I must recall a television programme in which I interviewed an American musician named David Tudor about the Prepared Piano. This was a device invented by John Cage and was being presented by his pupil and friend.

After a moment of introductory chat we looked inside the piano, and the amazed viewer saw that steel bolts had been screwed between pairs of strings. There were also strips of rubber placed over one string and under the next. (Tudor had brought a letter from Steinway in New York to assure my producer that no harm would be done to the B.B.C.'s instrument.) I asked my guest to play and he produced a *zinkazonk* sound, explaining that this was an episode in Cage's research into percussion. We then took the bits and pieces out of the piano and proceeded to treatment No. 2. In this the strings were hand-plucked, the keys were elbow-banged and the iron frame was struck (the right pedal being held down at the time) with a tympani stick. This, I have to say, produced a rather fine sound.

I asked if there was any rhythmical beat in this music and was told that each phrase was timed on a stop-watch.

I then recalled that when we had first met on the previous day David Tudor had said something concerning manuscript paper. Not quite understanding the point he was trying to make, I brought to the studio a sheet of manuscript paper in pristine condition and asked for an explanation. He took the sheet, held it up to the bright lights of the studio, and pointed out the slight flecks and marks—defects in paper manufacture—not normally visible. These, he said, were sources of inspiration for John Cage.

End of programme. But there was something that the viewer had not seen. In the studio, before transmission, the producer had declared his total non-comprehension. He said to me quietly, 'Look, there's no melody, no harmony, no rhythm, and, well, no sex, if you know what I mean.' Before he had finished his sentence our guest came by and could not help hearing what was not intended for his ears. He took it quite calmly. 'Oh, but I assure you, it is most romantic.'

Until then I had thought that I understood how a great pianist might be a great lover.

---

25. *Despite Everything*

The world was no longer kind to pianos. The technology of electronics that killed the player-piano wellnigh killed the piano altogether. Why should amateurs struggle to play the piano at home when the wireless and the radiogram provided all that most of them needed in the way of music? Why should devoted committees of voluntary workers struggle to organize provincial music societies when audiences were comfortably staying at home and listening to every kind of music from the Emperor Concerto to late-night dance music from a smart hotel?

The young pianist who passed an audition and 'got on the B.B.C.' was making his way in a new medium but also helping to kill the established concert system in which he might otherwise have made his name—as I remember.

At a different level the arrival of 'talking pictures' meant unemployment for hundreds, thousands, indeed tens of thousands of picture-house pianists.

When economic historians talk about the troubles of the twentieth century they never mention the music industries. Understandably they talk about unemployed miners and shipyard workers and farm workers. The communist–fascist riots were not staged by cinema pianists. But the tribulations of pianists and piano-makers can be a poignant footnote to a terrible history.

And there was a conflict in the hearts of many musicians when, trying to hold out a helping hand to refugee pianists, they wondered whether competition for engagements and pupils would now become worse.

Nothing, of course, abated the ambitions of gifted young pianists. Nothing ever does. If Vladimir Horowitz could succeed, why not they? But the world had harshly changed. When I was a child I knew that wherever I went there would be a piano in the house and I would be asked to play. Suddenly the pianos disappeared. 'We're moving into a small flat. It takes up too much room. It disturbs the neighbours.'

The 'little woman round the corner' had no more pupils, the piano shop took to selling radio equipment and records. More than one piano factory went bankrupt.

Yet, strangely, the piano still held a certain magnetism. I must add a few lighter touches to a gloomy picture. There were still families in which the children did their practice. There continued to be held those competition festivals in which my colleagues and I listened to hundreds of youngsters playing little 'teaching pieces' with titles like 'A Marching Tune' or 'Sailing My Boat on the Pond' while their older brothers and sisters waited to play Beethoven's 'Für Elise' or, for the Senior Championship, a group of three pieces by, perhaps, Bach, Mozart and Chopin.

Examiners from the Associated Board of the Royal Schools of Music in rivalry with other examiners from Trinity College of Music travelled to the principal cities of Australia, New Zealand, Canada, South Africa and to Hong Kong, Singapore and other territories that looked to the British for cultural guidance.

Even in the Latin-and-cricket schools there began to be a more tolerant attitude towards pianists, and the state education system found room for music advisers.

Pianos might be got rid of, but the image of piano-playing as something enviable and desirable remained bright. And it grew ever brighter when the war came. Precisely when piano factories were given over to making parts for aeroplanes and new pianos were totally unobtainable, pianists were in demand.

Popular symphony concerts were a sell-out and the principal box-office magnet was the big romantic piano concerto. I could draw at length on my memories of playing such pieces with the London Philharmonic Orchestra all round Britain but I am bound to say that there were other pianists who were bigger names than I—Moiseiwitsch, Solomon, Eileen Joyce, Cyril Smith—who untiringly and with unflagging skill and power travelled under great difficulties from one concert platform to the next, playing on pianos that were kept in as good condition as bad circumstances allowed.

For my part I often played on appalling pianos when I was sent far and wide by the Regional Committees for Education in His Majesty's Forces. I could easily have followed the example of most of my colleagues by taking records and a player to the ack-ack batteries, the airfields, the ships that survived the convoys, but I preferred to be the best player of bad pianos, and I discovered all over again the curious power that lies in a pianist's hands. Never mind the moth-eaten, worm-eaten instrument, again and again people would say, 'I do envy you.'

And I realized, if I ever needed to be told, that a pianist is a privileged person.

Playing to paraded audiences I could not assume any knowledge of serious music, and when question time came I was expected to show at least a little knowledge of light music. This was no great problem for me since, as a student, I had to some extent earned my way through college by playing light music and was one of the few people in the country who could give a convincing performance of Gershwin's *Rhapsody in Blue* with orchestra.

I have to admit, however, that real jazz was another world,

almost as though there was a separate kind of instrument called a jazz piano.

Rachmaninoff used occasionally to go and listen to the playing of some great jazz pianist. Neither could have played the other man's music. A jazz player owes nothing to Clementi or Czerny for his technique, nothing to Field or Chopin for his *cantabile* or his *rubato*. He may, indeed, be totally unable to read music, and he has no intention of playing 'as written'. He invents and plays in his own style and is nearly always very much imprisoned in that style. It is his call-sign, his trade-mark and, in performance after performance, his improvisations explore a very limited territory.

A few conservatory- or university-trained musicians have become good jazzmen and they nearly always then abandon the music they were trained to play because theirs is essentially the art of the self-taught.

For my part, being a pianist with a reasonably wide range of styles, I am irked to find myself unable to play jazz. I can listen to a record over and over again and perhaps imitate some other pianist's style for a few moments, but no jazz comes from inside me.

A well-known jazz player once asked me to give him lessons. 'Yes, on condition you give *me* lessons.' He pursued the matter no further. Maybe I am too old a dog to learn new tricks but it is equally likely that I am a dog of a different breed.

I must not make too much of the great divide. André Previn can play highly professional jazz, and Jacques Loussier can play jazz versions of Bach that emphasize once again how open Bach's music is to new possibilities, but there are two worlds and few can inhabit both.

Once, on a visit to New Orleans, I spent as much time as possible at Preservation Hall and heard white-haired old-timers play whore-house jazz. I got them to autograph their records and I keep these in a sort of Preservation niche. I remember they used a tall, rough-toned upright piano with its front removed, and I am convinced that a concert-grand Steinway would have made performance impossible.

This is not true for the modern player. He takes a leaf from Duke Ellington's book and asks for a piano of size and quality.

But through the era of evolving jazz, composed jazz, modern jazz, the jazzman must preserve a relationship with those old boys of New Orleans just as we preserve a relationship with Beethoven or Liszt. So much is this so that it was widely believed for many a year that only a black man could play real jazz.

It was equally widely believed that a black man could never play Beethoven.

We now know differently. We live in an age when an aspiring young pianist no longer looks for the patronage of the rich and powerful (though their patronage is not to be sneezed at) but rather to the great international competitions. It is now beyond question that anyone who comes top in, say, the Tchaikovsky competition in Moscow is made. It is also beyond question that the top pianist could be black, brown, yellow or any other colour that is alternative to pink-white.

When a winner is announced the recording companies and the concert promoters come running, and the young pianist's only danger lies in too much success too soon.

The breakdown in prejudice is recent. It was assumed that, of course, the Russian teachers knew best how to produce winners, and when the young American, Van Cliburn, came top his fellow countrymen were so astonished that, forgetting his brief association with Commies, they gave him a ticker-tape procession down Broadway.

It will never happen again. Why shouldn't anyone from any country come top? Even the easygoing and self-deprecating British have managed to produce two winners, neither of them a forced plant from an oh-so-artistic hothouse.

Neither John Ogden nor John Lill is much like Paderewski and I am sometimes asked whether the great personality pianist belongs to the past.

Nothing is more mysterious than personality. How can one account for the never-failing magnetism of Artur Rubinstein? Yes, he is a wonderful pianist, one of the greatest in history, but there is something else. It has nothing to do with eccentricity or showiness. He disdains gimmickry or over-personalized interpretations.

I have had the privilege of talking to the great man. I have also talked to an old lady who remembers Rubinstein when young. It would be easy to write a 'piece' about warmth and sex-appeal and experience and authority. It would be a waste of time and paper precisely because—and I must say it again—music is non-verbal and, in the last analysis, defies words.

I cannot believe that Rubinstein, though unique, is the end of the story of those Great Pianists who constituted a kind of musical royalty, but the world changes much too fast for anyone to dare to make prophecies.

Pianists change: so do pianos. The French industry, for one, has virtually disappeared. Gone are Érard and Pleyel and Gaveau, though instruments bearing those names are marketed by the German firm of Schimmel and catalogued as *grandes marques réunies*. Some of the great European concerns are under new ownership. Bechstein now belongs to the American Baldwin company, and a pianist can travel through the States playing Baldwin pianos and in Europe playing Bechstein. Bösendorfer of Vienna is also American-owned.* Blüthner remains German in East Germany where ownership has a special meaning. Steinway has its pianos well established all across the world—I saw one in Moscow when I went there for an Education–Music conference—and Steinway pianists who want Steinway service know better than to flirt with rival makes. Even Steinway is not quite its old self. It is part of the Columbia Broadcasting System conglomerate.

Alas for the days when a piano-making family made pianos for royal families. I do not sigh for the days when a king could say 'Off with his head' and my temperate royalism is confined to constitutional royalty, but there must have been something special about the craftsmanship that went into making a piano for a Grand Duke. ('Take your time, Heinrich, you know what His Highness is like.')

At the biggest piano factory in the world, the Yamaha factory in Japan, there is a production line of grand pianos four abreast, 300 yards long. (*See Plate 10.*)

---

* The Jasper Corporation (Indiana, U.S.A.) is a big name in lumber and furniture. It makes the Kimball piano in America, it provides piano-actions for many British manufacturers from its English subsidiary, Herrburger Brooks, and it owns Bösendorfer.

Yamaha are a portent. They make every size of piano from a basic upright to a concert grand of very high quality. Their output is 160,000 for their home market and 41,000 for the rest of the world, and the figures are growing. It is not perhaps part of our story to mention that they make every kind of musical instrument and that on every highway you will find a Yamaha motor-cycle, but what does concern us is their Music Foundation that influences nearly half a million children and catches them very young.

One curious fact remains. Russia, the land of many great pianists, never made a great piano. However, there now arrives in the west the 'Estonia'. I have tried a concert grand and am reasonably impressed. I am also startled, since the action (the Schwander action) is made in England by Herrburger Brooks. This would not in itself be extraordinary were it not for the fact that Herrburger Brooks for some time past has been owned by the Jasper Corporation of Indiana, U.S.A., an enterprise known for lumber and furniture and the not specially distinguished Kimball piano (not to be confused with the British Kemble—*see Plate 9*). The plot thickens when we remember that the Jasper Corporation also owns Bösendorfer of Vienna and that the 'Estonia' has been launched by the Russians (who have their own notions of profit and loss) at a temptingly low price.

Here are wheels within wheels, and perhaps one day the Chinese will throw a spanner in the works, since they, too, must surely attempt to make a high-quality concert grand and show it to the world.

26. *Teachers of the World Unite!*

Piano professors are generally treated with respect. Even the 'young student of today' is usually willing to admit that this teacher knows a thing or two. Nevertheless there is some tendency for people outside the conservatories to think that we are a reactionary lot. It is a blanket condemnation. No doubt there are some who 'teach piano' merely as they themselves were taught, but most of us do a good deal of rethinking. As for repertoire, we have, over the years, studied Schoenberg and Messiaen and Stockhausen and have found it is our students who are sometimes reactionary.

Methods are not much in vogue even though one may legitimately refer to a certain teacher's method of tackling a specific problem. A Method seems to suggest that there is a right way of teaching everything, whereas we all know that we may teach two different pupils in different ways. No doubt it is flattering to be quoted, but I tremble when anyone says 'I once heard Sidney Harrison say . . .'. This easily turns into 'As Sidney Harrison always says . . .'. Whereas Sidney Harrison, despite his pet sayings, is constantly contradicting himself—apparently. My students arrive with several years of study behind them. How can one teach a piano-basher in the same way as an ivories-tickler? After giving a lesson to a highly cultured person with no muscles, how shall one teach a highly skilled piano-operator who has never once heard an opera?

We teach in a multitude of ways and when we talk shop there are no great areas of disagreement.

Am I talking only of the London scene? Not at all. I am a fairly widely travelled man and I pick the brains of my rivals wherever I go. In this I am not unique. I remember a distinguished teacher from Israel who sat in my room for the best part of a day and then, for several days in succession, sat in my colleagues' rooms at the Royal Academy of Music. If I had nine lives I would follow her example in every conservatory in the principal centres of musical learning.

One proof that there is now widespread agreement lies in the fact that at international competitions the juries are brought from various countries without fear that the Viennese school of thought will be totally opposed to the Parisian or the New Yorkist.

However, a very powerful witness in this matter is Heinrich Neuhaus who, before his death in 1964, wrote *The Art of Piano Playing*. Since he counted Richter, Gilels and Lupu amongst his pupils at the Moscow Conservatoire we may surely take him seriously. Though he is a highly serious artist he takes himself lightly, and the book gains from his willingness to be a bit self-contradictory, to reminisce about his own feelings, and to allow himself some flights of fancy. I warm to him for two reasons. One is that he spent his life torn between concert-giving and teaching. He played in public a great deal, not without success, but simply had to rush to help any young person whose playing was faulty. The other is that he rejects the idea that people can be made into pianists by some settled course of study. Though he was Director of the Moscow Conservatoire he resigned from the post in order to teach more, and he complains that an organized time-table interferes with his work. Just when a lesson is going well, the student has to rush off to play viola in the third orchestra. (I wish I knew the answer to this problem.)

I have a slight feeling of disagreement with him about exercises. He hates them and I am no lover of them, but I do think that there are students who need a bit of piano drill and who may even find it exhilarating. However, I quite agree that, better than an Exercise in Octaves, is an attempt to play a Bach Two-Part Invention in octaves—which is what a harpsichord produces when you use couplers. It is an exercise: it is also music.

Neuhaus is intent on realizing 'the whole image of the music': 'The child should be made, at the earliest possible stage, to play a sad melody sadly, a gay melody gaily, a solemn melody solemnly, etc. and should make his musical and artistic intention completely clear.'

Quite so: if 'The Merry Peasant' does not sound merry and rustic there is no merit in passing an examination on the basis of neat fingerwork and a careful observance of the rests. And in a work devoid of any picturesque title we must still sense the succession of incidents and the sensations of joy and sorrow. The 'whole image of the music' is arrived at slowly by most students: it is arrived at immediately by the greatly gifted. What they do is to give a performance at sight and *then* practise. Practising after rather than before performance seems strange to most people, but that is the way of prodigies.

Neuhaus, like any other teacher, has had to think about muscular action, physical sensation, arm-weight and so on, and he has found a quasi-scientific way of communicating his thoughts about this. He talks of *F, m, v* and *h*—Force, mass, velocity and height (Force, for some reason, with a capital F). This is not science as understood by, say, an expert in ballistics, but I do not doubt its effectiveness. If other teachers prefer to talk of timing and aiming, or even of sinking into the upholstery of the piano, they may well be talking the same language in essence.

Although Neuhaus likes practice to be directed towards artistic image he does not discount other possibilities. He advocates a well-known practising device which is to switch off all emotion and quietly and slowly go through the motions of a piece—which is quite different from stamping one's way through slow practice as generally understood by the diligent. He also notices something else that surprises everyone but piano-teachers.

> I have noticed that every great virtuoso—I mean particularly the virtuoso who plays in large halls with very large audiences—at some time or other in his youth was extremely fond of banging and thumping; the future great virtuoso sowing his wild oats, as it were. Richter, too, used to thump away when he began his concert career, and Vladimir Horowitz, when he was seventeen or eighteen, used to bang so mercilessly that it was almost impossible to listen to him in a room.

In my own view, this explains why juries sometimes put the best man second.

No teacher has all the answers for every student. Every now and again someone leaves me for a teacher who, he thinks, will wave a more effective magic wand, and equally frequently a colleague's pupil will come over to me.

And talking of magic wands I notice that Neuhaus finds it necessary to use the motions of a conductor to transform mere time-keeping into rhythm. I use a pencil and make more gestures with it than marks on the page. I also keep a ruler handy and use it as a baton, not as a means of rapping knuckles.

The point that arises from all this is that teachers are more and more becoming an international brotherhood. It still remains true that a student, once he is mature, should have the chance to study abroad, if only to get right away from mummy, daddy and teacher. (A maestro is not a teacher, you understand.) But the days when a Leschetizky could dominate the piano-teaching world are over. No doubt, in any country, there will be a certain mystique surrounding the teacher who can scarcely speak the language, particularly if his fees are twice as high as anybody else's, and no doubt there will always be great travellers ready to assure us that there is a truly fantastic teacher in Patagonia; but we live in a world where American pianists can win a major British contest, and British pianists can win a major Russian contest, and where one of my own pupils can win a major American award against stiff opposition from Juilliard.

In fact, one of the problems of our age is an over-competitive atmosphere. The first-place winner is 'made'. The second man —second by a whisker after anguished discussion in the committee room—is very much an also-ran. The first man's fees are multiplied by ten and he has more engagements than are good for his playing: the next man's fees go up by a mere 50 per cent.

What is almost frightening is the drive towards ever-more-efficient ways of teaching. Even the amiable Neuhaus thinks that his book would be all the better if it could be accompanied by tapes of different kinds of playing; and if he had lived longer he might have asked for video-tape. As for what goes on in Japan, where Suzuki seems to be able to make a hundred toddlers play a violin concerto in unison while strolling about, I wonder when a hundred Yamahas will be placed in some vast arena so that a thousand little fingers will be able to play the Fugue from the Hammerklavier.

Curiously there is a dearth of people who play the piano 'rather well'. There are too few amateurs who play the piano as enthusiastically as other men play golf or go sailing. It is to be hoped that, in the age of leisure that economists are constantly foretelling, the musical evening at home will revive.

It may be that educational psychologists will discover something more about learning and memory. What *is* teaching? What *is* learning? What *makes* us forget (and what prevents us from forgetting)? Every performer has a guardian angel who urges him to play better. But the moment the angel has flown back to heaven, a mocking devil says, 'And I'll see to it that you don't.'

Does language hinder explanation? I once said to a conference of musicians, 'I sometimes think that there are too many teachers who are deaf but unfortunately not dumb; and I wonder whether good lessons might not be given by a teacher who was dumb but fortunately not deaf.'

Who should come to me soon afterwards but a Chinese student whose language I certainly could not speak and who had hardly a word of English. No problem. I pointed, I gestured, I nodded, I shook my head, I conducted, I sat down and 'illustrated'.

No more words.

⁕⁓⁕⁓⁕⁓⁕⁓⁕⁓⁕⁓⁕⁓⁕⁓⁕⁓⁕⁓

27. *Before the Public*

Exploitation is an ugly word and conjures up pictures of dark, satanic mills. Yet there must be many an ambitious young pianist whose secret cry is: 'I wish someone would exploit me.'

How to be exploited: that is the question.

The 'own-risk recital' is a conventional way of starting a public career. Take a hall, print posters and leaflets, invite the critics. Include in your programme something, perhaps a first performance of a new piece, that might interest the gentlemen of the press. Steel yourself to endure anything that they may write and do not be surprised if a quality daily says you are full of faults while a heavy Sunday paper praises you to the skies. Either way, do not expect a rush of engagements: you have a thousand rivals as good as you are.

Try for auditions with radio and television, play to anyone who will listen, be seen around, join societies of professionals, team up with singers and string players, and never miss an opportunity to compete.

Grind your teeth at 'those stupid critics' but never publicly criticize them. They are very thin-skinned and hate criticism even more than you do. After all, you invited them to the concert, didn't you? Or your agent did.

Agents. Promoters. Do not confuse one with the other. They are not the same.

In only one thing do they agree. You had better be a success before they will help you to become one.

An agency is a glorified post office. If a pianist has a degree of reputation he may be telephoned and hear something like 'We have had an inquiry from the North East Midlands Music Society to know whether you would be free to give a recital for them on such and such a date . . .'. The agency will negotiate a fee, making it as high as possible to increase their percentage, or making it as low as possible to keep a client, or making a nice balance between the two.

The bigger the pianist's reputation, the higher the fee, the tougher the negotiations. Where the volume and price of business is high, an artist will usually have a sole-agency arrangement.

An international celebrity may have a personal manager devoted only to his interests—the negotiation of concert engagements, recording sessions, radio and television programmes, booked far ahead, perhaps even several years ahead. If your celebrity is not to have a nervous breakdown he must insist that certain times of the year are inviolate with no engagements whatsoever.

His manager may have a number of dealings with promoters. A promoter does not 'pass on' an engagement and take a percentage: he organizes a concert in the hope of making a considerable profit and may do so in two ways. One is to pay a big fee and take everything that is left after the fee and expenses have been paid: the other is to make a profit-sharing arrangement with the artist.

One well-known promoter told me of a famous pianist on just such an arrangement who, in the first interval of the recital, asked the promoter what the receipts were. The promoter mentioned a figure. The pianist challenged it. The promoter, nettled by this, produced the box-office book. The pianist shook his head and said that the figure for the number of people in the audience was wrong.

Said the promoter: 'How do *you* know how many people there are in the hall?'

'I counted them during the slow movement.'

All over the world there are agencies and concert-promotion organizations. Whereas Chopin obtained letters of introduction from lords and ladies as a means of making his way in a strange city, your modern pianist must be in with a whole network of men and women in the music business. How does one get *in*?

There is no easy answer. Lords and ladies and tycoons can be useful. Titles and money still carry influence. Luck plays a part (though the lucky will never admit it), and the luckiest thing in the world is to have the nature that attracts luck. You may think that quality comes first and such characteristics as persistence and ambition come second. No doubt they do, but they will never bring talent to fruition without magic.

The fact is that a pianist giving a recital is asking for serious attention over a considerable period of time and he must be seen to have the right to make this demand. He must be like the Ancient Mariner who, accosting the wedding guest, 'fix'd him with his glittering eye' after which there was no escape from the story that was to follow. Mysteriously some people have this power. A bow, a few notes . . . yes, that's *it*. *Him* we'll listen to.

Once this has been established the agents and promoters will lend an ear—an ear that can be surprisingly deaf to most other pianists.

Pianists are not always quick to recognize this magic in one another, which is why a music-business person should be included in a panel of judges in any big competition. It could well be that while eminent musicians are arguing as to the awarding of a prize, a concert promoter will know quite certainly where he would place his money as an investment. I could even imagine such a person not listening to the performance but scrutinizing the faces of the audience.

It is no longer the policy of the big piano manufacturers to promote tours, but recording companies and concert promoters are known to work hand in hand.

The laws of the market place operate very stringently. One man has great difficulty in selling his wares: another is in demand and can make breath-taking claims in the way of fees and conditions. Suddenly a young star is in the ascendant and he is travelling to a new engagement every day of the week until the public begins to say 'Not *him* again!' There is an element of absurdity in the way one particular artist will be the rage for a while, but this state of affairs is nothing new, and it will not alter.

Certain older artists become unassailable, beyond criticism. They are the acknowledged great pianists and seem to be part of the history of music . . . until they die, when they are soon forgotten.

It might be thought that records will preserve the memory of what they are like, but old records, except in a few cases, lose their magic. It is the performance that we shall never hear, the performance by Beethoven or Liszt, that is magical.

28. *Take Care*

What of today's pianos? Essentially they are the same as yesterday's. If you want a good one you must make room for it and pay a decent price. Short grands and low uprights can never achieve the highest quality. For that the maker must stretch long strings very tightly over a big sound-board, install an expensive action and lavish special craftsmanship on every job. Since a very grand piano can be maintained in fine condition for a lifetime it is a good investment even if the initial price makes the customer catch his breath.

For the home, even for a stately home, the concert grand is too large and too expensive, but all serious pianists like a piano of some size.

However, for the average family, the upright or the small grand is the obvious choice. I cannot help a certain disdain for very short grands, and I see no point in a very squat upright since a taller piano, with longer strings, takes up no more floor space. If anyone says that a piano takes up too much room I always answer that it is the furniture that takes up too much room. At the risk of seeming chauvinistic, I assert that for musical parents of modest means and for children taking lessons there is no better value for money than a British piano.

The demand is world-wide, and one may wonder why manufacturers do not expand their factories. The problem is not simple. There is no pool of piano craftsmen waiting for jobs, and youngsters will not undertake the training unless they see good wages ahead of them. Higher wages are matched by higher costs of materials. Hardwoods and ivory come from countries that have learned to drive a hard bargain, and even expensive grands now have plastic 'ivories'.

The wood for sound-boards is now kiln-dried, with control of moisture content, not seasoned in the air as in former times. We need not sigh for the older method, but I do sometimes regret that pianos now look so plain. Nobody applies gilt or marquetry to casework, which is why decorated beauties in fine preservation fetch high prices.

Customers want their pianos tuned, and tuners are not plentiful. The more knowledgeable customer wants his piano regulated every few years, to make sure that every note has exactly the same character of sound, the same feel, as its neighbouring notes. Regulators are even scarcer than tuners.

After he has had a piano for many years an owner may wonder about a thorough reconditioning. If the piano bears a distinguished name, if the sound-board has no cracks and is still alive to vibration, if the frame is sound, the piano may be worth rejuvenating, but he should take the best of advice and employ none but a firm of repute. The piano must go into a well-equipped workshop and be the subject of devoted attention by people who will know whether it is worth while to fit new strings and new hammers. But the result can be an extraordinary transformation into youth and beauty. It will all cost money, but a new piano of the same size and make might cost six times as much.

All pianos must be defended against moths, worms, ants and other such enemies—also against the excessive dryness of centrally heated rooms. Every piano-dealer ought to sell a humidifier with a piano.

Pianos age very gradually and like to be kept reasonably busy: they should be neither neglected nor worked to death. They should not be used as cake-stands or covered with ornaments: their only permissible burden is a pile of music.

Municipal authorities nearly always need educating in respect of pianos. They think it quite proper to place a clapped-out old piano in a million-pound new town hall and to provide a piano-stool that pretends to be adjustable but in fact rocks from side to side with an audible click. They should, in fact, provide two pianos: one for dances and galas and jumble sales, and another (normally locked out of sight) for serious music. Architects should take advice before designing a concert platform. They should be *made* to take advice. They should also measure a concert-grand piano before deciding on the width of doors.

A piano should be an object of worship. As I say to my students: When you go shopping, look for the most expensive piano you can afford. Then buy something dearer. Once you have acquired the piano of your dreams, look for a house suitable to put it in.

And take care to marry a suitable partner.

Index

Abel, Friedrich, 41
Aeolian (pianos), 215, 229, 236
Agoult, Countess Marie d', 125,
  148–9, 151–2, 155–6, 160
Agricola, J. F., 28
Albeniz, Isaac, 212–13
Albert, Prince, 130, 155
Alberti, 34
Alexander (pianos), 105
Alexander I, Tsar, 113, 115
Alkan, 193
American Piano Co. (Ampico),
  231–3
Angelus (pianos), 235
Arco, Count, 50–1
Artraria, 91
Astor, John Jacob, 90
Auguste II of Poland, 161
Austen, Jane, 101–2
Austria, Empress of, 43

Babcock, Alpheus, 125
Bach, Carl Philipp Emanuel, 29,
  31, 34, 48, 56, 67, 82, 91
Bach, Johann Christian, 31, 34–5,
  41, 43, 50
Bach, Johann Sebastian, 17, 19, 21,
  28–30, 32–3, 35–6, 41, 54–5, 105,
  112, 123, 128, 134–5, 146, 175–6,
  191, 203
Bach, Wilhelm Friedemann, 31
Backhaus, Wilhelm, 215
Baldwin (pianos), 172, 254
Balzac, 144
Bartók, Béla, 13, 213, 243–4
Bechstein, Carl (pianos), 45, 170–2,
  186, 195, 215, 237, 254
Beckett, Walter, 153
Beckford, Peter, 51–2

Beecke, 46
Beethoven, Ludwig van, 11, 58, 60,
  65–6, 69, 71ff., 82, 85, 88–9, 91,
  93, 95, 98, 101, 103, 105–7, 110,
  115, 121, 123, 129–30, 146, 152,
  165–6, 175–6, 203ff., 253, 263
Belaief, 209
Berg, Alban, 210
Berger, Francesco, 210
Berger, Ludwig, 54
Beringer, Oscar, 186
Berlin, Irving, 216
Berlioz, Hector, 105, 123, 127, 148,
  151–2, 159, 194
Bernhardt, Sarah, 239
Bizet, Georges, 181, 212
Blessington, Lady, 155
Blüthner, Julius (pianos), 171–2, 254
Bösendorfer, Ignaz (pianos), 171–2,
  254
Brahms, Johannes, 58, 93, 176ff.,
  187, 200–1
Brandenburg, Elector of, 33
Branson, David, 126
Breitkopf & Härtel, 62, 85, 179
Breuning, 69
Brinsmead (pianos), 172
Broadwood, James, 159
Broadwood, John, 40, 80, 84, 88,
  104, 124, 172
Brunner, 113
Bucholtz, 115
Bülow, Hans von, 170–1, 190, 194
Burney, Dr. Charles, 23, 25, 33, 35,
  40, 83, 104
Busoni, Ferrucio, 203–5, 207
Byron, Lord, 104, 109

Cage, John, 246, 248–9

267

Carpentier, J., 229
Carus, 110
Caruso, Enrico, 239
Catalani, Angelica, 112
Challen (pianos), 172
Chappell (pianos), 172
Charles X (of France), 161
Charlotte, Queen, 41
Cherubini, 121, 142
Chickering, Jonas (pianos), 125, 172, 194
Ching, James, 223, 226
Chopin, Frédéric, 11, 46, 58, 72, 82, 92, 101, 104, 107–8, 111ff., 121, 123ff., 130, 133ff., 139ff., 150, 157ff., 173, 180, 193, 207, 225, 240, 252, 262
Christie, Winifred, 214
Coleridge, 23
Collard, F. W., 40, 63, 86, 88, 90, 100, 129, 172
Clark, Alfred Coming, 202
Clementi, Muzio, 51ff., 58, 60, 62ff., 73, 80, 82ff., 100–1, 104, 106, 124, 126, 129, 130, 145, 147, 191, 225, 228, 252
Cliburn, Van, 253
Clutsam, 213
Constantine, Grand Duke, 112
Cornelius, Peter, 182
Corri, 63
Cortot, Alfred, 188, 211, 224–5
Cramer, Johann Baptist, 82, 106, 122, 124, 142, 145
Crisp, Samuel, 38
Cristofori, Bartolommeo, 24–5
Crosby, Bing, 48
Cuisinié, 24–5
Czartoryski, 112

Debussy, Claude-Achille, 210ff., 234, 242, 247
Deichmann, 179
Delacroix, Eugène, 148
Dent, Professor Edward, 205
Deppe, 192–3, 217
Devrient, 128

Diabelli, 140
Diviss, Procopius, 235
Dlugosz, 113
Dolge, Alfred, 195
Dudevant, see George Sand
Dumas (fils), 156
Duo-Art (player-pianos), 236
Dupin, Aurore, see George Sand
Duplessis, Marie, 155
Dussek, J. L., 67–8, 82, 105
Dvořák, Anton, 13, 181, 200, 210

Edward VII, 239
Elgar, Sir Edward, 121
Elizabeth I (Queen), 17
Ellington, Duke, 252
Elsner, Joseph, 112, 120, 143
Erard, Sébastien, 64, 80, 85, 105, 172, 215, 254
Esterházy, Prince, 121, 152

Faversear, 86–7
Fay, Amy, 184ff., 194, 217
Ferdinand dei Medici, 24
Fétis, François, 68, 127
Field, John, 81, 86–7, 100–1, 106–7, 126–7, 142, 144, 252
Fontana, Juljan, 115, 162–4
Forkel, 29
Foster, Stephen, 238
Franck, César, 248
Franklin, Benjamin, 67
Frederick the Great, 29–30, 56
Fricken, Ernestine von, 135
Friederici, C. E., 39
Fux, J. J., 49

Gallenberg, Count, 117
Gát, Josef, 227
Gaveau, 254
Gay, John, 31
George I, 122
George III, 41
Gershwin, George, 98, 116, 251
Gieseking, Walther, 215
Giesemann, 177
Gilels, Emil, 256

Giordani, Tommasso, 82
Givens, Larry, 232
Gladkowska, Constantia, 118ff., 141, 143, 158
Glinka, Mikhail, 100, 127, 156
Gluck, C. W., 12
Godowsky, Leopold, 202–3, 213, 215, 235
Goethe, 175, 178
Gorlitz, 201
Gottschalk, Louis-Moreau, 174, 185
Grabowski, 115
Graff (pianos), 80, 116–17, 139
Grainger, Percy, 101
Granados, Enrique, 212–13
Gray, Thomas, 39
Greville, Fulke, 38
Grieg, Edvard, 13, 200–1, 234
Grotrian-Steinweg (pianos), 170
Grzymala, W., 173
Guicciardi, Countess Julie, 73
Gyrowitz, 112

Hallé, Sir Charles, 151
Handel, George Frideric, 31–3, 55, 115
Harding, Rosemond, 26
Harrington, Dr., 86
Haslinger, 116
Hawkins, J. I., 83
Haydn, Joseph, 32, 43, 52–3, 60ff., 69, 70–2, 82, 85, 121, 129, 175
Heath, Edward, 239
Hebenstreit, see Pantaleon
Hedley, Arthur, 113, 163
Heine, Heinrich, 137, 150–1
Hemerlyn, 113
Herrburger Brooks, 27, 172, 254–5
Herz, 106, 117, 125, 142
Hess, Myra, 219
Hickman, Dr. Clarence, 233
Hindemith, Paul, 242, 244
Hoecke, 86
Hoffmann, Josef, 202, 208
Hoffmann, Professor, 113
Hoffmeister, 113
Hohenlohe, Cardinal, 183

Holland, Frank, 234
Horowitz, Vladimir, 250, 258
Hummel, Johann Nepomuk, 89, 91, 106, 113–14, 120, 122–3, 140
Hussarjewski, 116

Ibach (pianos), 172, 214
Irving, Sir Henry, 239

Jacquard, Joseph-Marie, 229
Janko, Paul von, 214
Jarvis, Charles, 90
Jasper Corporation, 254–5
Joachim, Joseph, 177–8, 187
Joseph II (of Austria), 239

Kalkbrenner, Friedrich, 106, 113, 117, 134, 142, 145
Katzwarra, 103
Kauntz (Count), 56
Kemble (pianos), 255
Kimball (pianos), 255
Kirkmann, J., 39
Klavarskribo, 216
Krzyzanowska, T. J., 111
Kuntsch, J. G., 109, 112

Lanner, Josef, 139
Legouvé, Ernest, 146
Lehár, Franz, 98
Leipzig Conservatorium, 132
Lenz, W. von, 164ff.
Leschetizky, Theodor, 196–7, 199, 201, 219, 259
Lichnowski, Count, 117
Liszt, Franz, 21, 72, 74, 82, 93, 101, 107–8, 116, 120ff., 124ff., 137–8, 144ff., 170–1, 178–9, 182ff., 192, 194, 199ff., 207, 212, 243, 247, 263
Loesser, Arthur, 101, 105, 195
Logier, J. B., 105
Louis XIV, 17, 25, 161
Louis XVI, 64
Louis XVIII, 161
Louis Philippe, 120
Loussier, Jacques, 252

Lupu, Radu, 256

Macdowell, Edward, 201
Maelzel (metronome), 74
Maffei, Scipio, 24
Mahler, Gustav, 244
Malfatti, Dr., 139–40
Marie Antoinette, Queen, 68
Marius, Jean, 24
Marxsen, Eduard, 176
Mason & Hamlin (pianos), 172
Matthay, Tobias, 197, 218ff., 242
Medtner, Nicolas, 210
Melba, Nellie, 239
Mendelssohn-Bartholdy, Felix, 21,
    54, 82, 100, 107ff., 110, 114, 121,
    124, 128ff., 134, 143–5, 200–1
Mérimée, Prosper, 161
Merrick, Frank, 196
Messiaen, Olivier, 247, 256
Metternich, Prince, 121
Meyerbeer, Giacomo, 92, 143, 148,
    167–8
Mickiewicz, 148, 160–1
Montez, Lola, 156
Moór, Emmanuel, 214
Moscheles, Ignaz, 106, 109, 117–18,
    122, 124–5, 129–30, 132, 145
Mozart, Leopold, 49, 52, 108, 199
Mozart, Wolfgang Amadeus, 17, 26,
    32, 34, 38, 41ff., 51ff., 62ff., 69,
    70, 72–3, 95, 98, 101, 105, 108,
    112, 114, 121–3, 129, 133, 146,
    152, 155, 168–9, 186, 198
Müller, Matthias, 83
Musset, Alfred de, 161
Mussorgsky, Modest, 210

Napoleon (Buonaparte), 64, 73, 81,
    92, 95, 111, 229
Needham, Elias, 229
Neefe, C. G., 69
Neidhardt, J. J., 36
Neilisson, 168
Nelson, Admiral Lord, 102
Neuhaus, Heinrich, 256ff.
Nicholas I, Tsar, 116, 157, 166

Nourrit, 148

Offenbach, Jacques, 98
Ogden, John, 253
Opienski, 112
Ord-Hume, A. W. G., 230, 233
Ortique, Joseph d', 127
Ortmann, Otto, 223

Paderewski, Ignaz, 196–7, 201–2,
    238–9, 253
Paer, 142
Paganini, Niccolò, 116, 123, 132,
    135, 147, 180, 240
Paliarino of Modena, 23
Pantaleon, 24, 114
Pape, Jean-Henri, 124
Paris Conservatoire, 81
Peters (publishers), 200
Pilsudski, Marshal, 239
Pirani, Max, 215
Pixis, J. P., 118
Pleyel, Ignaz, 104, 113, 124–5,
    163–4, 172, 215, 254
Pohlman, 40
Pot, Cornelius, 216
Potocka, Countess Delphine, 169
Potocki, 112
Poulenc, Francis, 212
Previn, André, 252
Prokofiev, Sergey, 205, 219, 242

Quantz, J. J., 29

Rachmaninoff, Sergey, 74, 189,
    202–3, 207ff., 234, 238, 240ff.,
    244, 252
Rachmanov, 127
Radziwill, Prince, 112–13, 144
Ravel, Maurice, 183, 210ff., 247
Reicha, Anton, 74
Reményi, Eduard, 177
Richter, Sviatoslav, 256, 258
Ries, Ferdinand, 106–7, 113
Rimsky-Korsakov, Nikolay, 210
Rochefoucauld, 133

Roehl, Harvey, 235
Rogers (pianos), 172
Rolston, Thomas, 206
Rossini, Gioacchino, 125–6, 142, 144, 152, 194
Rothschild, Baroness, 144
Rousseau, Jean-Jacques, 37–8, 168
Royal Academy of Music, 130, 186, 189, 215, 256

Saint-Saëns, Camille, 212
Salamon, 67
Salieri, Antonio, 120
Salzburg, Archbishop of, 43, 49–50
Sand, George, 157, 160ff., 148–9, 151
Saphir, 151
Sayn-Wittgenstein, Princess Carolyne, 178, 182–3
Scarlatti, Domenico, 17
Schiedmayer (pianos), 172
Schimmel (pianos), 254
Schindler, 74ff.
Schlesinger, 164
Schmitz, E. Robert, 224
Schnabel, Artur, 196
Schoenberg, Arnold, 213, 217, 244–245, 256
Scholes, Percy, 218
Schonberg, Harold C., 74ff., 105, 199, 237
Schroeter, J. S., 22
Schröter, C. G., 22
Schubert, Franz, 11, 72, 94ff., 101, 107, 110, 115, 121, 137, 162, 175, 206
Schumann, Clara, 89, 132, 135ff., 151, 157, 170, 175ff., 185
Schumann, Robert, 82, 93, 107–8, 109ff., 114, 116, 121, 123–4, 125, 132ff., 143, 145ff., 154, 158
Schuppenzigh, 116, 118
Scriabin, Alexander, 209–10, 248
Serov, Alexander, 156
Seytre, C. F., 229
Shakespeare, 18–20, 205
Shostakovitch, Dimitry, 248

Shudi (Tschudi) Burkhardt, 39
Silbermann, Gottfried, 28
Simrock (publishers), 69, 182
Sitwell, Sacheverell, 153
Skarbek, 111
Späth, 44
Spencer (pianos), 172
Spohr, Louis, 86, 106
Spontini, Gasparo, 114
Stamitz, Jan, 34
Stassov, 156
Staufer & Haudinger, 213
Steibelt, Daniel, 64ff.
Steigermann, 195
Stein, Andreas, 26, 44–5, 49, 80, 116–17, 132
Steinway & Sons, Henry, 45, 170, 172–3, 194, 202–3, 254
Stern, Daniel, 149
Stirling, Jane, 169
Stockhausen, Karlheinz, 217, 246–247, 256
Stoddard, Charles, 236
Stokowski, Leopold, 205
Strauss, Johann (the elder), 32, 92, 98, 104, 139
Strauss, Johann (the younger), 98, 104, 181, 203
Strauss, Richard, 12, 234, 244
Stravinsky, Igor, 213
Streicher, Johann, 80
Sullivan, Sir Arthur, 98, 138
Suzuki, 105, 259
Swieten, Baron von, 55–7

Tabel, 39
Talleyrand, Prince, 68
Tausig, Carl, 185–6, 192
Tchaikovsky, Piotr Ilyich, 103, 180, 200, 209, 210, 240
Thalberg, Sigismond, 118, 149, 151
Thun, Countess, 50
Tomaschek, 66, 68
Tosi, P. F., 47–8
Tovey, Sir Donald, 215
Tschudi, see Shudi
Tudor, David, 248

Verdi, Giuseppe, 156, 205
Viardot, Pauline, 166
Victoria, Queen, 130, 155
Vincent (Heinrich Winzenhörlein), 214
Vogl, J. M., 96–7, 99
Vogler, Abbé, 9
Voltaire, 29, 35
Voynich, 112

Wagner, Cosima, 149
Wagner, Richard, 32, 145–6, 148, 171, 186, 210
Wainwright, David, 172
Waldstein, Count, 69–70
Walewska, Maria, 111
Walter, Bruno, 215

Weber, Carl Maria von, 91ff., 95, 101, 107, 110
Webern, Anton von, 246
Wells, H. G., 234
Welte-Mignon (player-piano), 232, 236
Werckmeister, Andreas, 36
Wieck, Friedrich, 132, 135, 187
Wodzinska, Maria, 111
Wood (father), 38
Woyciechowski, Titus, 115, 119, 139, 143

Zelter, Carl Friedrich, 114, 118
Zumpe, Johannes, 26, 40
Zywny, Adalbert, 112–13, 118